Van Pelt Seminar Workshops available:
    The Compleat Courtship
    The Compleat Marriage
    The Compleat Parent

For further information contact the author
by writing to:
    Better Living Programs, Inc.
    P.O. Box 1119
    Hagerstown, MD 21741

Published jointly by
REVIEW AND HERALD® PUBLISHING ASSOCIATION
Hagerstown, MD 21740

PACIFIC PRESS PUBLISHING ASSOCIATION
Boise, ID 83707
Oshawa, Ontario, Canada

Train Up a Child

A Guide to Successful Parenting

Nancy Van Pelt

Dedication

To my three champion children—
Carlene,
Rodney, and
Mark

who no doubt wish I could practice
more of what I preach!

ISBN 0-8280-0241-X
ISBN 0-8280-1028-5

Printed in U.S.A.

Acknowledgments

This book is the product of the thought and works of the many people with whom I have counseled as well as of the experts in the field of parent education upon whose experimental and clinical research I have drawn.

My deepest gratitude goes to: Judy S. Coulston, who heads my "ways and means committee" in a most brilliant, creative manner, is a writer's guild, a human dynamo, and an architect of the written word—all gift-wrapped into one beautiful package dedicated to the God she joyfully loves to serve; Leslie Morrill, retired school administrator, teacher, and experienced writer, for his ever-willingness to read the copy and offer helpful criticism and encouragement; Dr. Hervey W. Gimbel, outstanding family physician, for his unparalleled common-sense insight into human relationships; Roger Ferris, pastor, for his suggestions and interest in promoting Christian family life; Richard O. Stenbakken, U.S. Army chaplain and family counselor, for reference material supplied from his experience; Dr. Jack Hoehn, family physician, for teaching skills which were a valuable aid in developing the subject of self-respect; D. Douglas Devnich, minister and educator, for his sermons on the home which enlightened my thinking; Ethel Befus, for her typing skills; all the instructors and graduates of the Parent Education Guidance program, for sharing with me their experiences, and all their children, who verify that these principles work; my husband, Harry, for his insights which have enriched my thinking and for his patience with my mental and physical preoccupation during the months of writing this book.

Several professionals have greatly influenced my thinking and confirmed as valid many concepts I originally held. I pay special tribute to Dr. James Dobson for his many insightful books. I frequently refer to myself as "Dr. Dobson's greatest fan." It was a day of special honor for me when he invited me to participate with him on his Focus on the Family radio broadcast to discuss the subject of discipline. In my estimation no one has made a greater contribution to the stability of family life than has

Dr. Dobson through his personal ministry, radio programs, films, and books.

Others whom I know only through the written word but through whom I have gleaned many important concepts are Dorothy Corkille Briggs, Rudolf Dreikurs, Thomas Gordon, Clyde Narramore, Letha Scanzoni, as well as others too numerous to mention. Since I wrote this book primarily for parents rather than scholars, I will not cite instances where I rely on such writers, but those who are familiar with their works will recognize my dependence on their original concepts. To all these professionals I personally owe tremendous gratitude.

And last, but certainly not least, special thanks to my editor and friend, Richard Coffen, whose special touch to my work makes it so much more readable.

Train Up a Child Study Program

A new approach to parenting is difficult, especially if you must work alone. You are more likely to receive maximum benefit from the *Train Up a Child* Study Program if you can study with your partner in parenting, a friend, or a group of parents. If you cannot attend a *Train Up a Child* Workshop, organize your own. You'll find the experience most rewarding. Let the book be your teacher. Your task will be to put the principles learned to work at home with your child.

The following guidelines will help you:

1. Study the material chapter by chapter in order of its presentation. Jumping ahead or out of sequence will promote confusion. Complete all exercises and projects as you move along. The course is organized for study over an eight-week program as follows:

   Week 1: Chapters 1 and 2   Week 5: Chapters 6 and 7
   Week 2: Chapter 3   Week 6: Chapters 8 and 9
   Week 3: Chapter 4   Week 7: Chapter 10
   Week 4: Chapter 5   Week 8: Chapters 11, 12, and 13

2. Stick with the program. Most parents when deciding to change their approach to child rearing go in all directions at once. This creates more problems than it solves. It is a better plan to work on one area at a time in sequence.

3. Purchase a notebook for exercises and projects. If you do not wish to write directly in this book, purchase a notebook for each person participating in the study program. Each person should also have a copy of the book.

4. Schedule a weekly time when you and preferably a friend or a parent study group can meet for discussion. Discuss major concepts, responses to exercises and projects, as well as personal concerns. A one-and-a-half to two hour time frame is ideal.

5. Anticipate resistance from your child. After beginning to implement some of the ideas presented in *Train Up a Child,* you may notice your child becoming more difficult than ever. This is not a signal that

what you are doing is incorrect or that your methods should not be used with your child. It may simply be your child's reaction to try to force you back into your old role. Your child may like the attention he received previously and may continue to test you again and again. Please note: When your child's behavior becomes worse after trying a new method, it is a sign that your new method is working. Take heart!

6. Exercise self-control during this difficult period. Try hard not to lose complete control. Gain composure so you can employ your new method in a controlled, friendly manner. Count to ten, take a walk, go to another room—do whatever is necessary to bring yourself under control. When your child realizes that you will no longer accept his old behavior, he will change.

7. Do not attempt to solve your most serious problems first. Your most serious problem is probably most closely connected to your attitudes, values, or uncertainties. Begin instead by choosing an area in which you can experience success quickly. Success here will provide incentive to continue the program. As you achieve success in the more basic areas you can then move on to other goals.

8. Have courage. Don't give up after just a few tries. Just as your child's poor behavior was not learned overnight, new behavior will not be learned overnight. Just as it took time to learn the old behavior, it will take time to unlearn it. Each day offers another chance to succeed with your child. Accept your failures and move courageously on. You cannot profit by your mistakes if you continuously wallow in discouragement. *You can change your behavior and that of your child!* Commitment to the task is the key.

9. Allow yourself to be human and even to make mistakes. Your child can accept your imperfections and still love and respect you. There is no such thing as a perfect parent.

10. If you wish to proceed with the study program, please commit your-self to the task by signing your name and dating your commitment. You'll never regret the effort expended!

I agree to participate in the *Train Up a Child* parent education program for a period of eight weeks from the date of signing in order to improve my parenting skills and enrich my relationship with my child.

_____   _____
Date   Signature

Preface

As director of Women's Programs for the Health Education Center in Calgary, Alberta, Canada, I first recognized the need for a solid program in good parenting. Classes on happy marriage, discipline, sex education, communication, and many other facets of family life already glutted the market, but I could not find a course that combined in one package all the essentials of parenting. So I began to dream of producing such a class.

After months of research, I combined the results of my study into a program which we christened PEG—short for Parent Education Guidance. The amazing response of the public and the success of the classes provided the impetus for this book.

I have prepared this book with three groups of readers in mind. First, for young people who are seriously preparing for marriage and parenthood. Not only is preventing problems before they arise the best method of family-life education, but it is also much easier to prevent trouble in the home than to cure it once it has gotten a stronghold. Second, for average parents who are jogging along fairly well with no serious problems. Many parents who assume that things are going satisfactorily are later disappointed in the results of their training. I have tried here to help average parents widen their horizons within their homes so that they can see hitherto-unrecognized possibilities within this relationship. We already have too many mediocre homes with mediocre children. Third, for parents who are distressed and discouraged because their dreams for a happy home have not come true. I hope that this book can help guide disenchanted parents out of their troubles.

Finally, I have prepared this book for use as a guide in group sessions for parents bent on improving the parent-child relationship. Many parent-education classes are springing up throughout the United States and Canada, and group sessions, conducted under the direction of a competent teacher, offer added value. As problems are alleviated at the root—the home—juvenile delinquency, divorce, and many other difficulties will be well on their way to extinction.

I earnestly hope that this book will help clarify your understanding and increase your joys of parenthood.

From Cover to Cover

Chapter at a Glance

Chapter 1

Are There Chinks in the Links of Your Family Circle?

Billy Graham tells a story about a college girl who was critically injured in a car accident. As she lay dying, she said to her mother, "Mom, you taught me everything I needed to know to get by in life—how to light my cigarette, how to hold my cocktail glass, how to have intercourse without getting pregnant. But you never taught me how to die. Teach me quick, Mom, 'cuz I'm dying."

The police arrested a 17-year-old boy and sent him to a detention home to await trial, where he suddenly went berserk. He wrenched a piece of radiator pipe loose, broke every window he could reach, and then banged on the pipes for four hours—

until subdued by tear gas. Later, when questioned about his spree, he said, "I had nothing to lose. I have already lost the only thing that could have kept me, and that was my parents."

Another boy writes, "I'll tell you why we teen-agers grab our drinks and crawl into a bed with a girl. You parents start wars and set a terrible example regarding morals and honesty, yet you expect us to be angels. We are only copying you. Why don't you practice what you preach?"

A girl collapsed at the counselor's office. "I'm the saddest girl in town," she moaned. "I go to work, come home, and have nothing to live for. I have to keep my

---

IV. **Today's Parents Need a Change**
  A. The behavioral sciences help by providing information about—
    1. human relationships
    2. motivation
    3. communication
  B. Parents can learn good techniques
    1. They can learn the essentials of character building
    2. They can learn ways to effective communication
    3. They can learn ways to successful discipline
  C. Change begins with us
    1. A different parental response can change a child's behavior

    2. All parents make mistakes
      a. They should not dwell on their failures
        i. Most parents do remarkably well
        ii. Guilt feelings do not produce good parents
      b. They can learn how to improve
    3. God is on the side of parents

parents from killing each other and my baby brother from beating up my sister." And with tears she added, "We used to have a happy home. My dad went to church with us, and we all got along fine. Then something happened to Dad. He got tired of it all and bored with Mom, so they started fighting. He began to drink, and she went out with other men. Now I hate being home, but I feel I have to stay to keep everybody from killing one another."

Today's Parents Need a Change

Never before has the family structure been in such grave peril. Half the marriages in North America end in divorce. The same pattern holds true in places other than North America. Some observers predict that in a few short years the family, as we know it now, will be a thing of the past. The future life style, they predict, will involve group marriages and communal living. And how will this affect children? Few care to even speculate.

Yes, times have changed, but human relationships which form the roots of character growth have not. Children still need parents, for these close early relationships establish the beginnings of humanness. Youngsters still need guidance, forms of restraint, along with support and encouragement as they grow away from the shelter of the family and into adulthood.

But nature is a little careless about whom it allows to become mammas and papas. Producing a child—in or out of wedlock—does not require a test or license. Young married couples often find themselves saddled with children, but they have had no training in the principles of parenthood, discipline, character building, or communication. These parents don't intentionally make mistakes, but the children suffer the consequences just the same. Millions tackle the job of parenthood every year. Yet one of the most difficult and challenging tasks in life is to take an infant, a totally helpless little person, and assume full responsibility for raising him so that he'll eventually be a self-disciplined, productive member of society. Most parents, however,

stumble along, left largely on their own with occasional hints from such psychologists as Dr. James Dobson—author of the best seller *Dare to Discipline.*

Most parents bravely battle toy-strewed rooms and furious cries of "No! No!" and the next day they deal with pinching and tattling and who gets the wagon. Although the problems change, they never end, and parents plunge on doing their best. They invest time, energy, and money. They spare no effort—proper food and clothes, expensive toys. Yet, despite all their good intentions, some parents are disappointed in their youngsters' behavior. The children may fail in their classes, sass, or disobey. They may whine, throw temper-tantrums, wet the bed, or argue. They may be lazy, uncooperative, or disrespectful. They may demand attention, fight with each other, or try patience to the limit.

Parents with good intentions may rightfully ask, "How can my children be so disobedient when I have tried so hard?"

Other parents hear about rising rates of juvenile delinquency, drug addiction, venereal disease, and dropouts. Uneasy thoughts cross their minds. "Am I doing as good a job as I think I am? Have I really given my child all the help he'll need to guide him through this maze?"

Today's parents need a change, yet most of them rely on the same methods of child raising and problem solving used by their parents, by their parents' parents, and by their grandparents' parents. Yet the behavioral sciences have collected much information about human relationships, motivation, and communication. But in addition to more information and principles, parents need help in developing techniques that will work for them in their home with *their* children.

This book teaches easy-to-learn, easy-to-use methods of effective discipline. It emphasizes the importance of training during the first five years of life and insists that self-respect becomes the determining factor between success and failure in life. Along with the essentials of character building, it teaches how to effectively communicate with and discipline children of all ages. Parents who take the time to read, understand, and then conscientiously apply the methods and principles presented in this book will be richly rewarded as they watch their children mature.

Although I cannot offer ready-made answers for every parent, nothing is more practical than the attitudes and principles you will explore here. If you allow these attitudes to color and determine your behavior, in the end the things which you

learn will prove of value to you as you absorb them and put them to work.

Of course, if changes need to be made, these changes must begin with us. This is true of any relationship whether it be parent-child, husband-wife, or friend-friend. "Behavioral psychology" has discovered that when you break your habitual response to any given situation, your change can and will modify the entire situation. For example, if you respond

"I've had it! I'm through! Let him take care of himself!"

The Good Parent Test

Are you a good parent? Are you really successful in dealing with the problems that arise daily? Here's a fun test that will measure your current knowledge and ability. Don't take the test too seriously. Just enjoy it!

There are few all right or all wrong answers, but if you study the responses carefully you will find one more nearly correct than the others.

If you have children at home, answer each question according to how you would respond now, not how you *think* you should respond. If you plan to be a parent someday, answer the questions as you think you would function. If your children are grown, answer as you acted then.

Circle the response that most closely approximates your feelings. Choose only one reply.

1. If you were in a pediatrician's office and had to wait before seeing the doctor, what would you likely do while waiting?
   (1) Supervise my child's play.
   (2) Visit with someone in the waiting room.
   (3) Read *Time* magazine on the table.
   (4) Read *Parents* magazine on the table.

2. The most valuable gift I as a parent can give to my child is:
   (1) self-respect.
   (2) love.
   (3) discipline.
   (4) quality time.

3. I frequently discuss and seek child-rearing advice from:
   (1) no one.
   (2) friends and relatives.
   (3) books and seminars.
   (4) Numbers 2 and 3.

4. If my child frequently cried because the kids at school didn't like him, I would:
   (1) help him find a specialty or compensating skill.
   (2) talk with his teacher about it.
   (3) spend more time with him.
   (4) talk with his friends about it.

5. Positive feelings of worth in your child can best be built by:
   (1) utilizing natural consequences.
   (2) talking and listening more.
   (3) spending quality time with your child.
   (4) helping your child feel special, loved, and a secure part of a personal family.

6. On the average, how much time per week do you spend communicating with your child one-to-one without TV or other interruptions?
   (1) More than one hour.
   (2) 31 to 60 minutes.
   (3) 11 to 30 minutes.
   (4) 10 minutes or less.

7. If my child moped around the house complaining there was no one to play with and nothing to do, I would likely:
   (1) send him to his room to play.
   (2) give him a job to do.
   (3) stop my work and play with him.
   (4) listen to the feeling behind his complaints.

8. If I were watching my favorite show on TV and my child,

without asking permission, switched channels, I would likely say:
(1) I feel very irritated when my favorite TV show is interrupted because this is the only relaxation I get today.
(2) Hey, let's be considerate of one another. Please change it back to my program.
(3) Change it back to my show or you'll get a spanking.
(4) Can't you see that I am watching a special program, you meathead?

9. If I called my child for dinner and she continued to play rather than coming, I would:
(1) go to her and forcibly bring her to the table.
(2) threaten her.
(3) call her again.
(4) allow her to miss the meal and go ahead without her.

10. If my child were to throw a temper tantrum I would likely:
(1) ignore her.
(2) imitate her by throwing one too.
(3) deprive her of a favorite activity or toy.
(4) spank her.

11. Parents tend to blame themselves for their child's behavior and rightly so because the outcome of a child is mostly dependent upon:
(1) heredity.
(2) using proper child training methods.
(3) parental example and environment.
(4) individual temperament type and how parents relate to it.

12. In order to instill pure character traits a parent must develop in a child:
(1) moral excellence.
(2) a pleasing personality.
(3) talent and/or genius.
(4) pleasant disposition and individuality.

13. Responsible behavior and better habits can best be accomplished through:
(1) natural consequences.
(2) consistent rules.
(3) parental example and a loving home.
(4) rewarding positive behavior and ignoring negative behavior.

14. The best way of controlling a 17-year-old's choice of questionable peers is to:
(1) invite the questionable friends to your home.
(2) move the family away from them.
(3) restrict privileges.
(4) forbid the association.

15. If my 15-year-old failed to clean his room and accept responsibility for common household tasks, I would:
(1) clean the room and do chores for him.
(2) allow natural consequences to take over.
(3) send an "I-statement" about my feelings.
(4) try to motivate him through a contract system that manipulates privileges.

16. The most effective means of keeping a youngster from

experimenting with drugs is:
(1) to provide the security of a loving, well-adjusted family life.
(2) to send him to Christian schools.
(3) to select his peer group carefully.
(4) to know the physical symptoms connected with drug abuse.

17. It is now common knowledge that there is a direct link between delinquency and poor nutrition. Which of the following can be attributed to faulty nutrition?
(1) Reading problems.
(2) Hyperactivity.
(3) Running away and vandalizing property.
(4) All of the above.

18. The best way of handling sibling rivalry is:
(1) let children settle their own disputes
(2) love each child equally.
(3) listen to both sides before punishing.
(4) protect young children from older ones.

19. The diet our Creator chose for us consists of:
(1) meats and poultry.
(2) grains and nuts.
(3) fruits and vegetables.
(4) 2 and 3.

20. Your 7-year-old asks you where babies come from. You would likely respond:
(1) Babies are made when the daddy puts his penis into the vagina of the mommy. During certain days of the month the mommy can become pregnant, and a baby begins to grow in her uterus.
(2) When parents want a baby, they love each other in a special way and they'll have one.
(3) I'll tell you about it when you get a little older. Remember to ask again.
(4) Babies come from the cabbage patch.

21. Your 5-year-old asks what it is the two of you do after you close the door of your bedroom at night. You would likely respond:
(1) I never asked my parents questions like that when I was a kid!
(2) Ask your mother (or father)!
(3) We sleep mostly. Why do you ask?
(4) Sometimes we sleep and sometimes we love each other in a special way and we want a private place to do it.

22. Bringing children into the family:
(1) produces added stress for couples throughout child-rearing years for those not prepared for the task.
(2) decreases material satisfaction particularly during the children's teen years.
(3) is more satisfying to women than men.
(4) automatically increases marriage satisfaction.

Turn to page 238 for **Scoring the Good Parent Test.**

differently to your child's behavior (or misbehavior), his behavior will change. And this is what the whole topic of parent education is about—changing parental attitudes and behavior toward the children.

Many of you will undoubtedly say to yourself, "I wish I had had this information years ago! Jeannie is already ten, and I can see the mistakes I made with her during the formative years. I don't want to repeat it now with little Julie!" Please don't feel guilty or blame yourself for past mistakes. You could have your Ph.D. in psychology and still make a multitude of mistakes in raising your children—like the psychologist who had six theories on rearing children and no children and then ended up with six children and no theories! Considering the fact that most of us have received absolutely no training in parenting, we do a remarkable job, and it is a wonder our youngsters turn out as well as they do.

Guilt feelings do not produce good parents, and the fact that you are studying to become a better parent shows that you truly care about your children. Poor parents rarely make this effort or else make it when it is too late. So don't dwell on your failures, and don't reproach yourself when you fall back into old habits. Instead, reinforce your own self-respect by recalling the times you have succeeded as a parent. Recognize your inclination to make mistakes but do so without threatening your own personal value as a parent or person. This will help you keep up your courage. Perfection in parenting is an unattainable goal. Improvement, however, is realistic. Watch, then, for little improvements. Learning how to apply all the principles delineated in this book will take time, but each small improvement is a step forward. So when you try a new method, and it works, be happy!

Since sin entered the world, Satan's calculated plan has been to do away with the home, for he knows that he can destroy nations by destroying homes. Yet while most of us seem ignorant of his devices, he intrudes into every department of the household—perplexing, deceiving, seducing, and breaking up families.

Eternal Consequences

God, who is also concerned about our families, rallies sincere parents to defend their homes, and if our homes are built on solid foundations, we need not fear the future. The pivotal factor that determines in whose image a child develops centers on whose image the parents reflect. Do you belong to God or to the enemy?

Further reading you will enjoy . . .

Abrahamson, David.	*THE EMOTIONAL CARE OF YOUR CHILD.*
Bernhardt, Karl S.	*BEING A PARENT.*
Menninger, William C. et al.	*HOW TO HELP YOUR CHILDREN.*
Smith, Sally Liberman.	*NOBODY SAID IT'S EASY.*

Chapter at a Glance

Chapter 2

Reflections on Your Child's Self-respect

He was the fourth of eight children born to an immigrant family who had moved from Poland to Michigan four months before his birth. Father worked for the city sanitation department, and mother took in laundry. The family moved frequently during those early years. Times were hard, and their dreams of finding a better life were disintegrating. When he was only 12 the boy's mother died shortly after giving birth to her eighth child. She was the one person who might have cared for the boy, the one person he might have cherished. At this tender age desertion and rejection totally enveloped him. The father was never able to get ahead. Burdened with his own problems, he remained unresponsive to his family's needs. Eventually the father remarried, and the family settled on a small farm.

The boy's childhood was impoverished. No one cared about him, and he retreated to a lonely life of self-loathing and personal misery. Eventually he completed five and one-half years of schooling and became known as the studious one in the family. But his retreat into the silent world of magazines and newspapers allowed him to nurture an extreme shyness. He had no close friends except for one brother. He was obsessively neat and possessed an extreme hostility for cruelty—even to insects. In the house he

"And what is your name, little boy?" "No-no Billy."

would catch flies in his cupped hands and carefully carry them outdoors, where he would surrender them to the wind.

At 13 he signed up for work in a bottle factory, followed by a dreary job in a wire mill. A loner, he had difficulty making friends of either sex, but he especially had difficulty in establishing lasting relationships with women, never having a girl friend. He was relatively short (five feet seven inches) and slight (140 pounds).

He was a good worker, though unsociable. He never quarreled, but sequestered himself so he could read the many radical newspapers and magazines that he had learned to enjoy. He also attended many Socialist meetings. Doctrines of anarchism became his consuming interest. His work was menial and his life as bleak and rigid as the wire he made.

When he was 25 years old his personality changed sharply. The *apparently* healthy normal factory worker vanished, and in his place stood a pale, agitated potential villain. Later that year he quit his job and moved onto his parents' farm, where he spent an abnormal amount of time sleeping. When awake he devoted his time to reading anarchist propaganda.

Prescribed medications to alleviate his adverse symptoms proved of no avail. His mental condition continued to deteriorate. His was a daily diet of despair, wanting to be left alone, always fighting with his stepmother, day after day becoming more and more withdrawn and irritable. He began to take his meals separate from the rest of the family—eating alone in his room. An abnormal thirst for sensationalism caused him at one point to read every night for weeks on end one particular newspaper account of an assassination.

When he was 28 he decided to leave the farm, and he wandered aimlessly to several cities, where he attended more anarchist meetings. The final blow to his self-esteem came when he tried to join one such club, but the group rejected him. By now his concept of failure and self-hate was deeply reinforced within.

One day he read in a newspaper that the President of the United States planned to attend the Pan American Exposition in Buffalo early in September, and personally greet people. He read these reports with deep interest. During that time this sullen loner went to the exposition in his solitary, secretive way. The silent, unsmiling figure spent the days that followed walking the grounds of the exposition. Sometimes he would sit and listen to Sousa's concerts. Many people saw him, but no one remembered him. He carefully studied all newspaper accounts of the President's forthcoming visit. At this time he made his preparations with utmost calm. He purchased a short-barreled revolver and practiced folding a handkerchief over his hand to hide the weapon.

September 6 dawned. It was a hot day, and no one paid any attention to the small man in a neat gray suit—just a working man come to greet his President along with thousands of others. During this public reception the President would shake hands with the crowds for ten minutes. Seven or eight minutes elapsed before the young man approached the President. While thousands of people were enjoying a Bach sonata, the young man extended his left hand. The President saw the supposedly bandaged right hand and attempted to shake with his left. The assassin slapped the President's hand aside and fired twice through the handkerchief at such close range that the powder stained the President's vest.

President William McKinley rallied at first but died eight days later as he mumbled the words of "Nearer, My God to Thee." Leon F. Czolgosz's trial was held four days after McKinley's funeral. It lasted only eight and one-half hours. After deliberating only thirty-four minutes the jury found him sane and guilty. At 7:12 A.M., fifty-three days after he had shot McKinley, Czolgosz was strapped into an electric chair at the state prison, and the switch was thrown.

Czolgosz had listened to McKinley as he addressed an audience of an estimated fifty thousand at the exposition on the day before the killing. He told the court, "I saw a great many there saluting him, bowing to him, and honoring him. It was just not

Self-esteem Evaluation for Adults

This Self-esteem Evaluation measures your current level of self-esteem. Answer these statements according to how you actually *feel* or *behave*, rather than how you *think* you "should" feel or behave.

Score as follows (each score shows how true or the amount of time you believe that statement is true for you):

0 = not at all true for me
1 = somewhat true or true only part of the time
2 = fairly true or true about half of the time
3 = mainly true or true most of the time
4 = true all the time

SCORE

_____ 1. I don't feel that anyone else is better than I am.
_____ 2. I am free of shame, blame, and guilt.
_____ 3. I am a happy, carefree person.
_____ 4. I have no need to prove I am as good as or better than others.
_____ 5. I do not have a strong need for people to pay attention to me or like what I do.
_____ 6. Losing does not upset me or make me feel "less than" others.
_____ 7. I feel warm and friendly toward myself.
_____ 8. I do not feel others are better than I am because they can do things better, have more money, or are more popular.
_____ 9. I am at ease with strangers and make friends easily.
_____ 10. I speak up for my own ideas, likes, and dislikes.
_____ 11. I am not hurt by others' opinions or attitudes.
_____ 12. I do not need praise to feel good about myself.
_____ 13. I feel good about others' good luck and winning.
_____ 14. I do not find fault with my family, friends, or others.
_____ 15. I do not feel I must always please others.
_____ 16. I am open and honest and not afraid of letting people see my real self.
_____ 17. I am friendly, thoughtful, and generous toward others.
_____ 18. I do not blame others for my problems and mistakes.
_____ 19. I enjoy being alone.
_____ 20. I accept compliments and gifts without feeling uncomfortable or needing to give something in return.
_____ 21. I admit my mistakes and defeats without feeling ashamed.
_____ 22. I feel no need to defend what I think, say, or do.
_____ 23. I do not need others to agree with me or tell me I'm right.
_____ 24. I do not brag about myself, what I have done, or what my family has or does.
_____ 25. I do not feel "put down" when criticized by my friends or others.

_____   Turn to page 238 for scoring instructions.

This Self-Esteem Evaluation #69 is reproduced with written authorization of copyright holder, Lilburn S. Barksdale, President and Founder of The Barksdale Foundation, P.O. Box 187, Idyllwild, CA 92349.

right.'' In his jail cell prior to his execution, he wrote out his confession: "I killed him because I done my duty. I don't believe one man should have so much ceremony [attention] and another man should have none." And so, because no one had ever respected, loved, esteemed, or paid attention to him, Czolgosz snuffed out the life of one of America's most beloved Presidents, until that year of 1901.

Although not every child reared in neglect grows up to become an assassin, we can almost guarantee that such a child will have problems with feelings of personal worth. The individual may not respond as aggressively as Leon Czolgosz, but on every hand we witness the results of those who feel inferior. The self-doubt and feelings of inadequacy handicap the person for the rest of his life. Why do so many people grow up disliking themselves? Parents have not understood how to structure the child's environment so that self-respect can be built instead of destroyed.

Who Feels the Sting of Inferiority?

Nearly everyone suffers from feelings of inadequacy. We see evidences of this mass tragedy on every hand—in every neighborhood, church, and school. Although feelings of inadequacy are evident in small children, it becomes particularly apparent during adolescence. Most teen-agers are bitterly disappointed in who they are, what they look like, and what they are accomplishing.

But teen-agers are not alone in this dilemma. People of every age group face their own particular brand of inadequacy. A child of 5 can tell how important he is to those around him. Many adults face severe feelings of inferiority. Senior citizens also feel that sting in a world that worships youth and beauty.

Heart and blood-vessel disease is the greatest disease killer in America today. More than 1,000,000 men and women succumb annually. However, a greater killer of human life stalks the earth. A lack of self-respect plagues more people, cripples more lives, and renders useless more

individuals than the world's greatest health problem.

Let's get personal. Your child's future happiness depends on his mental picture of himself. Everything else between these covers is predicated on this fundamental fact. *How your child feels about himself will determine his success or failure in each of life's endeavors.* How he perceives himself will influence his behavior and his grades—also his choice of male and female friends, schools, and career. Ultimately it will even affect his outlook on moral issues and spiritual matters. His view of himself, in short, influences every decision he will ever make.

The purpose of this book is to reveal the comprehensive ramifications involved in developing your child's self-concept. As you read the ensuing chapters, you will notice that every word, action, and method of child training you now employ either builds or destroys your child's self-image. The far-reaching effects of this one subject can hardly receive enough emphasis.

The Illusive Sense of Self

Current research has demonstrated that children as well as adults who possess self-respect will function well rather than stumble and grope through life. But exactly what is self-respect? It is the mental picture

29

of oneself formed by feedback accumulated from others over the years and through the experiences of life.

People who possess self-respect, like themselves, have confidence in their abilities, and are satisfied with their life and work. Since they have confidence in their abilities, they are able to risk attempting new things. If they encounter failures, they have the ability to deal with them without whipping themselves mercilessly with guilt. They can move out of a failure pattern and begin anew. Those with self-respect not only feel innate value, but they also know they have an important contribution to make in life. They feel loved and, therefore, can genuinely love others. Because they feel good about themselves, they are able to respond positively to people and life situations.

A good self-concept allows individuals to accept their appearance—even their distinctive features. These people are free to throw their energies into solving problems rather than fainting under their weight. They can accept the value of their accomplishments without becoming conceited. Persons with healthy feelings of worth are able to appraise their abilities realistically. They realize that they are not perfect—that they make mistakes and fail in life's endeavors from time to time. However, after appraisal, they also realize that they have sufficient good qualities to counterbalance their negative traits. Consequently, they feel *equal* to others and able to measure up to others' positive opinions of them.

Self-respect is not "self-love" in an egotistical, prideful sense. In fact, bragging and boasting about oneself and one's accomplishments are classic symptoms of low self-worth. Persons who can appreciate their individual worth have little need to impress others with their abilities or possessions.

Self-respect cannot be measured through talent or capabilities. Many people who possess tremendous talent and ability may still have a crippling self-concept. History tells us of many intelligent and gifted individuals who became alcoholics, drug addicts, or suicides in order to escape from a self they grew to loathe.

Where Do Negative Feelings Originate?

How are opinions of self formed? What makes a child think about himself the way he does?

It all begins in the tender years of childhood. Most parents cannot stop with a plain No to a child when his behavior infringes on the rights of others. The typical

parent feels he must continue: "No, you naughty child. That was a bad thing to do. You are just plain mean." Words such as *bad, slow, ugly, stupid, naughty, dumb, ridiculous, clumsy,* and *retarded* downgrade a child's feelings of worth. Phrases such as, "You never do anything right," "I'm ashamed of you," or "What's the matter with you? Are you stupid or something?" help mold a child's image of himself. Subjected to a constant barrage of put-downs, along with nonverbal disrespect or emotional neglect, a child begins to grow up feeling ashamed of, and dissatisfied with, himself. The seeds for thoughts such as "I'm no good" or "I can never measure up to what my parents want from me" begin to sprout.

Unfortunately, the structure of society is designed to promote such feelings. Competition to be "the best" permeates every classroom. Awards and rewards go to the winners of sports and other activities. Prizes await the champions of contests. Fierce competition for popularity dominates the teen years. The advertising world tells us that we must use certain products if we want others to accept us. Brothers and sisters slug it out for top honors within the family circle. Wherever there are winners, there must also be losers. Those who play the game and lose feel the pains of unacceptance and inferiority. Belittling remarks at home added to the competition-packed society sets the stage for a child to belittle and refuse to accept himself.

The origin of self-disrespect lies in childhood. Parents fail to render the support needed for feelings of adequacy to develop during the tender years. This has the potential of initiating a lifetime of self-castigation, self-recrimination, and self-unacceptability. Such feelings begin during the formative years and are nurtured by a performance-oriented society. The devastating results dog a person for the rest of his life.

Dimensions of Self-respect

By the time the child blows out that one little candle on his first birthday cake, his self-respect is already vulnerable. When an infant is only a few months of age, he can distinguish between censure and praise. He senses his importance when he receives attention, and he sees himself as having less value when he is treated roughly. He identifies with how he perceives his parents feel about him. His awareness of their love and respect lays the crucial foundation for his own self-respect.

As a child nears his third or fourth birthday, his world widens to include a community of people. Nursery, preschool, or day-care classes, attendance at church, television viewing, and listening to books being read increase his exposure to others. By the time he turns 7 or 8, when his social life enlarges again, a child may already be wrestling with feelings of inferiority. Contact with playmates exposes him to teasing and ridicule. Children are frequently frank, cruel, and heartless in their dealings with one another. Almost every day the growing child encounters experiences that could assault his own self-concept. And feelings of inadequacy accelerate to maximum levels during the teen years.

But is there more to developing self-respect than refraining from calling a youngster belittling names? Yes. Three factors must always be kept in mind when discussing the development of one's self-image.

1. *Self-respect must be learned.* Self-respect is a learned response to the total combination of life's experiences. A child is not born feeling good about himself, although tendencies toward either positive or negative feelings about oneself may be inherent. Self-respect generally evolves from a child's daily interactions with others. Through the total input of life's experiences, then, a child develops either positive or negative feelings of worth.

Charlie Brown, star of the ever-popular "Peanuts" series, has *learned* that he is inferior to others. Put him next to a drinking fountain, and he knows it will spray him. On the pitcher's mound he is a total and complete flop. He has no friends. "Nobody likes me; nobody cares if I live or die," he frequently comments. His "friend," Lucy, constantly belittles him and reminds him of his inferiority. How does Charlie Brown know these things about himself? It has all happened before! Every time he attempts any task he fails. Experience upon experience has taught him of his total incapacity to measure up. Everybody and everything are against Charlie Brown.

Just as Charlie Brown learned to be down-in-the-mouth, so also your child will learn negative or positive feelings of worth. The more positive experiences you provide for your child and the more positive the feedback he receives from you, then the greater the chances that he will *learn* that he is a person of worth and adequacy.

2. *Self-respect must be earned.* A worthwhile task done well will foster feelings of adequacy. Wealth and possessions can be inherited, but feelings of respect are learned. As a result, questions about performance and ability weave their way into the very fabric of a child's life.

Spoken or unspoken, "How am I doing?" lurks in every child's subconscious mind. Regardless of how well a child is performing a task, most of us believe that he could have done better had he only tried harder. If you feel that way about your child, it will come across either verbally or nonverbally. You cannot hide such feelings for long.

Productivity, performance, and creativity promote feelings of worth. A child could never like himself if he thought that he couldn't do anything well. Therefore, every child needs a "specialty"—a skill or ability through which he can *earn* self-respect. By developing skills and abilities a child can enhance his sense of adequacy. Carrying out household chores and duties in a responsible manner also contributes to a child's positive feelings about himself.

Parents can reinforce this aspect of self-respect through verbal comments such as: "You did a fine job of making your bed this morning" or "You're improving in arithmetic" or "You're showing real talent in drawing." Feelings of accomplishment promote feelings of adequacy.

3. *Self-respect must be experienced.* You can repeatedly tell your child, "I really love you. I think you are great. I like you." But if he doesn't *feel* your warmth and acceptance, your words will not convince him no matter how many times you repeat yourself. You can talk all you want about respect: "Of course, dear, we respect you. We think you are wonderful." But if your actions don't reinforce your words, your child will not develop self-worth.

A child can sense that his parents love and care for him and still not believe they feel he is worthy. The mother of a drug addict may love her son yet loathe what he has become. Likewise, a child can conclude in his mind, "You say you love me, but you have to because I'm your child. You only take care of me because you have to. I can tell you aren't really proud of me. I'm not really important to you. I've failed you in some way. I haven't turned out the way you wanted me to."

You convince your youngster of this every time you speak up for him when someone asks him a question, when you tell him what and what not to say before going to a friend's house, and when you send other subtle messages that reinforce the thought that he might make you look bad to others. He can tell whether you really "like" or accept him.

Loving your child is not enough. Your child must *feel* your acceptance of him as a person—*feel* your appreciation of his individual worth whether or not he accomplishes anything great in life. Love is not the greatest gift parents can give to a child—self-respect is. A child is not capable of experiencing or returning love until he first learns to respect himself.

Self-respect, then, is a positive attitude toward oneself gained by *learning, earning,* and *experiencing.*

A Blend of Three Feelings

Three feelings that a child senses significantly affect his comprehension of self-worth: *uniqueness, belonging,* and *human love.* These three feelings combine to give stability and support to the structure of the self-concept. If any one of these three aspects is weak, to the same degree the developing self-concept will also be weakened.

1. *Uniqueness.* Every person is unique, and the specialness of a child deserves respect. Children are never carbon copies. Whether you have two or fifteen children, each will have his own individuality. And each child must recognize that he is unique and can make a contribution to the family that no one else can. This uniqueness can be found by being the oldest, middle, or youngest child, or through a special talent or ability. I enjoy thinking back on the unique characteristics that each of our children contributed to our family. Carlene was the organizer and the creative one. Rodney excelled in school and won top honors. Mark excelled in sports and working with young children. Recognize in each of your children the uniqueness he brings to your family, and feel that he can fill an important spot in your life.

2. *Belonging.* A child senses whether Mom and Dad are happy when he is around. He senses whether he "belongs" in the family. The child who feels that he is an unncessary appendage or believes that he is a "fifth wheel" or "unhappy accident" will have a difficult time feeling respected.

We all have a basic need to be "a part of" or "in with" a group. A child is no different. He needs to experience a "we" feeling in his family. Such a feeling is fundamentally established in infancy. As the parents adequately care for a baby's needs, when they affectionately hold him, he develops a sensitivity to being loved. Soon he establishes a basic trust in people. From these early beginnings the entire foundation for his future relationships with all people is structured.

3. *Human love.* Love is defined here as a valuing of your child, a tender caring. It means that your youngster remains special and dear to you even if you don't approve of all he does.

We all know that children need love, but many of us assume that our children automatically know that we love them. On the one hand, countless children feel unloved even though their parents care deeply. On the other hand, some young-

sters never hear the words, "I love you," yet feel deeply cared for.

Often parents feel they demonstrate love by setting aside their own interests for their child's, watching over him, providing advantages, or spending abundant time with him. But this doesn't necessarily make a child feel loved. Warm affection fosters growth, but it doesn't guarantee that a child will feel loved. A child needs to be certain he is loved.

Innocently, sometimes, parents convey to a child that he is not loved or cared for. "If you are a good girl, Mommy will love you. If you aren't a good girl, then Mommy can't love you." "If you will be Mommy's little helper, then I'll love you." "I'll love you if you will sweep the kitchen floor for me." "If you will mow the lawn for me, Son, I'll love you." All this makes love conditional on good behavior.

Other common sayings are: "Mommy won't love you if you act like that." "If you wet your pants, Mommy won't love you anymore." "If you don't eat your vegetables, Daddy can't love you anymore." "If you don't stop that whining, I can't love you." "You told me a fib, and I can't love you." Love here is withheld during misbehavior.

Most importantly, love your child because he is yours. You must love little Johnny, not because he is behaving right now, not because he gets good marks in school, not because he excels in sports, not because he is an obedient child, but because he is yours. You love him because he is Johnny. There is no security in the world which can compare with this kind of love. When you love your child in this manner, he will sense that he belongs, that he is needed, and that he is respected, and these inner feelings of security will help him grow up into a sound, mature person.

False Values

Our society has created a false value system that effectively destroys human worth. We need to understand these destructive forces if we wish to help the younger generation through the formative years of life.

1 *Beauty.* If your child is born beautiful, he or she has a distinct advantage. Human society highly prizes beauty. By 3 or 4 years of age a child has learned what good looks can do for him. The beautiful child knows that adults respond favorably to him. People smile at him, tell him how "cute" he is, and make a fuss over him. But the unattractive child is overlooked while better-looking siblings and friends get all the attention. You too have probably cooed and gushed over the more attractive child and paid little or no attention to the less attractive brother or sister. It's human nature.

In his bestseller *Hide or Seek* Dr. James Dobson refers to an article from *Psychology Today* (March, 1972). The article, titled "Beauty and the Best," reported some startling biases against homely youngsters:

1. Evidence seems to indicate that the attractiveness of the student influences academic grades.

2. When shown a set of children's pictures and asked to identify the child who probably created the classroom disturbance (or some similar misconduct), adults most often selected an unattractive child as the offender. Likewise, the ugly child was thought to be more dishonest than his cute peer. As the authors put it, "For all the talk about character and inner values, we assume the best about pretty people. And from grade school on, there's almost no dispute about who's beautiful."

3. According to the findings of Karen Dion, the way an adult handles a discipline problem is related to the attractiveness of the child. The same misbehavior is likely to be handled more permissively for the cute youngster and more severely for his less attractive peer.

4. Most importantly (and correlating with my observations), the impact of physical attractiveness is well established in nursery school! Cute 3-year-olds already enjoy greater popularity among their peers. And unfortunately, certain physical features, such as fatness, are recognized and disliked at this tender age.

During adolescence the problem increases. It doesn't take the physically attractive girl long to find that she has the world at her feet. Quickly the handsome, athletic boy learns that he is on top of the heap. The rest of the crowd trails along in their blue jeans and braces, nursing terminal cases of acne. In spite of the cruel way Mother Nature has treated them, they hope and pray someone will notice them. What a distorted value! To judge a person's worth on the basis of physical attractiveness is a false value indeed!

2 *Intelligence.* Another critical factor by which we measure the worth of an individual is his innate intelligence. Parents are highly sensitive and vulnerable if it is ever implied that their child might lack something in mental abilities.

Parents are interesting creatures after

Building Feelings of Worth

Check your response in the appropriate column.
T—TRUE   F—FALSE   U—USUALLY

1. My child feels reasonably secure.   T F U

2. I avoid transferring any of my personal fears or apprehensions to my child.   T F U

3. My child fears my marriage will end.   T F U

4. I make it a practice to hug and kiss my child daily.   T F U

5. I do not compare my child with others.   T F U

6. I am not an overprotective parent.   T F U

7. I treat my child as a unique individual.   T F U

8. I give my child some personal quality time each day.   T F U

9. I introduce my child by name to visitors to show I think he/she is important to the family unit.   T F U

10. I allow my child to speak for himself/herself when asked a question by an adult.   T F U

11. I encourage positive feelings of self-worth because I possess positive feelings of self-worth.   T F U

12. I respect my child's opinion.   T F U

13. I refrain from using such terms as *bad, slow, ugly, stupid, naughty, dumb, clumsy,* or *retarded* when addressing my child.   T F U

14. My child's feelings of worth are being promoted through productivity, performance, and creativity.   T F U

15. My child is experiencing daily positive feelings of worth by residing in our family.   T F U

16. My child feels unique and feels he can fill an important spot no one else can fill in our family.   T F U

17. My child feels as though he "belongs" in our family rather than a fifth wheel or an unhappy accident.   T F U

18. My child feels loved just for being himself without having to achieve or measure up to anything.   T F U

Check up on your honesty in responding to each of these statements by having your partner in parenting, or an adult close to your family, also score you.

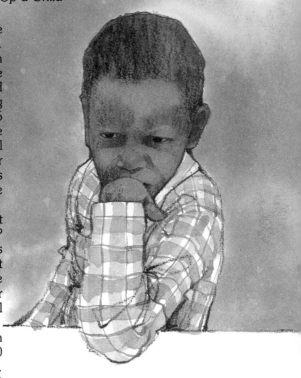

the birth of a baby. It is almost as if they are in competition against all other parents. They want their child to be the first in everything. Bragging is the name of the game—cutting her first tooth (as if the child could help it!), sitting up at 4 months, saying "Dad da" at 5 months, and walking at 6 months. As if all this gives the child more worth! The earlier the baby performs all childhood feats, the greater our esteem for the youngster. To a large degree, parents evaluate the worth of their child by the baby's ability to make them look good.

What happens to the child who cannot measure up to the parents' expectations? (Remember that parents' expectations merely reflect society's expectations.) What happens to the child, for instance, when he gets to school and is only average or perhaps less than average in intellectual ability?

Approximately 22 percent of all children in the United States have IQs between 70 and 90, a range denoting the slow learner. By the time these children leave the first grade they will already have developed deeply ingrained scars of inadequacy. One-fourth to one-half of all children battle feelings of never measuring up to the group standard as they proceed through twelve years of school.

The child with intellectual deficiencies may be able to survive the early years with his self-respect intact, but when he reaches school the picture changes drastically. It is now that he will be measured and compared with the others in his grade, and it doesn't take him long to discover that he can't measure up to his brighter friends. His parents may have been able to protect him thus far, but now he will experience crushing insults from peers who may make fun of him, call him names. This "new light" brings overwhelming darkness to the tender spirit. He'll be the last one chosen to play a game, the one who always flubs or loses. And guess who wishes he could run away and hide from the world? How many tragic tears have been shed in silent seclusion!

Parents of slow learners should de-emphasize the importance of academic excellence and focus instead on the child's strengths and good qualities. In the light of eternity, there are more important things in life than report cards with straight A's. They will help this child develop a specialty that will compensate for his weaknesses. Slow learners are often good with their hands. Wise parents will help him find a skill he enjoys and provide the opportunity for him to master it. Slow learners need positive feelings of worth, too.

The passing years may have dimmed the recollection of our own experiences when we felt incredibly dumb. But most of us can remember the shame and humiliation we felt the day we gave a foolish answer, and the whole class burst into deafening laughter. Remember the day you lost the game for the team? Or the day you flunked a test?

During the course of the years, every child will experience the sting of rejection and ridicule, but some children—because they lack beauty or intelligence—live with it every day of their lives. The child who lacks average mental ability may find himself caught in a whirlpool of depression—the wasted victim of another false value created by our society. The worth of an individual must not be measured by his IQ!

3 *Other problems.* Circumstances beyond their control predispose some children to having emotional problems. Factors such as physical deformity or oddity can almost ruin a child's life. Financial deprivation can seriously handicap a youngster's peer acceptance, particularly if his clothing does not fall within acceptable norms. A child from a poor family or from a family where parents are unaware of peer pressure to conform through dress could become a social outcast. A child with rheumatic fever or other health problems that keep him from entering into normal school activities may begin to believe that he is defective.

A social blunder or mistake during the early years can sometimes haunt a person all the days of his life. Other youngsters may have been socially deprived—reared by parents of foreign descent or having grown up in a mission field or in a rural area. Other factors affecting self-worth include: being brought up in a single parent home, having an alcoholic parent, having a mentally or physically disabled sibling, or being part of a different race or religion. Unloving relationships cripple other children.

What can a parent do who does not have a magic wand to bestow instant beauty, wealth, or talent on his child? People often naively assert that all a child needs is love and he will develop satisfactorily. No! Love is not enough. You may be able to control factors inside the home, but you cannot control the world outside your home. Your child must be able to function adequately in spite of the problems life has dealt him. No pill or inoculation yet invented will prevent your child from receiving rejection outside the home. It

hurts to be made fun of, laughed at, put-down, called names, ridiculed, ignored, or snubbed by others.

None of us particularly wishes our children to experience these incidents. However, we can hardly prevent them. Our job as parents is not to protect our children from every hurt in life, but rather to prepare our children to accept the inevitable hurts and nobly rise above them. In other words, we can teach our children how to cope with the false values that stem from society or to allow the words and reactions of others to destroy them. How important, then, to teach them to grow emotionally through problems!

Inferiority caused by the types of problems we have discussed can completely crush and destroy an individual or it can provide a springboard to prove oneself through achievement and success. It is just such feelings that can drive a person toward achievement and excellence. The need to prove oneself worthy, to find feelings of competence, drives people to success.

Your example will mean a lot. If you can laugh at your own shortcomings and mistakes, this will go a long way in helping your child over some of the rough spots of life. Teach your child to remember his failures with a smile.

Let your child know you will not allow him to depreciate himself or anyone else. Begin this policy early in life and enforce it. However, if you belittle yourself, the entire concept will crumble. Eliminate comments such as, "I never do anything right." Constant self-depreciation can become a bad habit that is difficult to break. Those with low self-esteen commonly love to recite their own inadequacies.

Charlie Brown frequently worries about himself out loud to his friends. If Chuck would only learn to keep still about his inadequacies, probably no one else would notice them. When Lucy learns about one, she delights in ridiculing him about it. The success of the "Peanuts" series revolves around two factors: Charles Schulz' ability to recreate the many blunders and failures we recall from childhood, and our personal identification with Charlie Brown.

Roadblocks to Self-respect

Most feelings of inadequacy can be traced to unfortunate childhood experiences. Parents are frequently unaware of the effect of their words and actions, yet it all either builds or destroys self-worth.

A critical parent arouses in his child feelings of rejection. "You stupid idiot. Can't you see that screw doesn't go there? Anyone with any brains at all could figure that out!" Yelling, screaming, and constant criticism tell a child that you do not love him or care about his feelings.

Parents with low self-esteem particularly have a compulsive need to find fault with everything a child does. Soon the child feels that it is impossible to please this parent or to measure up to expectations. If the child receives additional censure and condemnation at school from teachers and peers, the blow is even more devastating. Please note: Feelings of unacceptance do not always have to be verbalized to be experienced. *A lack of appreciation or recognition speaks as loudly to a child as if it were verbally announced.* Whether spoken or unspoken, criticism is by the far the most common and destructive cause of low self-esteem.

An adult's domineering or bossy attitude implies to the child that he isn't capable of completing an assigned task unless his parent is there to supervise. A parent spends much time in telling a child what to do, when, and how to do it. Authoritarian parents weaken self-worth. A child who is constantly told what to do develops few inner controls and lacks faith in his own abilities to carry out tasks by himself. A child needs training and guidance, but not in an overbearing manner.

Overprotectiveness or excessive sheltering can also make a child feel rejected because he never has an opportunity to make decisions for himself. During the very early years of a child's life, you can control his environment. But from age 3 or so he begins interacting with others—neighbors, your friend's child, and schoolmates. It may tear your insides out to have your child laughed at, called names, or ignored. Your first reaction may be to hold him close—shielding, defending, and smothering him. But such an approach would only inhibit your child's progress. His emotional growth will be strengthened by learning to cope with small problems. A mother who fights all the neighborhood battles in order to protect her "precious" from the cruel world inhibits his progress toward a positive self-image. Such an overprotective parent is also likely to tackle any teacher who tries to discipline her little darling.

Or perhaps the overprotective parent attempts to show everyone how much he loves his child by spending much time with him. Parents are advised to spend more time with a child, yet it is not quantity but quality time that is important. I know a father who spends hours with his boys on projects and games and on the surface looks like the epitome of devotion, but his comments sound something like this: "Stop dawdling over your turn, John. Hurry up." "You're not holding that drill right, Tom. How many times have I told you to hold it like this!" "I wish you'd watch your brother more closely when he bats. You've got to learn to get your whole body into the swing." "You sure botched up this wax job. I'll have to do it all over. Watch me this time. When you do something, learn to do it right the first time." In essence, this father is telling his sons that they are not competent, and the more time the boys spend with him the less adequate and less loved they feel.

Still other parents show rejection through lack of interest. In effect they send the message: "Don't bother me with your troubles. I've got problems of my own. Hurry and grow up and get out of here." Some of the most crippling effects arise from parents who don't have time or who have been emotionally handicapped themselves by unloving relationships.

Furthermore, our attitudes of acceptance or rejection vary along with our moods. If we feel happy with ourselves, we can tolerate a lot of misbehavior from our child. However, when we've had a tough day, are dead tired, feel ill, or are unhappy with ourselves, our "acceptance quotient" will dip to a very low level.

Some parents are more accepting and loving than others by virtue of their emotional makeup. Since they like themselves, they possess an inner security. Other parents are unaccepting by nature, and they often nurture rigid notions about right and wrong.

Our accepting and rejecting attitudes also depend on where we are and who is watching—the old double standard. Most of us tend to be less accepting at a friend's home, in a restaurant, at church—anyplace our child's public behavior reflects back on us. And when friends visit in our homes, we may get upset over manners that we would accept at other times.

Many of us fall innocently into some of these traps. We love our children deeply, we care for them, we'd even give our lives for them. And yet in the day-to-day struggle for existence some of our love gets lost.

The key is the ability to accept the *child* at all times, while perhaps not accepting everything he *does*. Just as God hates sin but loves the sinner, so parents should differentiate between the child's behavior and the child himself if they want him to build a positive self-image. Statistics indicate that a child cements a principle in the mind far more easily through repetition in song than merely by rote memorization. One of the verses in the song "Jesus Loves Me" beautifully teaches unconditional love and acceptance.

> Jesus loves me when I'm good
> When I do the things I should;
> Jesus loves me when I'm bad
> Even though it makes Him sad!

Sources of Parental Rejection

During a workshop we were giving in Las Vegas, we began discussing reasons why parents reject their children. Immediately a parent abruptly and loudly interjected, "Why all this talk about rejecting a child? I don't know any parents who have rejected their child!"

With equal fervor a social worker from the other side of the room quickly responded for us. "Every day of my life I deal with battered and abused children. I am here to testify that there is a sick world out there, and many parents are rejecting their own kids for many different reasons."

Ann Landers, the popular columnist, confirmed this: Through her newspaper column she asked the question: "If you had it to do over again, would you have children?" Seventy percent of the people who wrote in said that if they had known what they know now, they would not have had children. The respondents fell into four categories: (1) young parents who were deeply concerned about overpopulation and the threat of nuclear weapons, (2) parents who stated that their children had ruined their marriage, (3) parents of grown children who had left home, showing little care or concern for their parents once they were gone, (4) parents of teen-agers in trouble.

What other reasons or attitudes may lie behind the rejection of a child?

1. *Wrong timing.* Many a child is rejected, not accepted, not appreciated or loved as he needs to be, simply because he came at the wrong time. Perhaps the child put in an appearance too early. Husband and bride were happy and just getting to know each other. All of a sudden she got pregnant. It can present a big problem.

Or perhaps the husband's business was going so great that finances were stabilizing and things looked good for the future. Suddenly the wife announced that they were going to have a little one. It was the wrong time. Not that he didn't want a child, not that he didn't like children—the child merely messed up his life.

When a child comes at the wrong time, it can lead the parents to unconsciously reject him. They do not reject him for anything he does, for any undesirable characteristics, or because he has no worth, but because he has come at the wrong time.

Other factors may be that there are too many children in the family already, that the child poses a threat to either of the parents' careers, or that one of the marriage partners did not want a child at all.

2. *Disappointment over the sex of the child.* Since it is a first child, and Dad wanted a boy, he can hardly face his baby girl. It may have been so important to him that he finds it necessary to reject the child as a girl and accept her as a boy. Perhaps he'll call her Bud, give her a baseball glove or a football, or encourage her to be "one of the boys."

A certain amount of exchanging sex roles is healthy. There is an allowance of interplay between Father and daughter or between Mother and son that is healthy and normal. It is a crossover of roles. But if these roles become blurred or indistinct, then the child becomes uncertain of his sexual identification. He will ask himself, "What am I supposed to be?"

Knowing one's sexual identity is a very important part of self-respect, for a child cannot respect himself if he doesn't know whether he is supposed to be a boy or a girl. If he is not sure of his role and place in the family, he cannot respect himself.

3. *Misconceptions in sex attitudes.* A child conceived before wedlock sometimes suffers from rejection even though the parents quickly marry. Many times the child's presence reminds the parents of their mistake, so they reject the child. The baby reminds mother of how "that guy" took advantage of her. The father wonders why she didn't stay him off a little bit. Guilt feelings about it can lead to rejection of the child, and the child feels he is not worthwhile because the parents don't feel worthwhile about themselves. They pass on their guilt because they cannot forgive themselves.

4. *Extra responsibility.* Some couples are so emotionally immature that they are totally unprepared for the responsibility of

parenthood. Bent on "doing their own thing," they reject a baby who costs money, makes work, and takes time. When the babysitter fails to show up, and they must miss an important evening on the town, they resent the child who caused them the inconvenience. They feel bitterly disappointed when they must give up a romantic vacation to a distant isle in favor of a $3,000 orthodontist bill. They end up walking the floor with a colicky baby when they really wanted to have fun and be young and free.

These parents do not mean to reject the child; they are not rejecting him because he is wicked or unworthy but because they lack the maturity that parents need to meet the heavy demands on their time and attention.

Other parents are so busy "doing their own thing" that they have little time left over for Junior. Dad has a business to run, and he'll get around to Junior if and when he ever has the time—some *extra* time! Since Mom holds down a full-time job outside the home as well, there seems to be little time together. Although the folks say that he is important and that they love him, Junior begins to realize that he is about three rungs below anyone else in the family. You'd have a hard time getting such parents to admit that they have rejected their child, but nevertheless Junior's self-esteem is going down the drain.

5. *Unrealistic expectations.* Many parents are secretly disappointed because their child is so average. They had hoped for a child with unlimited personality and talent. Many mothers dream that their daughters will be beautiful and popular—especially if they themselves weren't. When their daughters turn out to be neither, these mothers feel let down. Such moms rarely send direct verbal messages, but the constant urging to "fix up" or "get out and date more" lets the girls know that they don't measure up. Dads who never made the team or had the opportunity to attend college nurture secret hopes that their sons will succeed where they failed. Again nothing is said, of course, but the nonverbal messages come through loud and clear. Junior gets the message and feels inadequate and rejected.

Such a child may do well in several areas, but if the parents' dream, and goals for him are unreasonable, they may reject a very worthwhile child. He will grow up thinking he is not worthy because he didn't fit his parents' unrealistic expectations. What right do parents have to demand a superchild when they are so ordinary themselves?

6. *Extended family attitudes.* In some families, extended family members bring pressure on parents either to have children or not to have children; when to have them and how to have them; how to train them and how not to train them. They try to dictate in what religion the child should be indoctrinated, what schools he should attend, and so forth.

Let it be said that grandparents, along with other members of the extended family, can be a marvelous asset to the family. Families today are suffering owing to a lack of closeness with extended family members. Children are deprived of the warmth, love, softness, experience, and wisdom of the older generation. But at the same time parents must not allow grandparents to take

41

over child rearing. Although Scripture insists that parents must receive honor and not be neglected, the second chapter of the first book of the Bible says, "Therefore shall a man leave his father and his mother, and shall cleave unto his wife: and they shall be one flesh" (Genesis 2:24). Grandparents can cause no end of problems by meddling and interfering with parents or child. Consider the potential consequences. Laying pressure on parents or child to conform to a preconceived notion could result in a parent rejecting the child or increasing the child's rejection of self.

7. *Social Pressures.* Some theories prevalent in the world today urge couples to have no more than two children. Other parents are deeply concerned about universal hunger, overpopulation, the end of time, or the possibility that the world might be incinerated through nuclear war. A parent who accepts such ideals could reject a child.

Did you notice what lies at the base of these reasons for rejection? *Selfishness* is the root of all sin, unhappiness, marital discord, and broken families. As we work at being better parents and spouses we shall mature and, hopefully, lay aside our selfish desires by living for the good of others.

The Effect of Peer Acceptance

Parents are not the only ones who affect a child's respect. Any person who spends long periods of time with him helps to determine his self-image. This person may be a relative, neighbor, baby-sitter, brother, or sister. Teachers have a marked influence over a child because of their constant association. Even though the child is not as dependent on these people for his emotional needs as he is on his parents, they react continuously to him as a person and become an intimate part of his daily life.

About the age of 6, when a child begins school, he is no longer totally dependent on the family. He then finds that children outside his home value certain qualities. Boys place importance on sports, strength, and courage. Girls usually value their physical appearance and personality. Whether or not the child has these qualities affects how he feels about himself.

Tall, strong, well-coordinated Bart will feel differently about himself than his friend Leonard, who has a small, uncoordinated body. Leonard feels that he cannot offer what his friends want and, therefore, he sees himself as having less worth than Bart. Since all sports come easily to Bart, other children vie to have him on their teams, and parents and teachers take pride in his achievements. Hence Bart feels more adequate than does Leonard.

A child reacts emotionally to his growth, energy, size, appearance, strength, intelligence, friendliness, skills, and handicaps. He draws conclusions about himself partly from his comparison of himself with others and partly from how others respond to him. Each conclusion will add to or subtract from his feelings of self-worth. His successes in any given area will carry more weight if they are in areas he personally feels are important. A 12-year-old boy may be an accomplished pianist but a failure in football. However, piano playing means little to him if his friends do not value it. Every activity that a child participates in gives him more information about himself. Clubs, sports, church groups, school, and work all add to his collection of self-descriptions, and, hence, identity formation.

Even under the best circumstances, people outside the family contribute to a youngster's feelings of unacceptance, but the more acceptance he finds from his family, the more rejection he can withstand from outside. Thus, although parents are not totally responsible for a child's self-concept, they play a major role, because how they relate to their child during the early years at home sets the stage for his later success or failure.

Symptoms of Rejection

Perhaps you wonder at this point if your child might have feelings of rejection. Can parents tell if a child feels rejected? Yes. Fear of failure and criticism will dominate a child's emotions. Accusation and reproach will cause him to justify his existence by creating arguments for his own defense. Such fear and uncertainty exhaust a child emotionally and drain him physically. Therefore a rejected child exhibits certain signs or clues:

Symptoms of Low Self-worth[2]

1 Lacks decision-making ability

Hesitates to make even minor decisions
Fears to try new things even when help is offered
When asked to do something says, "I don't know how."
Will not ask for things he needs

2 Withdrawal or retreat to fantasy

Does not easily participate with others in games or activities
Does not initiate contact with others
Does not defend self by words or actions
Is afraid to ask or answer questions
Only answers direct questions
Displays a cool or nonaffectionate attitude
Spends an abnormal amount of time by self
Spends an abnormal amount of time watching television or reading
Prefers make-believe friends to real friends

3 Repeated deliberate misbehavior

Bites, hits, kicks, et cetera excessively
Habitually lies or steals
Hurts self or others
Seeks attention by doing something forbidden
Continually acts silly or disturbs others
Displays extreme competition with other children

4 Abnormal attempts to please

Constantly "gives" things to people in attempts to "purchase" affection or friendship
Brings things from home to get teacher's and friends' approval
Constantly asks, "Do you like me?"

5 Habitual easy crying

Cries or pouts or creates a scene when doesn't get own way
Complains "They don't like me" or "They won't play with me"
Shows fear when being left with a baby-sitter, new person, or teacher

6 Tension

Wets the bed
Bangs head
Bites nails
Stutters
Carries a blanket, pacifier, or same toy everyplace

7 Puts self and others down

Calls others names like "baby" or "dummy"
Is critical and judgmental of others
Blames others for own mistakes
Finds excuses for own behavior
Habitually tattles
Says things like "I'm better than you are."

8 Physical characteristics

Is grossly overweight
Speaks in weak, uncertain voice
Is careless and sloppy in appearance
Has sagging posture
Has a sharply turned down mouth and eyes that lack luster
Looks unhappy
Avoids meeting another's direct gaze

Before you leap to any wild conclusions, please remember as you take inventory that normal behavior can vary widely. Don't panic if your child occasionally displays a symptom or two. Look, instead, for patterns and consistency over a period of time. No attempt has been made to include an exhaustive list of symptoms, but rather to identify *tendencies.* If your child displays several of these characteristics in repeated patterns over a period of time, you will likely wish to look for methods to improve his self-image.

Please note: *The worse a child's behavior, the greater his cry for approval.* The more your child misbehaves—the more trying, withdrawn, or obnoxious he is—the more starved he is for attention and acceptance. The greater the defenses, the withdrawal, or misbehavior, the greater the need. Yet all too often these aggravating defenses cause parents *and* teachers to heap more punishment, correction, and negative comments upon the one who needs the most love and reassurance. The very defenses the child erects lessen the possibility of his winning the affection and acceptance he craves, and thus both parent and child are caught in a vicious cycle. Most defenses can be traced to a child's hidden conviction that he is bad, not worthy, inadequate, and unlovable, for we must protect weaknesses, not strengths.

Self-concepts Can Change

A child's self-concept is not forged for all time, although once established, it is not easily disturbed. For example, self-respect comes with feeling both loved and worthwhile, but being loved is the more basic of the two—his worth won't matter to him if love is missing. The child who is convinced that he is no good believes only messages that confirm this feeling. He ignores other messages, for no one can believe he is worthless and of real value at the same time. A girl may believe she is dumb even though intelligence tests show she is bright. She may feel ugly even though she is pretty. Once the picture has jelled in her mind it remains consistent, for changing the girl's view of herself means giving up the only identity she has known for years. Living with the familiar is safer.

Since feelings of worth are learned, earned, and experienced rather than inherited, attitudes toward the self can change when one encounters a positive experience with people and life. Parents who find their child lacking in self-respect discover if they provide a loving, accepting atmosphere, the child's self-concept will change over a period of time with consistent effort. However, the longer a child lives with a low opinion of himself, the deeper the roots of self-hate extend inward and the more difficult becomes the task of dislodging such feelings.

Strategies for Building Self-worth

If you detect that your child has some difficulty in accepting himself or if you wish to build more positive feelings of worth in your child, the following guidelines will equip you for positive results.

1. *Admit any lack of acceptance.* If you have detected symptoms of low self-respect in your child and if you feel you are responsible—even in part—your first task is to admit it. As long as you continue to deny knowledge of or responsibility for the problem, progress in your relationship with your child or in instilling self-respect will remain at a standstill. Most of us find it difficult to admit our mistakes, but it remains the first step toward growth.

2. *Identify the cause.* You may be totally unaware of why you have feelings of rejection toward your child. You may have to list the things you do not like about his appearance, personality, habits, or abilities. If you dislike things about him which remind you of yourself or your mate, or if he does not show traits or abilities in areas that would compensate for your weaknesses, it could be that you have never accepted yourself as a worthy individual or that you have never really accepted your mate. If you reject him because you did not want a child at all, because you preferred a different sex, or because you resent the responsibilities, unpleasant chores, and obligations thrust upon you, admit that selfishness is the real basis of your nonacceptance.

3. *Ask your child's forgiveness.* Often we think of children as too young to pick up certain vibrations from the home, whether it might be tension or an attitude of unacceptance. But children can and do feel these things. We need not feel that we have fallen from our "parental pedestals" when we ask our children to forgive our failures. Asking forgiveness involves three steps: (1) admit that you have been wrong, (2) identify the offense, and (3) ask, "Will you forgive me?" I would say it this way: "Mark, I've been wrong about something and I need to talk with you about it. I've made a serious mistake. I have not always had a proper attitude toward you. When you have done such and such, I have reacted by such and such. I know you have seen me do this. I'm not proud of what I've done. I'm sorry for it and intend to do better in the future. Would you forgive me?" This step can help draw both of you into a closer relationship.

4. *Ask God's forgiveness.* After confessing your shortcomings to your child, next ask God to forgive you for the selfish

45

attitudes you have had toward your child. Then thank God for giving this particular child to you. If circumstances allow, such a prayer may effect further mending of the relationship if the child is present as you pray. Recognize that your child is a special gift to you and that God has a special purpose for him. Now and only now are you free to help your child toward positive growth.

5. *Help your child develop a specialty.* Concentrate on helping your child develop the traits, skills, and habits that will harmonize with God's interests in his life. Help him redirect any negative traits into positive qualities for which he has a capacity. Some of you (perhaps most of you) will need to take this one step further. If your child is different from the "norm" or group in any way—if he is too short or too tall, too slim or too heavy, wears glasses, has protruding teeth or ears, has any distinguishing features, or in any way differs from what is important to his peer group—he will need a "specialty."

Having a specialty will counterbalance his weaknesses and help him capitalize on his strengths. It is something that he can do well to make up for those times when his peer group rejects him. And at some time in your child's life, he *will* receive rejection from the group, try as you may to protect him.

If you have a son who is small for his age or who is not good in sports (both size and sports skills are important to male peers), find a specialty for him. It might be carpentry, sailing, music, or photography. If you have a daughter who is overweight and wears glasses, help her find a specialty to build feelings of acceptance. She might learn to excel in swimming, sewing, drawing, or writing. By the time your child is 8 or 9 years old, he or she should have developed a skill or ability as a specialty. Then when the group rejects your child, he will hurt but can also say, "OK, you don't accept me. You're laughing at me and making fun of me. But I can do something you can't do." Specialties must sometimes change with the age and maturity of the child, but every youngster needs one skill to

carry him over the rough spots in life.

6. *Express verbal acceptance of your child daily.* This doesn't mean that you will praise your child for every tiny word or act. But it does mean that you will always speak positively about him—especially in his presence.

Reinforce your child's positive behavior by commenting aloud, "Thank you for remembering to change your clothes after school without being reminded. I appreciate that." Follow this with a wink or a hug, and you have demonstrated acceptance of your child in terms he can understand. Avoid empty flattery, but watch for daily opportunities to express genuine verbal praise of your child's accomplishments or behavior.

Avoid comparing him with others—brothers, sisters, neighbor children, friends at school, Dad, relatives, or you when you were his age. Like your child just the way he is. Mention those areas in which he fulfills your hopes and dreams. One of a child's greatest needs is to hear meaningful words of acceptance for him as a person, not in just the things he does.

The Rejected Child

Perhaps your child is suffering from rejection at school as well as from neighborhood peers. Tearful episodes and complaints that "the kids don't like me" occur almost daily. How should you tackle such a problem?

The typical parent might tell him that he shouldn't feel that way. Some parents might scold him for feeling the way he does. Avoid this mistake. Encourage him to express his hurt to you. Telling him that he shouldn't feel the way he does would be a "feeling stopper"—a denial of what he is experiencing. Instead, use the active listening skills you will learn in the next chapter. Don't attempt to solve the problem—not at this point. Right now he's too upset to listen to your solutions. But the freer your child feels to express himself, the more likely you will be able to discover the real source of the problem.

Through active listening you should be

able to find the root cause of the problem. Then you will be able to seek for a solution that will help your child develop whatever skill is necessary to receive the acceptance from his peers that he so desperately needs and yearns for.

Is your child lacking in some skill or attribute that might cause the other children to reject him? Is there something about him that promotes such feelings? Is your child being overly sensitive? Although you never verbalize these questions, seek the answers.

Go on to teach your child how to be a friend to others. You might invite one of his peers to spend some time at your home or to go on a picnic with your family. This might encourage the development of a genuine friendship.

If your child is overly sensitive, it signals low self-esteem. Work with your child to develop a specialty that can act as a compensating skill when he receives rejection. Teach him to cope, rather than mope!

Happiness Is Feeling Good About Yourself

The real place to begin in helping your youngster feel good about himself is with *you!* You provide a role model for your child, who quickly senses any lack of worth you might demonstrate. If you have low feelings of worth, they will likely contaminate your offspring like a deadly virus. He thinks to himself, "My mom and dad consider themselves 'inferior.' I guess I have to feel the same way about myself." In this way parents actually predispose their child to accept the same distorted concepts, values, and assumptions generated from their own low self-respect.

Low self-respect is often passed from generation to generation—from great grandparent to grandparent, from parent to child in a chain reaction. Each generation increases the severity of the malady and those who suffer from it. Case histories document that suicidal tendencies (suicide is the end result of a long period of self-hate) follow family lines. Unless parents take effective measures to break the vicious spiral, their own low self-respect may

cripple even the unborn.

The better we perceive and understand the all-encompassing effects of low self-respect, the more we will comprehend that it causes the vast majority of social ills. It is a major factor in mental illness, alcoholism, suicide, drug addiction, and crime. In addition, the rising divorce rate and the breakdown of almost all human relationships continue to levy a high toll. Building positive feelings of worth in ourselves and in our children is the only way out of these disastrous dilemmas.

You Can Make It!

By God's grace it *is* possible to repro-

Self-evaluation for Children

This is not a psychological test to determine if your child is "normal" or "abnormal." It is just intended to give you a better idea how he feels about himself.

1. The thing I can do best is . . .

2. The thing I do worst is . . .

3. I am most proud of my ability to _____ . Why? _____

4. One thing my friends do not like about me is . . .

5. The thing I dislike most about my looks is . . . Why? _____ .

6. When it comes to sports, I . . .

7. I feel important when . . .

8. If I could change one thing about myself and make myself different than I am now, it would be . . .

9. Three words that describe me are . . .

10. The best thing about being me is . . .

11. The people I dislike most . . .

12. It really worries me when . . .

13. I would have more friends if . . .

14. In order to be popular with other kids . . .

15. I feel awful when . . .

16. If you could make one wish and your wish could come true, what would you wish for?

17. If you had one hundred dollars and could do anything you wanted, what would you do?

18. What three things do you like best about yourself?

19. What three things don't you like about yourself?

20. If you could make one change about yourself and be different than you are now, what would you want to change?

Now study the responses carefully for negative feelings that showed up in your child's answers—things that he/she disliked about him/herself. What can you do to help your child overcome these negative feelings and develop healthier feelings?

gram a defective self-image. You see, God gives you the power to carry out His purpose and image in you as you behold Him—in His Word. Scripture substantiates this: "But all of us . . . reflect like mirrors the glory of the Lord. We are transfigured in ever-increasing splendor into His own image, and the transformation comes from the Lord." (2 Corinthians 3:18, Phillips).[3]

One girl found it difficult to achieve high grades in school. Turning her low self-image over to God, she at last captured the essence of 2 Corinthians 3:18. Each day she would repeat to herself these transforming expressions: "I can do all things through Christ who strengthens me." "Greater is He that is in me than he that is in the world." "I am more than conqueror through Him who loves me." She also continually reminded herself: "One with God is a majority." "I can make it!"

Anything fed directly into the subconscious mind is accepted as truth. No room for doubt. The teen-age girl's reprogramming campaign was a total success. Within a matter of weeks her whole level of functioning had taken a 180-degree turn—for the better! Whereas before she felt that she could do no right, now she was earning high honors. She knew for a certainty that God was giving her of His glory to carry out His purpose and image in her. Girl dejected was now girl triumphant.

You can make it too!

Taking Stock

It's time to take an intimate inventory of the emotional climate in your home. If you don't make the effort now, you will have to pay a high inventory tax later. Have you created an atmosphere of acceptance in which your child can nurture positive feelings of worth? Have you conveyed acceptance in terms your child can understand? Does your home contribute to the building of self-worth or toward the destruction of it? Have you met your child's emotional needs for acceptance today? Can you respect your child for what he is, or must he produce something of great value before he can win your approval? Must he make you proud before you can accept him? Does your home contribute equally to the self-worth of each family member? In the years to come how will your child look back on the heritage of worth you are contributing to his life now?

Happiness is feeling good about oneself, and the greatest gift you can give your child is a healthy self-respect. The word *love* can now be profoundly understood. This is the firm foundation for homemade happiness. Indeed, this is truly living!

Further reading you will enjoy . . .

Briggs, Dorothy C. *YOUR CHILD'S SELF-ESTEEM.*

Canfield, Jack and Harold C. Weils. *100 WAYS TO ENHANCE SELF-CONCEPT IN THE CLASSROOM.*

Dobson, James. *HIDE OR SEEK.*

Maltz, Maxwell. *THE MAGIC POWER OF SELF-IMAGE PSYCHOLOGY.*

Osborne, Cecil. *THE ART OF LEARNING TO LOVE YOURSELF.*

Schuller, Robert H. *SELF-LOVE—THE DYNAMIC FORCE OF SUCCESS.*

Trobisch, Walter. *LOVE YOURSELF.*

Wright, H. Norman. *IMPROVING YOUR SELF-IMAGE.*

Chapter at a Glance

Chapter 3

Special Communication to Harvest a Well-adjusted Child

Most parents nowadays view the generation gap as inevitable, yet they recognize that good communication is basic to maintaining good discipline and to establishing a sound system of values. They want to keep the channels of communication open or clear up those that have been clogged. But how? Although there is no pat formula which will succeed every time, there are principles and guidelines for parents to follow.

It is important, first of all, to establish what communication is, what it is not, and what a parent can expect from it. Some parents confuse verbal contact with communication. They think that if their lips

or their children's lips keep moving, they must be communicating. But communication is a two-way street—"a giving or exchanging of information" *(Webster's New World Dictionary)*. Communication consists of receiving information just as openly and willingly as it is given.

Kids often complain that no one ever listens to them, that no one understands how they feel, that they are nagged all the time. And many parents act the part of a drill sergeant barking out commands to the troops. Little wonder so many parents get written off and cannot communicate with their children.

Research and clinical psychologists

---

have learned techniques for more effective communication, techniques which parents can use in the home to open clogged lines of communication. One of their most important discoveries concerns an attitude that must be present before communication can begin. The attitude is called "acceptance."

Most of us assume that in order to develop our child's character, we must tell him what we do not like about him. We load our speech with preaching, admonishing, and commanding—all of which convey unacceptance. In many families, verbal communication consists only of criticism. Praise, appreciation, sympathy, and happiness are rarely expressed. Some parents even openly ask, "Why comment on good behavior? He's doing what I asked him to do!" Under such harangues, a young person finds it more comfortable to keep his thoughts and feelings to himself. Criticism makes a youngster defensive; so to avoid further complications he enters a silent world at home and communicates only with peers and well-chosen friends. A young person can speak freely to them, for he knows that anything he says will be accepted.

The American Institute of Family Relations reports the results of a survey on negative and positive comments to children. Mothers kept track of how many times they made negative remarks compared with how many positive comments they made to their children. The survey revealed that ten negative comments were made for every positive comment. In other words, 90 percent of their total communication was negative.

Apparently, teachers do a little better. A three-year survey in Orlando, Florida, public schools indicated that teachers were 75 percent negative. The same study also revealed that each negative comment had such a damaging effect on a child's self-image that it took four rounds of something favorable to undo it.

Parents recognize that "little pitchers have big ears," yet they frequently rattle on in an insensitive manner about the child in their presence. For instance, a friend of

Self-test on Communication

Let's evaluate how you communicate with your child. According to the scale of 1 - 5 as listed below score how it is you see yourself.

1. Never	2. Occasionally	3. Sometimes
4. Frequently	5. Always	

1. In our family we talk things over.   1 2 3 4 5

2. If I disagree with my child's opinions, I do so respectfully.   1 2 3 4 5

3. Before I make evaluations of any problem, I ask to hear   1 2 3 4 5
my child's point of view.

4. When listening to my child I maintain good eye contact   1 2 3 4 5
and frequently get on eye level with him/her.

5. I provide ample opportunity for my child to ask questions   1 2 3 4 5
and talk privately with me.

Discuss your responses with your partner or a friend.

mine had a rather difficult-to-manage 8-year-old. She constantly complained about how "impossible" Becky was, often while she stood within earshot. Such constant reminders encouraged Becky to build a mental picture of herself that read, "I am impossible." This self-image would now begin to affect her behavior at home, school, work and play in a most destructive, visible manner.

During our seminars, Harry and I are often besieged with parents who seek our personal opinions regarding the behavior of their child. They begin, "Ronnie this and Ronnie that" in rapid-fire sentences. All the while little Ronnie stands by listening wide-eyed. Parents sometimes seem oblivious to the damage they are doing to their child! From mother's latest description of him, Ronnie will add another detail to the mental picture he is constructing of himself. The more frequently such scenes are repeated, the more firmly the negative picture of self will become a permanent part of the psyche.

It is an act of love to accept another person just as he is, for to feel accepted means to feel loved. Feeling loved promotes growth of mind and body and is an effective therapeutic force in repairing psychological and physical damage. When a person feels truly accepted by another, he is then free to think about change—how he wants to grow, be different, or become more capable. Acceptance enables a child to actualize his potentials. But acceptance must be demonstrated so that he can feel it.

Communicating Acceptance—Is the Oxygen in the Family?

We can communicate our feelings and attitudes of acceptance to a child in a number of ways. Many times the lines of communication between parent and child are severed because the child detects feelings of rejection. Consequently the child will refrain from expressing his true feelings and thoughts to spare himself pain. And it isn't enough for a parent to *feel* accepting. He must be able to convey these feelings of acceptance in terms the child can readily understand. One of the easiest methods of conveying this kind of acceptance is by saying: "I understand what you mean" or "I see what you're saying."

Nonverbal messages or "body language"—gestures, postures, facial expressions, tones of voice—often speak louder and clearer than the voice. A pout, a sigh, a slammed door, can reveal feelings before anyone says a word. Many nonverbal messages set up barriers before conversation even begins.

Noninterference—another method of showing acceptance—can be shown a child by allowing him to play or participate in activities without interruption. To interrupt a child, to give instructions, to make suggestions, or to offer assistance while he is engaged in an activity reveals your lack of trust in the child's abilities. Dad may observe Stevie playing with an erector set. Dad may be able to spot trouble ahead in the construction if Stevie continues to build in the direction he has begun. However, if Dad stops Stevie and corrects the mistake Stevie may become resentful or discouraged. "I can never do anything to please my dad. What's the use?" Dad may not have meant to send a message of rejection, but he did. Very often forms of moving in, joining in, or checking up are really parental attempts to help their child measure up to their expectations. Noninterference during such times as these conveys positive, reinforcing thoughts such as: "I have confidence in your ability to complete this task satisfactorily." Meddling conveys unacceptance; noninterference conveys acceptance. Both affect the self-worth either positively or negatively.

Passive, interested listening can also communicate acceptance. The difference between passive listening and active listening centers in what you listen for. Passive listening simply means that as you listen for information you communicate your acceptance by saying nothing or very little. Professional counselors often use this technique to encourage the counselee to open up. No comments of judgment are conveyed, only acceptance. Here is a short example of passive listening.

Child: "Mommy, today at recess the teacher wouldn't let me go out to play."
Mommy: "Really?"
Child: "Yeah. She made me stay in and do make-up work."
Mommy: "H'mm."
Child: "I got all my work caught up, though."
Mommy: "Good."
Child: "From now on I'm not going to get behind."
Mommy: "Honey, I'm glad to hear it."

Mother could have said, "What did you do this time?" or "I'll call Miss Collins and talk with her about this." Such statements would close up the child. Passive listening allowed the child to open up, talk about the situation, and move toward solving the problem on her own. Her mother's passive listening along with her accompanying body language conveyed her interest and acceptance of her child's feelings.

Few parents have mastered this skill. They seem to feel it their duty to correct, refute, admonish, restate, or reinterpret everything their child says to them. This type of listening clearly signals to a child that you cannot accept his stories or feelings for what they are. Simple phrases used in passive listening might include: "How interesting," "Oh?" or "Really?" As a child is allowed to express his feelings in an atmosphere of acceptance he can more easily move toward solving problems on his own initiative.

However, parents cannot remain silent long in a good relationship. A youngster wants some type of verbal support, but the kind of response he gets will determine whether or not he will continue to open up to his parents. An effective verbal response is the "tell-me-more" invitation. This kind of communication is a door opener that does not communicate a judgmental evaluation of what the child is trying to say. It simply invites him to say more about the subject. Some simple "tell-me-mores" might include "No kidding," "How inter-esting," "I'm happy to hear that," "Good!" "Great!" "I see," "I understand."

More explicit "tell-me-mores" are "This sounds exciting! Tell me more," "I can see how important this is to you," "Tell me more about this," "I'd be interested in hearing what you have to say about this," or "I'd like to hear your point of view."

Such responses reveal your interest in your child, that he has the right to express his feelings on things, that you might learn something from him, that you'd like to hear his point of view, and that his ideas are important to you. They also keep up the conversation with him. He will not get the feeling that you want to take over the conversation and begin preaching, giving advice, or threatening. And the responses that you get from the "tell-me-mores" might surprise you, for this encourages a person to talk, move in, come closer, and share feelings.

Anyone would respond favorably to such attitudes. You feel good when others respect you, make you feel worthy, and indicate that what you have to say is interesting. And children are no different. We need to offer our children more opportunities to express themselves.

Parents who want open communication with their youngster must prepare themselves to hear some pretty threatening things. What good are you as a listener if you will hear only the good and the nice? Young people need to share their joys, yes, but they also need someone with whom they can share their problems, their heart-aches, their fears, their failures—someone who will not fly to pieces and shout incriminations.

More Than a Passing Acquaintance With Your Child's Feelings

Before we can learn how to listen, we must understand children's feelings. Suppose Sue runs to you and cries, "I wish I didn't have a sister! She's nothing but a tattletale!" You might reply, "Sue! What a dreadful thing to say! You know you really love her." You have just denied Sue's feelings. Wouldn't it have been better if you had moved in and eased her whopping case of jealousy?

Often when children share emotions with us, we proceed to tell them how they should or should not feel—as though our statements of logic can erase their feelings! We do this because we have been taught that negative feelings are bad and that we shouldn't have them. As a result, we feel less worthy or less mature when such feelings arise in us. Yet negative feelings are a fact of life. We cannot live from day to day without conflicts, and conflicts engender negative emotions. Unfortunately, most parents do not know how to release their own negative feelings or how to help their children channel their intense feelings.

Few people understand that the fastest way to get rid of negative emotions is to express them. If we store them up inside, they can form bitterness, which often leads to a resentment that will erupt later in unhealthy symptoms. Bill Gothard, lecturer and theologian of Basic Youth Conflicts, tells the story of a little boy who said, "My daddy made me sit down, but I'm standing up inside!" By telling children to calm down, not to be angry, or to stop the feeling, we push them from us. It tells them that a part of them—what they are feeling—is unacceptable, and they are terrible persons to have such bad feelings. Consequently, if they repeatedly strive to hide such feelings even from themselves, a mental disturbance may develop. Furthermore, repression of feelings plays havoc with self-respect.

When emotions surface, listen empathetically, accept the feelings, and provide acceptable outlets such as active sports, hobbies, music, drama, or even old-fashioned work.

Cornering the Market on Listening

Invitations to communicate open the door for mutual understanding, but parents need to know how to keep the door open. *Active listening* is an excellent skill for this purpose. Not only is information gleaned by active listening but, more importantly, the true feelings behind the words of the child

become discernible. It is best used when the parent picks up clues that the child is experiencing a problem or emotional turmoil. The parent should listen for the meaning behind the problem (the feelings) and then restate the feeling so there is no misunderstanding of the meaning. When you think you understand, you then put it into your own words and send it back to the other person for verification. If you have not identified the child's feelings properly, he will likely say, "No, that isn't what I meant" and correct you. At times it will be necessary for you to prod gently to uncover the feelings behind the words. The "tell-me-

mores" and gentle questions will help here.

As your child moves deeper and deeper into the problem he is experiencing, you must restrain the impulse to solve his problem or tell him what to do. Anyone in the grip of an emotional problem cannot think clearly, so by assisting your child to express the problem aloud, you help him learn how to handle negative feelings in a positive way. Your child will also learn that his feelings are safe with you, and you are thereby establishing a solid relationship with him.

Here are some short examples of parents who understand active listening.

Example 1:

Child: "Joanie took my book and hid it from me. She makes me so mad I just want to hit her."

Parent: "You're upset over this. It's no fun to have something taken away from you and then hidden."

Child: "It sure isn't."

Example 2:

Child: "Since Eddie moved away, I don't have anyone to play with. All day long there is nothing to do. I'm so bored!"

Parent: "You're lonely since Eddie moved away. It's no fun to lose your best friend and feel like you have no one to do things with."

Child: "You bet. It's terrible. And I'll never find another neat friend like Eddie."

Example 3:

Teen: "Dad, when you were a teenager and dating around, what kind of girl were you interested in? What appealed to you most?"

Dad: "It sounds like you're concerned about what kind of dating partner you'll be."

Teen: "Yeah. Here I am 14, and I've never had a real date with a guy. My other friends all have."

In each of the previous examples, the parents decoded the child's feelings properly as indicated by the child. But it isn't always easy to determine precisely what the feeling is.

Dr. Haim Ginott, in his best seller, *Between Parent and Child* (page 18), also stresses listening for hidden meanings. His classic example revolves around a young boy's first visit to nursery school. "Who made those ugly pictures?" the boy asked.

His mother tried to shush him, but the teacher broke in and explained, "In here you don't have to paint pretty pictures. You can paint mean pictures if you feel like it."

Then the boy asked, "Who broke this fire engine?"

Mother answered, "What difference does it make to you who broke it? You don't know anyone here."

The teacher responded, "Toys are for playing. Sometimes they get broken. It happens."

In each case, Dr. Ginott says, the boy actually wanted to know what happened to children who painted poor pictures or broke toys. The mother perceived the words and questions, but not the feeling behind them. The teacher picked up the child's feelings behind the question and then reassured him.

In the following example the mother consistently uses active listening to help Natalie open up, think the problem through on her own, evaluate herself and her friend, and begin to solve the problem.

Natalie: "I was with Jim Harder again last night, and he's really the greatest guy I've met in a long time. I really go for him. In fact . . .

Mother: [pauses as she weighs her words], I could *even* marry him!''

Mother: "Tell me about him." (A door opener.)

Natalie: "He's so considerate and mannerly. He treats me like a queen! He's not at all like the roughnecks around school."

Mother: "It made you feel good to be treated like a lady."

Natalie: "Wow, yeah! I've only been with him a few times, but last night we were together, and you know, he seated me at the table, helped me with my coat, and even opened the car door for me!"

Mother: "Sounds like you really enjoyed these attentions."

Natalie: "I really did. He's just great and a good conversationalist too. We never ran out of things to talk about. I could talk to him for hours."

Mother: "You really feel good after talking with him, huh?''

Natalie: "Yes. I really feel like something special when I'm with that guy, but you know something, Mom? He did mention something that bothered me just a little. He doesn't plan to finish high school. He's working at a store on the south end of town and he says he'd rather work there than go to school. It's a really good job though."

Mother: "Sounds like you're puzzled about whether he's doing the right thing or not."

Natalie: "Yeah, I did wonder about it. I kind of feel that everyone should at least finish high school. Not everyone should go to college, but I've always planned on going to college. Wonder how it works in marriage if the wife goes to college and the husband drops out of high school . . . ''

Mother: "Sounds like you have some real questions in your mind about this."

Natalie: "Well, it's not too serious but something to think about. And you know what else he told me that I'm kind of worried about? He feels it's perfectly all right to help his friends out with a few answers on an exam."

Mother: "You aren't too sure about this, it sounds like."

Natalie: "Well, I know it goes on all the time, but it really isn't quite fair, at least not to the kids who don't cheat. Maybe they're the ones who win in the end even if their grades are lower. Well, I gotta go get at my homework 'cuz Jim is calling me later, and I want to have plenty of time to talk to him."

During this active-listening exchange, Mother put her own thoughts and feelings aside to listen to Natalie's feelings. She showed an interest in Natalie's friend but refrained from judgment, which took real self-control on her part. Jim is a nice-enough fellow, but he comes from a family of "do-nothing" people. Mother really was hoping for someone a little more special for Natalie.

It bothered her to leave the conversation unfinished, because she felt that little or nothing had been solved. But as she reviewed the comments in her mind, she realized that Natalie had begun to move into the problem-solving stage by questioning some of Jim's shortcomings and habits that bothered her.

Natalie's conversation with her mother had allowed her to see Jim as she had never seen him before. Two weeks later Natalie quietly confided in her mother that she and Jim were still friends but that she wouldn't see so much of him. She reasoned, "Manners and good conversation are important, but they aren't everything!"

In the next scene the responses between father and son are restricted to attack and defense.

Dad: "Stan, weren't you supposed to mow the lawn today? That's one of your jobs, you know."

Stan: "I couldn't do it because I couldn't

Exercise in Listening for Feelings

DIRECTIONS: Children communicate to parents much more than their words imply. Behind words often lie feelings. Read each of the following typical "messages" and in the column at the right jot down the primary or main feeling you heard. A list of feelings is given below:

UNLOVED   COMPETENCY GUILT
FEAR   ANGER   FRUSTRATION
DISCOURAGEMENT GLAD   LONELINESS

1. Wow! Only eight more days till vacation. _____
2. Look, Daddy! I got a perfect grade on my science paper. _____

3. I don't want to go alone. Will you go with me? _____
4. Sharon and I had an argument. I was angry and said things I shouldn't have. _____
5. I've tried everything I know to please that teacher. The harder I try, the worse things get. _____
6. I'm never speaking to John again, and don't you dare let him in the house. _____

EXERCISE IN ACTIVE LISTENING

Active listening means responding to the "feelings" in verbal messages rather than the "facts." Circle the replies that you sense most closely respond to the implied feeling.

1. CHILD FALLS DOWN AND SKINS KNEE. SOBBING, SHE CRIES: "I FELL DOWN AND HURT MY KNEE."
   a. Stop acting like a crybaby. It isn't that bad.
   b. It will feel better soon. Don't cry. Let's go get a cookie.
   c. Don't be so clumsy.
   d. It hurts to fall down and scrape your knee. Let's put a band-aid on it.

2. CHILD COMPLAINS AFTER PLAYING WITH A NEIGHBOR CHILD. "I HATE JOHN. HE'S THE MEANEST KID I KNOW, AND I'M NEVER PLAYING WITH HIM AGAIN."
   a. Freddie, don't talk like that. You'll get over it.
   b. Calm down, Fred. You're so upset you can't even talk straight.
   c. It sounds as though you and John have had a misunderstanding.
   d. Shame on you for talking about John that way.

find any oil for it."

Dad: "Well, you better get the oil and do it tomorrow. And, do it right the first time while you're at it."

Stan: "What do you mean, do it right the first time? When I mow the neighbors' lawns they think it's OK, and they pay me without any hassle."

Dad: "Don't give me any back talk, young man. You did a sloppy job on our lawn last time. That's why you had to do it over two more times. You just do it right the *first* time, that's all."

Stan: "Do it right! Nobody can do anything good enough to please you."

Dad: "If you'd do something right the first time once in a while—that would please me."

Stan: "Sure! Like when I made the honor roll and you asked how come there were a couple of kids ahead of me! I'm not perfect, you know!"

Dad: "Watch your tongue!"

Stan: "How come you always yell at me? The other kids always get away with everything, and you never say anything to them, the brats!"

Dad: "That's not true, and you know it!"

Stan: "It is too!"

Dad: "Stan, take that back. Don't you talk to me like that. You're wrong, and you're going to tell me you know you're wrong."

Stan (silence).

Dad: "Stan, I *am* fair with you, and you're going to apologize, right now!"

Stan (cold, stony silence).

Dad: "All right! If you're going to be disrespectful and defiant on top of doing sloppy work, you're going to be restricted for a week unless you apologize right now."

Stan: "Yeah, see! You never restrict them. Just me!"

Dad: "That's enough from you. Go to your room. You're not going to sass me."

Stan storms down the hallway and slams the door to his room.

Dad (calling down the hall): "That will cost

you another three days of restriction."

Notice that the initial problem, the lawn, received only superficial attention. Since both father and son attacked, and since both defended their attitudes and statements, little was solved.

From the original subject, the topics wandered from Stan not doing things "right," to the neighbors and grades, to "no one can please you," to the other children, and to favoritism (perhaps not actual, but perceived this way by Stan). Topic-jumping, an unmistakable mark of poor communication, is similar to someone throwing a rock, then taking cover while ducking an incoming rock, and at the same time looking for another rock to throw. Stan and his father listened only for an opening in which to rebut or spew out. Neither listened to the undercurrent of "who is going to be the boss here," or "who is going to save face?" The responses were on the level of the *content* of the communications, while the anger, frustration, and other feelings went untouched. Hostility and recriminations were rampant.

As a result of not dealing with either the topic or the emotions expressed, both father and son went away with additional unresolved problems and unexpressed emotions. Stan left feeling put down, angry, and hostile. He also felt justified for his negative feelings; after all, "Who wouldn't be mad at someone who yells at you all the time like that!" Dad, on the other hand, felt frustrated, disobeyed, challenged, and angry. He, too, felt justified about his negative feelings. "So what can you do with a kid like that? He needs someone to take a firm stand with him."

The end results? A mutually frustrating stalemate. And it need not be that way. There were ample opportunities for each to listen to the words and, more importantly, the *emotions* behind them.

Five-year-old Anne-Marie brought home from school a ring which was not hers. The first version of where the ring came from centered upon a girl who "gave" it to her. Upon questioning, it finally came to light that Anne-Marie had found it in a wastebasket at school.

61

A few days after the incident, Anne-Marie asked if she could please talk to Mommy after supper. Mother agreed, and the two of them went to Anne-Marie's room, where she confided that she wanted to talk about "all kinds of things," which she did—friends, school, a particular teacher with whom she was having problems—everything, Mother knew, but the ring.

Mother finally opened the door to the ring subject by asking if she wanted to talk about the ring. She did! Anne-Marie was most worried about what she had done and whether it might be stealing. Mother relied on active listening, and Anne-Marie concluded that she would take the ring back to the room where she had found it.

Mother left the room, and Anne-Marie was joined by her sister with whom she shared the room. "Katie," Mother overheard Anne-Marie say, "when you get a thing that's bothering you, it's a good thing to talk it out with Mommy. It sure feels good to get everything out at once!"

Active listening does five specific things for the child:

1 *It helps the child learn how to handle negative feelings.* Your acceptance of your child's feelings will help him learn that negative emotions are a part of life and that he is not "bad" for having such feelings. It will also help him learn not to bottle up his emotions but to seek an acceptable outlet to vent his feelings.

2 *It provides a basis for a close relationship between parent and child.* Everyone enjoys the feeling of being listened to and understood by another. The experience creates a bond of closeness that will draw parent and child together in respect and trust.

3 *It helps a child move toward independent problem solving.* When a person is allowed the privilege of talking aloud about a problem he is facing, he can view it more clearly. This is one of the advantages of seeking guidance from a counselor when you have encountered a family problem. Being able to verbalize in an atmosphere of complete acceptance, being able to use another person as a "sounding board," helps us think more clearly and move toward a more acceptable solution. Children, as well as adults, will find communicating with an active listener beneficial when they must solve a problem.

4 *It teaches a child to listen to a parent and to others.* The earlier and more frequently you demonstrate to your child that you will listen to his ideas and problems, the more willing he will be to listen in return. If you feel that your child never listens to what you say, it might be that you are "modeling" this behavior to him.

5 *It encourages a child to think for himself.* Active listening encourages a youngster to think and to talk about problems rather than to run away from them. We as parents cannot follow our children all the days of our lives (or theirs) giving them advice, offering solutions, or making decisions for them. It is our duty as parents, however, to equip our child with the ability to deal with and solve the problems of life. Active listening provides the basis for a relationship of trust and warmth, whereas constant advice, solutions, warnings, and lectures destroy relationships.

Active listening is not a Band-aid to be pulled from the medicine cabinet whenever you think you can patch up your child's problems or manipulate his environment. It isn't as much a skill as it is an attitude. If the attitude of acceptance is missing from active listening, your child will recognize it. Your phony, mechanical responses will produce feelings of suspicion and resentment. Before active listening can be effective you must *want* to hear your child out and be willing to take the time to do so. If you are too busy, don't begin the conversation. Your mood is also important when you listen actively. If you don't feel up to listening, don't begin.

The key word in active listening is *acceptance*—acceptance of your child's feelings, ideas, or opinions in spite of how different they might be from how you want your child to respond to life. Feelings are transitory. They change, rarely remaining fixed in any of us. Demonstrate to your child that you trust his ability to handle his emotions and to solve his problems.

Every child will at some point in life experience problems at school or at home, with his classmates, teachers, siblings, or himself. Use active listening during such times. When your child learns that he can get the acceptance and support for solving problems on his own, he will develop feelings of worth and self-confidence. You will actually protect him from developing those disturbing emotional problems that others encounter. But don't wait until some serious situation arises. Use active listening every day in the little events that upset even very young children.

Bobby: "Mommy, Mommy, I want you. [Crying begins.] Come here!"

Mommy: "It sounds like you are upset over something, Bobby."

Bobby: (Still blubbering) "I want you to stay with me in my room tonight."

Mommy: "You're upset about having to stay in your room tonight. It's scary to be left alone in the dark sometimes."

Knowing that his mother genuinely understood and accepted his feelings immediately calmed Bobby—far more than all the adult logic she might have showered upon him.

Some typical responses that a more insensitive parent might have come up with include: "Bobby, stop that crying this minute! There's nothing to be afraid of." (A denial of his feelings) Or "Only babies are afraid of the dark. Are you a baby?" (A put-down) Or "It's silly to be afraid of the dark, Bobby. There are no monsters or bogeymen here. Now stop it!" (A denial and an order, which, by the way, cannot be enforced. There is no way mother can *force* Bobby to stop being afraid.)

In the example cited, mother realized that Bobby was frightened and had a lonely moment in his life. She accepted how badly he felt and how scared he was. Contrary to popular thought, crying can actually be defused by accepting the feelings behind it rather than denying it. When a child cries, he is often looking for validation of the hurt he is experiencing. Once he feels someone understands, the crying usually lessens or ceases.

It is better not to make a big thing over a small fear or hurt and to minimize the situation if possible. However, if a youngster is frightened or injured, this can best be accomplished through active listening.

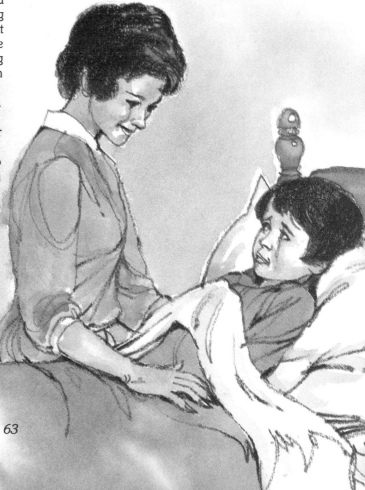

Safeguards Along the Way

However, active listening is not a way to guide a child to your view as the correct answer. If you feel you have latched onto a new method of manipulating your child's thinking, you don't understand the value of active listening. Although one of the main functions of parenthood is to guide a child and teach him values, this cannot be directly accomplished through active listening. It is neither the time nor the method.

Neither should parents encourage their child to express his feelings and then begin offering suggestions or attempting to set him straight. Children catch on to this method of being drawn out and consider it a put-down.

Don't get lost or confused by the facts—respond to feelings with feeling. Try to understand how your child feels when he is talking. Put yourself in his shoes. One father became discouraged after his first attempt at active listening. He said that his daughter told him to stop repeating everything she said. At first it may seem difficult to find the feeling but easy to merely parrot back what the child just said.

Be alert to times when your youngster just doesn't feel like discussing his problems. Don't probe after he's indicated he is through discussing the problem. Respect his right to privacy. And do not use active listening when a child asks for specific information, such as: "How much milk should I buy?" or "What time will you be home?"

Something may happen to you when you practice active listening. Your own attitudes or opinions may change as you really understand accurately how another feels. Opening yourself to the experiences of others invites the possibility of reevaluating your own experienc. And this can be scary, because a defensive person cannot afford to expose himself to ideas and views that differ from his own. A mature and flexible person, however, is not afraid of being changed.

Someone has aptly pointed out that we were created with two ears but only one tongue, and when parents learn to hold that one tongue and open their ears, they will find marked changes in dinner-table discussion.

Listen to your child. He is a small human being filled with wonder and curiosity and eagerness. Listen to his voice with your ears and eyes and heart. Sometimes his voice will be filled with singsong and chatter; sometimes with desperation and need, inquiry and indecision; sometimes with enthusiasm for a newfound shred of knowledge and youthful wisdom. Give him the greatest gift of all—yourself. Make your home a place for sharing ideas and thoughts without fear of humiliation and ridicule. Your children will start bringing up all kinds of problems that they never discussed with you before, and home will become a place for growth.

Not only is active listening an effective tool for communicating acceptance and developing a warm relationship, it is also an exceptional method of teaching your child to make choices and to be responsible for his own behavior. Since active listening does not try to influence your youngster's choices, he learns that you trust his ability to make wise decisions. Once you master the skill of active listening, it puts you in a position to help your child look more creatively at the problems he faces. Statements such as: "Is it possible that this happened because . . .?" or "What do you suppose is the reason behind this incident?" or "How do you think this whole thing got started in the first place?" may help a child think through a situation. Sometimes role-playing helps. You become the child, and your child becomes the parent.

Again it should be emphasized that you *must* become skillful at active listening *before* you attempt to enter this phase. If you try these latter suggestions before you have established a climate of acceptance and trust, your perceptive youngster will recognize it as another form of manipulation. Even in this phase of problem solving your motive should not be to try to influence, direct, or force your child to accept your solutions. Your purpose here should be only to help your child learn how to handle his feelings and to develop his ability to think clearly and solve problems.

Is This Any Way to Talk?

"How do we get him to listen to us? That's what I want to know," sighs a frustrated father. "How can we put across our ideas without irritating our child?"

Communication is a two-way street. Both parent and child need to send. But the timing is important. If listening doesn't settle the matter, then talk. But sending a message when a child is in an emotional upheaval simulates someone trying to put up wallpaper in a room full of steam. The paper just won't stick. It is much the same way with feelings. Your child can't hear you when he is churning with emotion.

Yes, parents must teach, persuade, use logic, share reactions, and even reassure their children, but the secret is the timing. Get the feelings out first. "Listen today; send tomorrow." And it isn't always necessary to wait a whole day. But wait at least a half hour after the issue has cooled.

Parents must also develop effective methods of communicating their needs to their children, for parents have needs too. Children often annoy, disturb, and frustrate us. They can be thoughtless, inconsiderate, destructive, noisy, and demanding. They often cause extra work, delay us when we are late, pester us when we are tired, or mess up a clean house.

When a child causes his parent a problem, there are several options to consider. Depending on the situation, a parent might decide to ignore the misbehavior, use active listening, employ natural or arbitrary consequences (see description in the chapter on discipline), or send the child what is called an "I-statement." Most frequently, however, parents take over the situation, crack the whip, and *make* the child do what they want him to do. Parents who assume this role might be termed commanding officers. They attempt to

Exercise in "I-messages"

The following exercise will help you practice the skill of sending "I-messages." Read the situation on the left and the "You-message" in the middle, and then write your own "I-message" to the right.

Situation	instead of saying . . .	say . . .
1. Father is watching a special on TV. Child thoughtlessly begins noisy play.	"Cut out the racket! Go to your room and make that kind of noise!"	
2. Child keeps getting up after he has been put to bed.	"If you don't stay in bed, you're going to get a spanking!"	
3. Parent is making an important phone call when children begin disruptive behavior.	"Every time I get on the phone you begin acting like savages. Now stop it!"	
4. Child fails to vacuum living room before company arrives as asked.	"You never do anything you're asked to do. You're the laziest kid I know."	

"If I'da knowed you'd like me to tell my side, I'da planned a speech."

dictate, threaten, or direct their child toward forced obedience. The commanding officer sounds much like this: "I said you'd better get busy, and I do mean *now!*" "You had better never do that again, or I'll tan your hide!" "Don't you *dare* speak to me like that *ever* again!" "You do it now or else!" The commanding officer does not wait for the child to initiate considerate behavior. He hops right in and *tells* the youngster what he must do.

Perhaps you are thinking, "What else are parents for if it isn't to tell their kids what to do, especially when they are misbehav-ing and causing the parents difficulties?" Telling children what to do creates "parent deafness." Children resent it when they are told what they must or should do. This kind of communication sets up roadblocks to effective communication and implies that you don't think the child is capable of initiating good behavior on his own. It also insinuates that he is not on a par with you since you require instant and unquestioned obedience.

Another group of ineffective phrases are put-downs, which accuse, reproach, and denounce through negative evaluations:

"You're the slowest child I know." Put-downs involve name calling: "You're such a dummy!" Ridicule and humiliation are also a part of put-downs: "How can you be so stupid!" or "Don't you have any brains?" Other put-downs that ought to be banned from the parental lexicon are: "Can't you see I'm busy?" "I've told you a hundred times. . ." "What's the matter with you?" "Are you deaf?" "Where in the world. . ." and "How many times do I have to tell you . . ."

As a long-range result, the child who is repeatedly put down by being called stupid, lazy, mean, or ignorant comes to picture himself as a no-good. Eventually he will accept that judgment and try to live up to it. When borne from early childhood, feelings of worthlessness tend to follow the child into adulthood, often handicapping every aspect of his life.

Putting It Across Effectively

Perhaps you are wondering what method you can use to communicate your frustration when the child is misbehaving or causing a problem. In learning the difference between ineffective and effective communication during such situations, you will need to become acquainted with "You- and I-statements." Most commands and put-downs contain strong evaluations of the other person. If you go back to a previous page where the "commanding officer" puts down his child and circle all the "yous" involved, you'll discover a devaluation of the child.

If you could simply tell your child how his unacceptable behavior makes you feel, it would be what is referred to as an I-statement. "I can't watch television when there is so much noise here." "I really get upset when I find that your chores have not been done." "I can't fix supper when there are blocks all over the kitchen floor."

Notice, the parent selected *suitable* words to let the child know that parents have feelings too. For the parent who is tired and does not feel like playing, "You are such a bother" is a poor selection of words to convey tired feelings. I-statements

contain an explanation of how the parent *feels* about the annoying behavior. They do not condemn the child but refer only to the youngster's unacceptable behavior, differentiating between the child and his behavior.

I-statements are much more likely to produce positive behavior changes and to reduce those feelings of resistance and rebellion that often accompany you-statements. The child interprets you-statements as a judgment of his worth, whereas I-statements merely refer to the parent's feelings.

An effective I-statement has three parts:

1. A statement of how the child's unacceptable behavior makes you feel.

2. A nonblameful description of the child's behavior (it is acceptable to use the word *you* in this description).

3. An explanation regarding the tangible effect of that behavior on you.

The format of an I-statement, then, would be: "I feel __(1)__ when you __(2)__ because __(3)__.

Here are more examples of effective I-statements. Notice that they contain no commands and no put-downs. The parent does not tell the child what to do.

Example 1: Father is napping on the couch after supper but is awakened by quarreling between two brothers. "I can't sleep with so much noise going on. I've had a tough day, and I want to relax without listening to all this bickering."

Example 2: Mother is sewing. The young child has discovered the plug and keeps pulling it out of the socket. "I don't have much time to sew today. It really slows me down when I have to keep replacing the plug. I don't have time to play now."

Example 3: Son, who often forgets to brush his teeth, appears all smiles for supper with his teeth coated with food debris. "I love to see you smile, but I can't stand to look at dirty teeth while I'm eating. It makes me lose my appetite."

Example 4: Teen-ager is listening to music of which parent doesn't approve. "I can't stand music like that. It affects my nerves and makes me jumpy and irritable."

I-statements can bring out some startling results. It surprises children to learn how their parents really *feel*. Often they say, "I didn't know that it bugged you so much" or "I didn't think you really cared if I . . . " or "How come you never told me before how you really felt?" Even adults are often unaware how their behavior affects others, and children are not unlike adults. We are all basically selfish in pursuit of our own goals, but children are particularly self-centered. Irresponsibility will frequently turn into responsibility once children understand the impact of their behavior on others.

A family was traveling in their station wagon on vacation, and the children were getting quite boisterous in the back. Finally Father reached the end of his rope, abruptly pulled the car to the side of the road, turned around, and declared, "I can't stand all this noise. This is my vacation too. I want to enjoy it, which I can't do with all this noise. I get nervous, and headaches come on from so much horsing around. I have a right to enjoy myself too." The kids, who had been carrying on in their childish ways without thinking of others, became apologetic and much more cooperative.

When our son Rodney was 13 he was doing something that really irritated me. In accordance with what I teach, I sent an I-statement. "I really get irritated when you do that because it causes extra work for me." He hardly gave notice that he heard me. I repeated the same statement. This time I thought what I had said might be penetrating his gray matter, but it still bounced right off him. And so I stated it a third time before he finally changed his behavior.

Some of you are probably asking, "Why repeat something over and over when you could tell him once to cut it out and get the same results?" First, Rodney *chose* to change his behavior in respect for my needs. He was learning to respect the rights and needs of others. Second, and most important, he *chose* a right course of action without being *told* what to do. And *every* time a child can make a right choice without instructions, he is moving toward self-control and maturity—the ultimate goal in child training.

Please note: I-statements can effectively change a child's unacceptable behavior, but that is not the main purpose for sending one. The main reason for using I-statements as opposed to you-statements is to release *your* feelings of irritation before you get angry.

More about I-statements: (1) Use them when you are first irritated. Don't wait till you are angry. (2) Avoid sending a solution or telling your child what to do. (3) If your child does not respond to your first I-statement—as may often happen when you first begin to use them—send another one that is perhaps a little stronger, louder, or with more feeling.

I-statements communicate more effectively because they place the responsibility with the child to change his behavior. They help him learn responsibility for his own behavior. They tell him that you trust him to handle the situation constructively and to respect your needs.

Over a period of time, I-statements can do more to encourage a child to change his unacceptable behavior—without damaging his self-respect or hurting a relationship—than all the rewards, punishment, or nagging most parents have unsuccessfully used.

Where's the Volume Switch on Your Voice?

Arnold Bennett said that when you talk to someone else, you actually speak twice: once through what you say and again in the way you say it. He is certain that 90 percent of the friction in life is caused by the tone of voice used.

Often when we speak to our children, we use a tone which indicates that we already know they have no intention of doing what we asked them to do. Other times there is a threatening tone in our voices which warns, "You had better not do that if you know what's good for you!"

Exhausted parents frequently speak irritably to a child through outbursts of scolding or menacing threats. This manner of speech excites feelings of anger and resentment within the child, and as a result, he becomes irritable also, and all are miserable. The parents blame the child, thinking him disobedient and unruly, when they themselves have caused the trouble.

If Communication Has Broken Down

If communication has broken down in your family, it is up to you to do something about it. If it hasn't, see to it that it doesn't, for it is an unhappy home that lacks interaction. Keep little differences from growing into big ones by caring for them while they are tiny and can be handled. Don't let your child keep his anger with you buried inside to fester and erupt in later years. The Scriptural admonition, "Let not the sun go down upon your wrath" (Ephesians 4:26), holds for children and parents. Heal the wounds while they are scratches and easy to mend.

The initiative for restoring broken communication rests in your hands as the mature adult. It hardly matters what the child did to kindle your wrath. You have erred since you allowed the breach to remain and widen without repairing it. Find a way that will reach your youngster. At first you may want to rely on the nonverbal language of kindnesses—tangible loving acts which tell the child that you love him. To most youngsters, actions speak louder than words. Later use active listening and I-statements.

Perhaps after experimenting with active listening and I-statements, you still haven't solved all the communication problems that exist in your home, but if you can discover, maybe for the first time in your parental experience, that you are really in touch with the way your child feels about his problems and yours, you have succeeded. Genuine communication with young people doesn't necessarily mean a daily rehash of every event. It does imply daily pleasant association. Many parents feel that they have lost communication with their children because there isn't endless chatter in their homes, but endless chatter may be a cover-up for a deep-seated problem. Genuine communication has taken place if you are in touch with your child and are increasing your ability to accept him as an individual with rights, needs, and values of his own.

There are no magic cure-alls once communication has deteriorated, and even the best communication requires careful daily nurture. But when parents and children treat each other with respect and can recognize each other's feelings, then the generation gap is on its way to being bridged.

Further reading you will enjoy . . .

Dinkmeyer, Don and Gary McKay. *RAISING A RESPONSIBLE CHILD.*
Dobson, James. *DARE TO DISCIPLINE.*
Dobson, James. *THE STRONG-WILLED CHILD*, chapter 8.
Dreikurs, Rudolf. *CHILDREN: THE CHALLENGE.*
Ginott, Haim G. *BETWEEN PARENT AND CHILD.*
Ginott, Haim G. *BETWEEN PARENT AND TEENAGER*, chapters 3-6.
Gordon, Thomas. *PARENT EFFECTIVENESS TRAINING*, chapters 3-7.

Chapter at a Glance

Chapter 4

The Rewards of Discipline

Webster's New International Dictionary, second edition, defines discipline as "1. Teaching; instruction, tutoring." Yet many people think of discipline only as punishment. In this chapter, disciplining a child means not punishing him for stepping out of line but teaching him the way he should go. In fact, the word _discipline_ is related to the word _disciple._ Thus when you discipline your child, you are really training him to be a disciple or learner of you, his teacher.

Discipline and Self-respect

Early in the parenting process most parents recognize that they must limit their child's activities and teach him to control his behavior. They sense that if they do not begin early, their child may be well on the road to Tyrantville!

At this point, many parents make a common mistake. When they begin the discipline process, they label their child "bad" when in fact he is not bad at all. For example, a mother suffering from an intense headache might tell her son that he is a "bad boy" for slamming the door. In reality it was little more than childish exuberance that caused the door to slam. Parents and teachers frequently label a child naughty or bad for actions that may

B. Arbitrary forms of punishment
  1. Deprivation
  2. Isolation
  3. Spankings
C. Why spankings do not always work
  1. Inconsistency
  2. Strong-willed child
  3. Delayed action
  4. Too gentle
D. When not to spank
  1. Do not spank teen-agers
  2. Do not spank infants under six months
E. How to spank
  1. Using a hand or instrument
  2. Whippings are rarely needed

VI. **The Difficult Child**
  A. Temperament determines behavior
  B. Types of temperament
    1. Marvelous Margareta
    2. Difficult Darren
    3. Slow-to-warm-up Steve
  C. Do not give up on your child

VII. **Obedience Is a Must**
  A. A child should obey instantly
  B. Parents should not "give in"
  C. Parents should avoid disciplining for unenforceable matters
  D. Too much discipline is confusing

73

have caused the adult a problem, but this does not mean the child is bad. By constantly referring to negative behavior adults may cause a child to identify with his bad actions and thus induce in him negative feelings about himself.

Parental anger, aggravation, and impatience when disciplining reinforces the child's idea that they are punishing him because they do not like him. When parents become angry as a result of their child's inconvenient behavior, resenting the extra work the child causes and the price of parenthood, the child perceives that he is a burden rather than a blessing. Anger often forces a child to compensate for his feelings of low self-worth through defiance in order to establish his identity.

If a child feels respected when his parents correct him, he will not lose respect for himself even though he may have done something very wrong. He will feel bad about his mistake, but he will believe that he can overcome the problem. On the other hand, when a child is not respected during correction, he will tend to despair, and will not only learn to fear punishment but will also feel worthless and bad.

Never should discipline destroy self-respect. Yet how quickly and easily this is done, especially when a parent is caught off guard or embarrassed by a child's behavior. Take for example a mother who has caught her child hitting another youngster. Grabbing him roughly, she begins a tirade of criticism, "Why you little brat! You know better than to hit another child. What are you—a bully or something? I'll teach you never to hit again!" And mother proceeds to beat the frightened child.

Another mother handles the identical incident another way. "Jason, hitting others is bad, and I can't allow you to do it. Please come over here and sit on this chair for a few minutes. Then we'll talk about it." This mother distinguishes between the misbehavior and the child. Hitting was bad, but not the youngster. The child's self-respect has been preserved, whereas his bad actions corrected. She tells him exactly what it was that he did wrong, yet she does not personally condemn him.

If you attack your child's self-respect for poor conduct, he may well be motivated to defy you and harbor feelings of revenge. The less your child feels loved during these times, the more he will be motivated to defy your authority or to look for other deviant methods of getting back at you. The more you meet your child's basic need for self-respect during the disciplinary procedure, the less he will show defiance.

Discipline Is Not a Four-letter Word

The object of discipline is the training of the child for self-government. Parents' ultimate goal in disciplining a child is to help him become a self-regulating person. Since his self-concept will largely determine the extent of his self-regulation, discipline must not inadvertently attack his self-image. There is a vast difference between telling a child that he is bad for kicking you and saying, "Kicking is bad, and I won't tolerate it." It is relatively harmless to attack another's actions when he can learn to change. But it is disastrous to attack his self-respect, for he cannot become another person.

The Bible admonishes parents to "train up a child in the way he should go" (Proverbs 22:6). It does not teach parents to fulfill the wishes of their child, and a child may not always welcome training. In fact, he may stubbornly argue on every point. But, remember, you are the teacher, the trainer. He is the pupil or trainee. He does not decide the rules. He follows them whether he disagrees or not. And what if he refuses to obey and follow the guidelines you have established? Then you must help him learn to obey. The challenge and test of parenthood comes when a parent faces defiance, resistance, rebellion, and other similar reactions.

The Discipline Summit—Where's the Starting Point?

Discipline should begin the moment an infant begins to assert a determined will and choose his own way. This may be termed an unconscious education. Leland E.

Glover, a well-known psychologist, offers this advice to parents: "What years are the most important ones in human development? Experts in child care generally agree that, excluding the all-important prenatal period, the first year of life is ordinarily the most important one. Furthermore, the first month of the first year is the most important month, and each successive month is important to a lesser degree than the one that preceded it. Why? Because the human being matures most rapidly during the first month; and then, with minor exceptions, the maturation rate diminishes gradually in the next ten to fourteen years.

"What does this information suggest to you as a parent? It means that your child will probably need you more right now than he ever will need you again. Never again will he be as young or as immature as he is today. Never again will you have this opportunity to give your child a good start in life" (*How to Give Your Child a Good Start in Life,* p. 18).

Even an infant knows whether he can manipulate his parents, and if he can he will. If an infant is not taught to conform to a schedule that fits into the family routine by the time he is 6 months of age, he will train his parents to fit into his schedule!

Avenues to Well-Governed Children

1. *Gain and maintain respect.* The respect that a child maintains for his parents is in direct proportion to the respect he'll hold for the laws of the land, the police force, school authorities, and society in general.

Respect, however, is a two-way street. A mother should not expect respect from Jimmy if she doesn't respect him. She should not embarrass or belittle him in front of his friends. If Dad is sarcastic and critical of Jimmy, he should not expect respect back. Jimmy may fear his dad enough so that he dares not show his true feelings of hate and revenge, but they will emerge in future years.

Parents who gain and maintain their child's respect during early years will have his respect during teen-age years. And parents must realize that if they aren't worthy of respect, neither is their religion, their morals, their country, or any of their standards. It is in this matter of mutual respect that the real "generation gap" occurs rather than in just a breakdown of communication. Children are keen observers and exceptionally perceptive. You can never expect your child to grant you more respect than they see you give to your own parents.

The most important lessons learned in the home are not reading, writing, and arithmetic, as some suppose, but respect, obedience, reverence, and self-control. These must be taught patiently, tenderly, lovingly, and consistently every day so as to become a part of the child's character for the rest of his life.

2. *Set limits.* My hometown of Tacoma, Washington, is famous, among other things, for its ill-fated Narrows Bridge, which toppled a number of years ago. Shortly after the bridge collapsed, my father took our family to view the two towers and stumps of roadway which jutted into the air—all that remained after the tons of concrete gave way during high winds. A new bridge was completed eleven years later.

Let's imagine now that my family and I wish to return to Tacoma for a vacation and that one of the scenic spots we plan to visit is this bridge. As we approach the waterway, we notice that the bridge is intact except for one thing. For some unknown reason the

guardrails at the sides of the roadway have been removed. We are quite fearful to drive across it, even though we have no intention of driving off the edge—a drive that would plunge us into one of the choppiest and most treacherous channels in the world. The analogy to children and their behavior is simple: there is security within defined limits.

One of the first researchers in the field of child behavior experimented with a group of nursery school children on this point. He wanted to see if the children would experience more freedom if the chain-link fence surrounding the play yard was removed. The fence was taken down, but instead of feeling free, the children huddled together in the center of the playground fearing to venture even to the edge of the yard. None of the children attempted to wander.

A happy home always involves certain limits, for in order to maintain friendly relations, it is necessary to establish well-defined boundaries whenever two lives cross. Your child needs to know what you will permit and what you will prohibit. Specific limits ought to be as few as possible, and they should be reasonable and enforceable. Limits also need to be withdrawn entirely or modified as a child grows older. When a child is aware of the limits, he doesn't get into trouble unless he deliberately asks for it, and as long as he determines to stay within the limits, there is security and acceptance.

3. *Teach reason and obedience.* The long-range goal of parents is to teach a child to guide his own behavior, to make good decisions, to reason clearly about choices, to solve problems on his own, and to plan ahead. When a child understands the consequences of his behavior, he can make better decisions for himself when his parents are not there. A child who has been taught to follow rules will be a more responsible child. By giving a child reasons

Challenge to Authority?

Every time your child disobeys, you must take your brain off automatic pilot and decide whether it was childish irresponsibility or whether it was a direct challenge to your authority. If it was a direct challenge, you will wish to respond differently than if the child was just being childish. In the following situations decide the child's motives, and circle the correct response.

Situation	Childish Irrespon- sibility	Direct Chal- lenge
1. Child runs through the house and knocks over a lamp.	C I	D C
2. Child wets the bed.	C I	D C
3. Two-year-old child throws food on the floor.	C I	D C
4. Teen-ager comes home two hours after curfew without reason.	C I	D C
5. Twelve-year-old goes with his friend to the ballpark without letting you know where he is.	C I	D C

Discuss your responses with your partner, a friend, or your parent study group.

for his actions, parents help him to reason out the consequences of his own behavior.

In teaching a child to use reason, the steps are these:

a. *Tell him what it was he did correctly or why he is being punished.* "I am going to plan a surprise for you because you did such a good job cleaning your room." "You will have to miss TV tonight because you were late coming home from school."

b. *After your child has been given many examples of reasons concerning correct behavior and punishment, begin to ask him to state the reasons.* "Why do you suppose I am going to give you a special treat tonight?" "I'm going to have to punish you. Tell me what you did wrong." A child feels he has the right to know the reasons for punishment. If you take the time to help him understand the reasoning behind it, he will more readily accept and learn from it. When your child answers your question, say the whole thing back to him. "Yes, you've earned a special treat because you did such a good job of cleaning your room." "That's right. You didn't come home from school on time, so you will have to miss TV tonight."

c. *When he is able to tell you reasons for specific behavior, begin to work on general rules for behavior.* "Since you did the dishes on time, you will get to see your favorite TV program. When you do what you are asked when you are asked, good things happen." "You fell down and got hurt because you were not looking where you ran. It's dangerous not to pay attention to where you are going." When you explain carefully to your child what he has done wrong, it conveys more than "You were bad; don't do it again." It trains him to look for the general principles and to perceive his own behavior and intentions in these terms.

d. *When the child has learned certain general rules for behavior, these can now be used to make plans about actions to be taken.* Suppose you are taking your children to the amusement park, circus, or fair. In the past they have gotten overexcited about all the rides and food. You can't afford to let them have more than three rides and one treat. Discuss it ahead of time

rather than after they are all excited. Several days before the special outing Daddy should explain the situation: "On Sunday I'd like to take the family to the fair. You may have three rides, and you may choose the three you want. Each of you may also have one treat to eat. We can't afford any more than that. Do you understand?" The kids are excited about going, but the rule has been set ahead of time, and they have time to prepare for what is to come. When later one of them starts begging for "just one more ride," Daddy needs only to ask, "How many rides did we agree upon?" And stick to it.

Clear rules make day-to-day living easier. They provide guidelines for parents in consistently training their child. Through obedience to reasonable rules, a child learns trust in his parents. Rules also help a child to remember what is expected of him.

The rules we make should be short, easy to remember, and stated positively—especially must we state them positively. Children hear too many "Don'ts." Experiment with stating even a correction in a positive way. "You may turn on the television after you finish your homework." Not: "If you don't get your homework done, you can't watch TV." Everything we ask a child to do can be stated positively. Rules should also specify exactly what you want done as well as the consequence for noncompliance. "Make your bed before you eat breakfast." And rules should be stated so that they can be enforced easily. In other words, be specific. "You must clean your room before going out to play. By *clean* I mean all toys picked up, clothes put away, the floor vacuumed, and the furniture dusted." When the rule states the details of what has to be done, the child cannot make excuses for doing half the job. Adapt your rules to the child's age, ability, and living conditions—it is unlikely that you will teach a 2-year-old to make his bed or to wash the dishes. And finally, keep the rules at a minimum. A home with the best discipline and the fewest disciplinary problems will be a home with a few, simple rules. Allow your child to grapple with life under the rules. Allow him to make up his own

mind on many things. But the few rules you do have, apply consistently.

4. *Speak once; then act.* Mother takes her 10-month-old baby out to the sandbox for some fresh air and sunshine. The baby digs his hands into the sand and promptly stuffs it into his mouth. Mother catches him, digs the sand out, and goes back to reading her book. He does it again. This time mother scolds him and puts him back in the sandbox. This scene repeats itself many times in the course of a half-hour. Mother gets very little reading done, and baby gets lots of attention, for he has discovered a delightful way of keeping mother busy with him. A little action, not scolding, would have taught Baby not to put everything into his mouth.

Another mother handles it differently. When her baby stuffs sand in his mouth, she promptly picks him up and puts him in his stroller. She ignores all crying and protests and continues to read. When he is quiet, and not before, she puts him back into the sandbox to play. As soon as sand goes into

his mouth again, she quietly puts him back into the stroller. He soon catches on: sand in mouth—sit in stroller. He cannot understand Mother's words, but he can understand her actions.

Julie left her tricycle in the driveway and ignored all of Mother's requests to get it put away before Daddy came home. Finally Mother dragged her to the tricycle, then pulling the tricycle with one hand, she yanked Julie along with the other and began an angry outburst: "I told you to put that tricycle away, and that is just what you are going to do!"

A better method might have been for Mother to put the tricycle away where Julie could not retrieve it. Then when Julie asked for it again, Mother might say, "I'm sorry, Julie, but you cannot play with your tricycle now. You didn't put it away last time when you used it, so you may not have it now. You may ask again tomorrow though." The last remark allows Julie to try again.

Another method of training involves withdrawing when the child creates a disturbance. This technique is particularly useful in conflicts involving sibling rivalry, whining, and temper tantrums. Discord can result when parent and child disagree. If the parent removes himself from the scene, the child cannot continue—at least not for too long! And retreat to the bathroom, for it usually epitomizes privacy. Plan ahead by having a ready supply of magazines and books for such an occasion and perhaps a radio to drown out any protests that might arise. Now when Wendy throws a tantrum, Mother withdraws to the bathroom. Nothing needs to be said. By allowing the tantrum, you have respected Wendy's rights to express herself as she chooses. But by withdrawing, you do not give the desired attention. A child quickly learns that when he goes beyond his limits, the parent will withdraw. Often the child will then abandon his behavior and indicate that he is ready to cooperate again.

At first glance this may look like you are allowing the child to get by with something. But if you look closely at the situation, you will find that he wants attention. If you permit yourself to become involved in this

Speak Once: Then Act

Parents frequently talk too much and warn a child too many times. A constant barrage of words leaves a child "deaf." How much better to speak once, then follow through with action when the child does not comply. First read chapter 4 in the text: The Rewards of Discipline. Then for each of the common misbehaviors listed below, write down a proper method of action for follow-through.

Misbehavior	Action
1. Your child throws a classic temper tantrum.	
2. Seven-year-old Randy continues to watch TV after you have asked him to turn it off and get ready to go to town.	
3. Your child does not come in from playing outside when called.	

scheme, you are reinforcing negative behavior. We must aim our training at the root cause rather than at the surface problem. Few parents realize what is really happening beneath the surface of a misbehavior. Once they become aware of their mistaken concepts and the significance of the child's behavior, they can guide him into better conduct. If the child finds that his behavior does not yield notice, he will look for a new method by which he can gain the attention desired.

Often parental action in dealing with misbehavior should consist of little more than keeping their lips closed, even though they feel they must say something and correct the situation through words. But a child has a purpose behind his behavior and often has no intention of changing. He finds talk a bore and becomes "mother deaf." Parents of such children often sigh, "He never hears a word I say!" Yet they redouble their efforts and pile a barrage of warnings upon more warnings.

A good motto for parents caught in this bind might be: "In time of conflict, keep your mouth shut and act." Remain cool and quietly establish your right to require obedience. Be firm, and eventually action will bring respect. In fact, action will bring this about more quickly than words.

5. *Balance love and control.* Extremes are rarely helpful, and this is certainly true when disciplining a child. Avoid the following five extremes.

THE AUTHORITARIAN PARENT. Some parents assume that it is their duty to command, dictate, and control their child. The youngster is totally dominated under the rule of such parents. They heap punishment upon punishment, and the child lives in constant fear of retribution. Children who live under extremely authoritarian control where discipline is severe are often quarrelsome, disobedient, troublemakers at school, nervous, and quick-tempered. Because of constant domination the child never learns to make decisions on his own. Deep feelings of bitterness and resentment often take seed, which may later blossom into open hostility.

THE PERMISSIVE PARENT. Here the

Self-Test on Discipline

Score yourself on the following items as indicated:

1. Never   2. Occasionally   3. Most of the Time   4. Always.

1 2 3 4   1. My partner and I agree on disciplinary procedures.

1 2 3 4   2. I am consistent in carrying out disciplinary procedures in my home.

1 2 3 4   3. I handle misbehavior in public places correctly and confidently without embarrassing me or my child.

1 2 3 4   4. Clearly defined limits for behavior have been set in my home.

1 2 3 4   5. My child clearly understands both the rules of our home and the reasons behind them.

1 2 3 4   6. I speak once to my child and then follow through with action if my child has not obeyed.

1 2 3 4   7. I treat my child with respect even when I am irritated or correcting behavior.

1 2 3 4   8. I can allow my child to suffer the natural consequences of a situation without feeling compelled to step in and protect him from hurt or loss.

1 2 3 4   9. I tend to be an authoritarian (domineering or controlling) parent.

1 2 3 4   10. I feel I have found the proper balance between love and punishment.

1 2 3 4   11. I have planned an interesting and stimulating environment for my child along with proper play equipment for each stage of development.

1 2 3 4   12. I am able to individualize the methods of discipline I use for each of my children because I recognize that all children cannot be reared by the same rules.

1 2 3 4   13. I provide a living example of positive behavior for my child.

Discuss your responses with your partner, a friend, or your parent study group.

youngster is in control, and the parents bend to the wishes of their child. Since the parents cannot control their child's behavior and since the youngster has never learned to control his own behavior, discipline becomes a major problem. The child's uncontrolled behavior makes his parents the frequent object of others' jokes. As this child's frequent outbursts of uncontrolled behavior continue, the parents smart with embarrassment. Their nerves are shot, and more often than not they decide to stay home rather than hassle this "brat" in public. The child does not respect his parents, other persons, or the property of others. Eventually he may exhibit more emotional problems than does a child raised under authoritarian rule.

A child is not impressed with a parental permissiveness which conveys to him that they don't care what he does or how he turns out. He develops disrespect for parents who lack the strength of character to make the moral decisions that need to be made in day-to-day living. Don't imagine that you are helping your child by letting him do as he pleases.

THE UNLOVING PARENT. Many studies of children in institutions confirm the lasting importance of parental love and attention during the early years of a child's life. Dr. Rene Spitz, a New York psychoanalyst, spent three months observing the reactions of babies in a foundling home where the nursing staff was so busy that each child "had only one tenth of a mother." Dr. Spitz estimates that 30 percent of the babies died before they were a year old. "Without emotional satisfaction, children die," says Dr. Spitz. "Emotional starvation is as dangerous as physical starvation. It's slower but just as *effective.*"

Extreme cases of an unloving parent involve the total neglect of a child, abandonment, and cruelty. Juvenile courts are beginning to handle more and more of such cases. But a more commonplace and more subtle kind of rejection by too many parents disturbs sociologists far more: using severe punishment, constantly criticizing or nagging a child, seeing only his shortcomings, holding a child to unsuitable or unattainable standards, or comparing him unfavorably with others.

THE POSSESSIVE PARENT. Some well-intentioned but ill-advised parents refuse to allow their children to grow up and develop in a natural manner. Under the pretext of love and concern, these parents fail to allow their youngsters to take reasonable risks or to do things by themselves. Their guise is the constant "help" their children need. They want to keep their children as close to and as totally dependent on them as possible. Still others invest much or all of their hopes and dreams for the future in their child. Often this occurs in a family where a parent is not getting emotional fulfillment from other sources and so literally needs the child in order to function as an adult. A child *needs* a parent, but a parent should not "need" a child in the same sense.

Possessiveness, overconcern, or too much mother-love is a cover-up or compensation for unconscious rejection. A mother may feel guilty for the rejection she feels toward her child. She makes up for it by showing excessive concern and anxiety for him. We cannot protect a child from life, nor should we attempt to, but we are obligated to train him to face life with strength and courage.

OPPOSITE EXTREMES. One of the frequent problems brought up at our parenting workshops is what to do when parents have opposing ideas on how a child should be raised and disciplined. One parent may be harsh and overbearing. The other parent may try to be more balanced, easygoing, and less strict.

It is difficult to step aside when you feel your partner as a parent is not handling a disciplinary situation correctly. But stepping aside is exactly what you should do! Far greater damage is done to the child if he observes both of you disagreeing over how he should be handled. If you oppose what your mate is saying or doing, speak your piece *in private, never in front of the child.*

Though parents may differ in temperament, methods, and response, a youngster learns rapidly how to respond to each parent. He will learn who is strict and who is the softie, and he will adjust his behavior and responses accordingly. Different though the tactics be for raising this child, the child will adapt his behavior and will likely mature in a normal fashion as long as he learns that his parents will stick together on major issues! If he ever learns that he can "divide and conquer," he is likely to use it against you both. A youngster needs to feel secure, and this security will grow strong in the garden of consistent methods. His security will be deeply threatened if he sees one parent try to make up for the lacks of the other or if he sees one contradict, argue with, or undermine the stand the other has taken. As parents you might remember this motto when attempting to work together: "United we stand, divided we fall."

A child needs discipline in an atmosphere of love, and competent parents avoid extremes in either love or punishment. If you love your child with a nurturing love, then you can discipline him with the proper balance between love and control.

Setting the Stage for Self-reliance

Several methods of training will help your child to move toward the ultimate goal of self-regulation.

1. *Environmental control.* The more adequately you plan and arrange your child's environment, the fewer disciplinary problems will arise. Suppose you visited a school and found no books, blackboards, teaching materials, or play equipment. You would wonder how the teacher could educate the children, and you might wonder about all the disciplinary problems she would have on her hands.

In your home make sure you have proper play equipment indoors and outdoors for each stage of development.* A child is powerfully influenced by the "curriculum" of his home environment long before he begins his formal education in a classroom. If your house is a showplace full of adult things that your child is not allowed

---

*A comprehensive list of toys and play equipment for children of different ages and stages appears in Dr. Fitzhugh Dodson's book *How to Parent,* published by The New American Library, Inc., New York, 1970, pp. 329-341.

to touch, you are sure to have your share of problems. Provide an interesting and stimulating environment in your home and backyard.

2. *Individual attention to each child.* Children are not the same. We are aware of this fact, and yet we often try to use the same methods of control on all our children. Because the combination of genes and the environment ensures that each child will be different, parents need to use different methods of control with each child. A quiet, sensitive child needs to be handled differently than a boisterous extrovert.

3. *Allow a child freedom to explore his environment.* When your child grabs a spoon and wants to feed himself, forget the mess and let him do it. He is learning independence. If you continue to feed him, you will slow down the development of his self-regulation. It is the same with all his activities. As soon as he can dress himself, open a door, or pick up his toys, let him do these things by himself—even though it is faster to do them yourself.

4. *Parental example.* Parents are living models to their offspring, who innately love to imitate. We teach positive or negative traits of character through the silent language of our own behavior. If we are courteous and show a happy disposition, the child will be happy and courteous. If we show patience and determination during difficulties, he will. If we respect his rights and property, he will respect our rights and feelings.

5. *Natural consequences.* This is one of the most powerful teaching methods that parents possess, yet few parents use it. Eleven-year-old Arthur left his baseball glove at the ball field, and when he went back for it, it was gone. He begged his dad for a new one. Daddy wasn't very happy, since this was the third glove Arthur had lost during the summer. Dad scolded him and gave him a long lecture on money, on the value of things, on being responsible, and on taking care of belongings. But in the end, Dad relented. "All right. I'll get you another one tomorrow, but this is the *last one* this summer! Now promise me that you won't lose the next one." (Dad had said the same

thing when Arthur had lost the second one.)

In this instance Daddy had a golden opportunity to let natural consequences take over, but because he felt sorry for Arthur, who couldn't play ball without a glove, he protected him from the consequences of his actions. Dad could have told Arthur that he could buy a new glove with his allowance, and when Arthur bawled that he didn't have enough money saved to buy one, Dad should have told him kindly but firmly that he would have to wait until he did.

If natural consequences are pleasant, the child will continue to act the same way. If the natural consequences are unpleasant, the child will be motivated to change. Often parents protect the child from experiencing the natural consequences of his actions, and he begins to depend on his parents to protect him. But when parents deprive a child of the consequences of his actions, he loses the educational value of the experience and fails to learn how to stand on his own two feet.

One caution: Use common sense in this matter. Parents who let a toddler run into the street to teach him the results of natural consequences may end up with a dead child. In actions where serious or fatal injury may result, parents should prevent natural consequences from taking place. But when these only cause unpleasantness, then step aside.

Modern-day Tar-and-Feathering Techniques

It would be convenient if we could rely entirely on respect, setting limits, rules and reasoning, action, and natural consequences to discipline children. But such methods are not always sufficient. At times punishment is necessary. No children are so well behaved (at least no children I have ever heard of) that they need no punishment at all. Punishment is most necessary in three situations.

The first involves repeated misbehavior. You have talked to 3-year-old Kathy about staying out of the street and playing in the backyard. However, she continues to cross the street to play with friends. Since all warnings have failed, Kathy needs punishment to help her learn the lesson.

Second, punishment is necessary also when a child's safety is involved. If you find your child trying to climb over a fence to get to the swimming pool, a simple statement like: "We swim only when Mommy or Daddy are with you; you may not go to the pool alone," followed by a swat or two on the bottom can teach this lesson quickly. A similar approach may be used with all potential dangers: guns, knives, matches, or poisons.

Third, punish when your child deliberately challenges your authority. Every time your child disobeys you must take your brain off automatic pilot and ascertain the child's motives. Let's say your child forgets to feed the dog or has his bike stolen after leaving it outside or loses a library book. Such actions are not normally direct challenges to authority but result from a lack of maturity and experience. We do not want to punish a child for being a child and demonstrating childish characteristics.

However, if your youngster challenges and defies you, if he manifests a cool and calculated rebellion, it becomes necessary to choose an arbitrary punishment. Suppose that you have forbidden your child to swim while you are not home or that you have asked your child not to go near a certain area after school or that you want him to wait in a certain spot until you return. Unless your child complies with your request, these would represent blatant challenges to your authority as a parent.

Children begin to challenge authority at an early age. You can generally tell a challenge by the glint in the child's eye as he puts you to the test and pushes you to the limit. When a child responds in this manner he is really asking one question: "Who is in control in this home—you or me?" Parents need to settle this question for the child early or they will find themselves being repeatedly tested throughout all the years to come. And usually the tests will get "heavier" as the years go by, with the children becoming increasingly difficult to manage as they strive to push farther beyond the limits you have set.

There are three basic methods of arbitrary punishment. If the misbehavior is not a direct challenge to your authority the first two methods are probably satisfactory.

Deprivation. Deprivation involves the restriction or removal from the child's environment of something which is important to him. Suppose your 5-year-old scribbles on the walls with his crayons. Because there are no natural consequences for scribbling on walls, you must select an arbitrary one for this misbehavior. You might tell him, "David, you are old enough to know that you should not draw on the walls with crayons. I am going to take your crayons away for a few days. This will help you remember that crayons are to be used on paper, not on the walls. Here is a cloth with a special cleanser on it that will help you scrub the marks off the wall."

Try to make deprivation relative to the misbehavior. If Mary leaves her bike in the driveway so Dad can't pull in with the car, take away her bike. If there is bickering over a game of Sorry, put the game away. However, when depriving a child of something important to him, make the amount of time reasonable. To deprive a 5-year-old of television for a month is unreasonable. The punishment would become meaningless to him, and there is no incentive for him to improve so that he can watch television again. To deprive him of television for a few days would be reasonable and would also give him incentive to improve his behavior. A child recognizes the relevance and justice of punishment.

Isolation, another arbitrary method of punishment, includes sending a child to his room, standing him in a corner, or having him sit on a chair. Nine-year-old Barry disrupts a game with a group of neighbor children in the backyard. Mother might say, "I see that you are having difficulty getting along with others today. It upsets me to see children hitting each other, bossing, and pushing. I am going to send you to your room to play by yourself until you can tell me that you are able to control your actions."

Mother made her punishment "open ended"—as soon as Barry initiated good behavior he could rejoin the play. Don't make the child feel that he must remain in his room forever. The purpose of sending him to his room is to effect a change in his behavior, not to isolate him permanently. Let him know that as soon as he can change his actions and can play reasonably well with others again, he may come and tell you and then go back to his play.

Spankings are another arbitrary consequence of misbehavior that are sometimes necessary when other resorts fail. Most parents hesitate to admit it, but the main purpose in spanking a child is to relieve their feelings of frustration. And almost every parent who has ever lived has become frustrated by certain disruptive behaviors, gotten angry, lost his temper, and a swift spanking was the result. This may relieve the parent's frustration, but what of the child? Hostility and rebellion can quickly mount within a child when parents behave violently themselves. If parents yell and scream, lash out emotionally, or whip their child unmercifully for accidents and mistakes, they will serve as models for their children to imitate. This kind of parental violence is oceans away from a proper disciplinary approach.

However, if a child lowers his head, clenches his fists, and dares the parent to take him on, a proper parental reaction involves responding on the backside. Parents should not allow a child to gain an advantage over them in a single instance. A spanking administered in love can teach a child a valuable lesson, but a parent cannot be rational or loving in a state of anger. It may be necessary to go to another room to regain one's composure before administering the spanking.

Too often punishment and criticism go together. We scold, lecture, and label a child "bad" in an effort to correct him. Such punishment rarely corrects the behavior. It merely belittles the child. Restricting disobedience is enough punishment without need for calling the child bad or making him feel like a worthless person. And once he has indicated that he wants to change his behavior, allow him back into the good graces of the family without a word of humiliation or shame.

Sometimes parents confess that a spanking does not seem to work. This usually occurs for one or more reasons:

1. *Lack of consistency.* This is the biggest problem with parents. One day they will tolerate a misbehavior, and the next day they punish the child for it. It becomes difficult for the child to understand, even when spanking is employed, that a misbehavior will not be allowed, when one time he gets away with it and the next time he does not.

2. *Strong-willed child.* Some children are extremely strong-willed. In class we frequently ask how many parents have a strong-willed child, and usually half the class or more affirms with a raised hand. The strong-willed youngster may continuously repeat the misbehavior in order to gain control over the parent. Even though he is spanked time and again for the same misbehavior, he continues to defy his parent. This child is engaged in a power struggle with his parent. Thus, the parent needs to be geared for a long and strenuous battle. The parent must become stronger, more consistent, and patient—determined to outlast the child's stubborn behavior. It is a difficult experience to battle the strong-willed child, but tremendous rewards will be reaped in the years to come from efforts expended today.

3. *Delayed action.* Parents often allow small misbehaviors to pass unnoticed. A few months later they realize that yesterday's small problem has become a monumental problem. In an effort to correct the situation, they clamp down. They spank and spank, but see no results. Such parents need to remember that bad habits have taken root. These habits can probably be corrected, but only in time and with consistent, patient work. It may take the youngster time to realize that his parent will not permit this behavior again.

4. *Spankings that don't hurt.* Some parents are afraid of spanking their child for fear of hurting him. If it doesn't hurt, don't bother! A spanking utilizes pain as both a

punishment and a deterrent. If it doesn't hurt, it will hardly deter a child from repeating the misbehavior. The message a spanking should carry cannot usually be understood through several layers of Pampers, through heavy jeans or cords, or by gentle smacks of the hand. Never, never should a child be beaten into submission, but he should be able to feel the message.

To Spank or Not to Spank?

A parent should not use spankings as a cure-all for all types of misbehavior, or they will lose their effectiveness. Parents should learn to distinguish between what Dr. Dobson calls childish irresponsibility and challenges to authority.

However, when a youngster directly challenges your authority, when he displays attitudes of direct defiance or says in word and deed, "I will not do as you have asked me to do," or "You can't make me," he needs to be dealt with in a strong way. This is a time for action, not the time for a mild discussion on why it is important to listen to Mommy's or Daddy's opinions. This is not the time to put him in the corner to think about his actions. It isn't the time to put him down for a nap or to send him to Grandma's or to start him in nursery school.

When the child first challenges parental authority in a defiant way, parents must listen to the hidden question as well as the spoken question. When a child says, "I won't do it, and you can't make me," what is the hidden meaning? Probably he is asking, "Who is in control in this home? Can I be bigger and greater than you? Could I win this battle with you?" It is important that parents recognize challenges to their authority early and answer conclusively the question the child wants answered. If they don't, he will likely challenge them and test them repeatedly.

A child will often resist control, but he wants and needs it. You must earn the right to administer such control by taking a firm stand at the appropriate time. This will likely include a sound spanking from time to time when your child has deliberately challenged

your parental authority.

Parents frequently ask if a child should be allowed to cry after a spanking, and if so, is there a limit? I know of a father who would spank his child firmly and then demand that the child "stop crying this instant." He would stand above the child after the spanking and threaten more of the same if the child cried.

The crying and tears that accompany a spanking are a healthy release of emotions and should be allowed. However, real crying can quickly change from the hurt of the moment to a weapon the child uses against the "enemy." Rarely does real crying exceed much more than two to five minutes. Crying that continues beyond this point usually changes in intensity and tone and becomes protest crying. At this point it might become necessary to offer the alternatives: stop the crying or receive another and harder spanking.

A teen-ager should not be spanked. Your teen-ager may blatantly defy your authority and break all the rules, but a spanking is not the answer! Why? A teen-ager is entering the adult world. He considers spankings for babies, and deep resentments could grow from such an experience.

When our Rodney was 14, he not only defiantly disobeyed me but went ten miles beyond! I was furious to see such defiance. I remember him lying on his bed as my mind grappled with how to deal with such disobedience. In my frustration I could only think of whipping him, and I began searching for any instrument that might work. There on the floor I spied a broken hockey stick. As I raised it to teach him a lesson he would never forget, he spoke: "Mom, if you do that I'll never forgive you!" There I stood with the hockey stick in midair. The moment of decision came and went. *Consistency* has always been my byword.

I carried out the whipping, but not as severely as I had originally intended. When I had finished, I allowed him to cry. I felt most unhappy with my decision to follow through with the spanking. I had chosen the wrong course of action, and I knew it. I begged his forgiveness, and he refused to give it. I told him I would not leave his room until I received it. An hour or two later he finally forgave me, and we prayed together. I have never forgotten the lesson I learned that day. Spankings are a serious affront to teen-agers, a demeaning attack on their emerging self-worth. When a teen-ager defies authority he must also be dealt with in a firm way, but it should involve a loss of privileges (phone, car, allowance, going out with friends) not spankings.

Generally speaking, children under six months of age should not be spanked either. At this point, it might be wise to define what I consider a spanking to involve. A spanking is *not* a mild slap on the hand or bottom on a wiggling or mischievous child. A spanking is a series of swift swats with the hand or an instrument for the purpose of teaching the child a lesson and reforming his behavior. Children under six months should not be spanked in this manner because a youngster of this age does not possess the understanding needed to acknowledge wrong behavior and correct it. However, a mild or even a sharp smack on the hand or bottom can quickly change even an infant's behavior. But I do not consider this a spanking.

Some parents prefer to use their hands when spanking, and some prefer a paddle, a switch, a board, or a belt. The hand may be effective for a younger child, and the parent can then easily gauge how hard he is administering the punishment. However, it might be difficult to teach a hefty 9-year-old a lesson with only a hand. *It is better to have a chosen item in the house for this purpose.* The trip around the house to find it can be part of your cooling down process. Never spank a child with a split or broken board or anything with metal on it.

There is a padded area of the anatomy that readily lends itself to spankings. Since there are no blood vessels near the surface of the buttocks, the chance of injuring the child is minimal if you spank there. The legs may also be spanked. When spanking a child's hand always spank when his palm is up as opposed to hitting his knuckles, where blood vessels could be damaged. Never slap or spank a child on the head or face.

This could result in permanent damage to the head or ears.

Support the child's body over your lap, a chair, or bed when spanking. Avoid holding the child by one arm and flailing away at him. The back needs support. Teach your child early to accept a spanking when it is due. Do not allow your child to run from you, forcing you to chase him in order to carry out the punishment.

Dr. Dobson feels that a parent should have his or her child so well under control by age 8 or 9 that spankings would be needed only on rare occasions beyond that point. This is the goal toward which a conscientious parent should work—an 8- or 9-year-old child who can control his own behavior without the threat of spankings. Use spankings sparingly during the years of 9 to 12.

Whenever a severe whipping is necessary, carry it out in such a way that it will spare the child's self-respect. Spankings should not be given in the presence of other people. It is enough if other children in the family perceive the situation at a distance.

Public punishments develop within a child bitterness and loss of self-respect.

Most parents resort to spanking too frequently. If you find yourself constantly falling back to the use of your hand to control your child, perhaps you should reevaluate your entire disciplinary system. However, if milder measures prove ineffective, a spanking that will bring a child to his senses should be administered in love. Sometimes one such correction will be enough for a lifetime.

And remember that it is rarely necessary to whip a child in order to teach him a lesson. In dealing with children a little pain usually goes a long way. Before you spank a child make sure that he understands clearly why you are punishing him. He must know what rules he violated and that such disobedience results in punishment.

When his tears have subsided, he may often want to be held, which is an excellent time to have a heart-to-heart talk with him. You can tell him how much you love him, how much he means to you, how much God loves him, and how much it hurts God to see any of us disobey His laws. You can also explain what to do next time so he can avoid the difficulty. This kind of communication is not possible through other disciplinary means like sending a child to his room or standing him in a corner, for they tend to build up hostile feelings of resentment without a quick venting of feelings and the access to love and reassurance afterward.

The Difficult Child

Guilty as charged! Parents blame themselves for their child's behavior. Arlene Skolnick in *Psychology Today* (February, 1978) referred to this fallacy: "Most child-care advice assumes that if the parents administer the proper prescriptions, the child will develop as planned. It places exaggerated faith not only in the perfectibility of the children and their parents, but in the infallibility of the particular child-rearing technique as well" (p. 56).

From experience I have learned that there is more to rearing kids than parental training and proper use of methods. It took twelve years of personal research to excavate the missing dimension. How easy to pass hasty judgment on parents when we see them having problems with a child! But what happens to this theory when other children in the family develop into responsible, mature adults?

Researchers now tell us that a child's individual temperament type largely determines his reaction to life. *The temperamental differences that show up in infancy are good indicators of the child's temperament in later years.*

Dr. Carol Tomlinson-Keasey in *Child's Eye View,* who solved the mystery of the unknown ingredient for me, graphically describes Marvelous Margareta and Difficult Darren. Her views derive from the work of Thomas and Chess, who tested over 500 infants and identified three common patterns of temperament. Marvelous Margareta, the "easy happy child," adapts to all situations quickly and easily. She readily sleeps through the night and rarely fusses to get her way. She is prone to smile, coo, and giggle most of the time and rarely spits up. She will eat when you have the time and energy to feed her and is nondemanding in every way. Unfortunately, Harry and I were not blessed with a child in this category! But fortunately for the parents of the world, approximately 40 percent of all children fit into this pattern.

On the other end of the scale are the Difficult Darrens, who refuse to accept new situations, are very irregular in their life-style patterns, and are slow to adapt to any change. They can be classified as negative and sensitive in temperament. In short, they are difficult children. About one in every ten children could be labeled as a Difficult Darren.

The third category of children adjust to life more slowly than Magareta but more rapidly than Darren. This child might be labeled Slow-to-warm-up Steve. He meets his first experiences with a mildly negative reaction, but not as intensely as Darren or as easily as Margareta. This child quietly withdraws from new situations but will adapt in time. Parents should not pressure

"How come you didn't hang up your coat like she told you to?"
"Because she hasn't yelled at me yet."

such a child but should encourage him and deal with him patiently.

Thomas and Chess undertook their research to discover if the temperament determined in infancy could be used as an indicator of the person's temperament in later years. Would a Marvelous Margareta or a Difficult Darren still be Marvelous or Difficult 10 to 15 years down the line? By following 500 youngsters over a period of several months to 10 or more years, Thomas and Chess proved that the difficult infant is likely to be a difficult child later on.

When parents can early identify the difficult child, they can be given the extra amount of support, patience, and encouragement needed to cope. Dr. Keasey points out the futility of blaming parents because the child refuses to sleep through the night or screams when left with a sitter. Frequently parents of a Marvelous Margareta fail to understand their friends who must battle with a Difficult Darren. They confidently reason, "If you would only follow the guidelines of parenting, your child wouldn't behave like that." Parents with children of both categories must understand that a Darren will be difficult to control regardless of the parent's competence or the methods they use.

If you are struggling daily with a Difficult Darren, how can you cope? First, recognize that your child is not deliberately trying to destroy your life. Second, recognize that you are not the cause of your child's difficulties. Third, stop comparing your Darren with a Margareta. Then you can try to make changes in the child's life as painlessly and gradually as possible. Your child will frequently need more love and attention than other children. See that he gets it. Respond to him in much the same way you would to a difficult adult. Keep the stereo down, make changes gradually, feed him more often if necessary, keep calm when he is especially irritable, and enjoy him during his good spells. Another hint: Invest in a rocker. Don't underestimate the soothing power found in singing to and rocking a Darren.

If you are a full-time parent to a Darren, you should take time off from your demanding job. Leave him with a sitter at least once a week while you take a turn at something creative. If you are the parent of a Marvelous Margareta, you will have little need for these suggestions. But parents of "slow-to-warm-up" children might benefit from such suggestions as well.

A WORD OF CAUTION: Even though the difficult child will challenge your patience, tax your ability, stretch your proficiency, and test your creativity, *do not give up on this child!* Do not blame yourself for this child's problems. Exhaust your resources for learning how to cope with such a child, and then lean on a higher Power for strength and courage to meet the next problem.

The Operative Word Here Is Obedience

Ideally, a child should obey immediately, without asking questions and, if necessary, without explanations. If you are a law-abiding citizen, you obey the laws of the land because they are to be obeyed, not because you have tested or thought out every law. Likewise, a child who does not respond immediately is not really obeying.

A child learns rapidly how often a teacher will repeat a request before enforcing it, and he will inevitably wait for the umpteenth repetition of the request before complying. On the other hand, he learns with equal alacrity to obey when the teacher first speaks, if he knows the request will not be repeated.

Obedience should be carried out at once and without argument. A child should not be allowed to obey when he gets ready to or when he feels like it. If the timing is not critical, such as picking up a toy, saying Please or Thank you, you would be wise to time carefully your request and provide an opportunity for the child to *choose* to obey. Children are inexperienced. They often cannot see the necessity of doing immediately what they are told. They lack the wisdom to see from cause to effect. Work with your child wisely, patiently, and lovingly if the matter of timing is not crucial at that moment. However, certain matters need to be carried out at once—when an accident is about to occur, when you must meet appointments, and the like.

Never allow your child to argue about the "fairness" or "reasonableness" of a rule. When you suspect a rule or request is unfair or unreasonable, bring it up for discussion at a family conference unrelated to the incident. Once you allow arguments of fairness to succeed, your child may use the tactic against you *every* time an issue surfaces. And do not get trapped into making one exception after another. Stay cool, calm, and collected. Let the child know: "That's the way it is." Take the attitude that the rule will be followed even if you get nothing else done all day. You can last longer than your child. Protests will go away if you do not reinforce them by giving in.

Too many parents take the line of least resistance—anything to avoid a scene. "OK, I'll let it go this time, but you'll have to do it the first thing when you get home." We do not usually require enough of our children. We need to tighten or discipline and insist on better performance. Learn to tell a child something only once before following up with enforcement. If your darling has already become adjusted to years of chronic nagging, surprise him by limiting your requests to the "spoken only once" kind. Then either drop the subject or enforce it.

A hint to the wise: Avoid disciplining in matters which you cannot enforce. For this reason it is unwise to command a child: "Stop crying." "Go to the bathroom." "Go to sleep." In learning to instruct your child properly, choose the first lessons carefully. Pick subjects you are the master of, if only because you are bigger, and, until the child accepts your lessons as incontestable, avoid subjects which might reveal your weaknesses. If at some point you lose control and shout at your child, "Stop that crying this instant," just bite your tongue and change the subject. It does little good to pursue a lost cause.

Remember, too, that even the most brilliant student can master only a few new subjects at one time. Too much discipline, too much to learn at one time, results only in confusion and predictable failure, which can lead to a stubborn unwillingness to learn. Teach only four or five things at a time and continue to teach them until they are mastered. Then pause to let the child enjoy the fruits of his success before moving on to other lessons in discipline.

It takes real character on the part of parents to teach obedience, because a child is not always in harmony with parental decisions. But parents cannot take a popularity poll every week to see how they are doing in the eyes of their child. Parents are not running for an office. They hold an office, and it is their duty to fill that office.

On the other hand, we should tenderly forgive when a child confesses disobedience. Little feet are easily led astray. Little tongues wander naturally from the truth. Little hands find many things to get into. Let us not forget that in requiring obedience loving mothers and fathers teach mercy and kindness.

Discipline is almost a twenty-year project. The parents do their part along with the church, the school, community agencies, and society in general. Slowly during those twenty years, the parents relinquish control as their child gradually develops inner strengths. Eventually he can take full responsibility for his actions and enter society as a mature and responsible adult who can attain his long-term dreams without endless detours down dead-end lanes in vain attempts to satisfy every short-term impulse.

Further reading you will enjoy . . .

Dobson, James. *DARE TO DISCIPLINE.*
Dobson, James. *THE STRONG-WILLED CHILD.*
Dodson, Fitzhugh. *HOW TO PARENT.*
Dreikurs, Rudolf. *CHILDREN: THE CHALLENGE.*

Chapter at a Glance

I. What Is Character?
A. Character is not personality
B. Newborns do not have character
C. Long-term values count most

II. How Character Develops
A. It develops rapidly in infancy
B. Home atmosphere is important
C. Two essentials—
   1. Admirable traits
   2. Self-respect
D. How to teach a child right from wrong

III. How the Conscience Develops
A. Conscience develops gradually
B. Guilt plays a role
C. Consequences must be recognized

IV. Developing Self-control
A. Fear of punishment is not enough
B. Getting caught is not enough
C. Guilt is not enough
D. Choosing thoughtfully is the goal

V. Stages of Moral Development
A. Young children are hardly aware of rules
B. Between 5 and 10 years children

Chapter 5

Character Under Construction— Securing Your Child for Christ

Character. The very word evokes a myriad of nuances and diverse meanings. *Personality.* Now that brings another complex dimension into the picture. But is our picture truly in focus?

If we were to say that a child has a pleasing personality, we would mean that he is well-mannered, attractive, likable, or good-natured. His winning ways would have impressed us. Character goes far beyond such externals. A pleasant personality refers only to *outward behavior.* Character refers to moral excellence. It involves honesty, self-control, thoughtfulness of others, religious loyalty, moral ideals, conscience, and the ability to inhibit

impulses. The word *character* comes from the Greek word meaning "engrave." It is the mark of a person—the pattern of traits upon his life style.

A newborn baby does not possess character. However, an infant has potential or the raw materials for character development. Thus, active character development begins at birth. The various attributes that make up character must be developed in time.

All the attitudes and facets that go into shaping a child's character are *learned.* Therefore everything we know about the learning process should apply to character development. Hence the responsibility of

---

character development rests squarely on the parents' shoulders. Cop-outs such as "bad genes" won't hold up. When a child's character is defective, parents must blame either themselves or the environment in which the child was reared.

Because the results of building character do not appear immediately (many parents define the results solely in terms of whether a child obeys or not) parents frequently neglect (or carry out inconsistently or haphazardly) the task of character development. But it is the long-term *value* not the *immediacy* of the results that should be stressed.

During the early years of life, character development is most rapid and inherently most susceptible to guidance. Horace Bushnell admonishes: "Let every Christian father and mother realize that when their child is 3 years old they have already done more than half of all they will ever do for his character." Studies indicate that the first 5 or 6 years are the most formative period. Sometimes parents interpret that statement as meaning that they should force intellectual development on a child. Many parents who wish their child to shine before others for their own personal benefit attempt to stimulate the child's brain in many ways. They might attempt to teach him to read by the time he is 2, master typing by the third birthday, and speak a foreign language by age 4. Stimulation of particular interests may be in order, but at a machine-gun pace such forced performance may trigger frustration rather than nurturing a genuine learning environment.

Every parent can rest assured that the beginnings of character development are being laid and that a multitude of influences are already at work during infancy. All too frequently a mother falls into the trap of thinking, "My child doesn't need me at this stage. He doesn't know me from a baby-sitter." However, the child absorbs the very atmosphere around him.

The atmosphere of the home is particularly important to the child's budding development. If the parents do not respect each other, if they quarrel all the time or are jealous or untruthful, if they engage in power struggles of any kind, their child will suffer some distortion of development —regardless of how carefully they try to hide their own problems.

The main ingredient for a child's character development, then, is that the parents relate to each other with mutual love, respect, and appreciation. As surely as a mirror, the child will reflect the same character traits to which it is continually exposed.

Self-respect and Character Development

There is an intimate interrelationship between a child's developing character and his ideas and attitudes pertaining to himself. Repeated verdicts about being "bad" or "good" will now directly influence his character. Throughout his childhood, the many "shoulds" and "oughts" that he has heard begin to formulate the ideals and aspirations that he now decides to live up to. Hence, all indications of your child's standards of behavior are nurtured by repeated positive reinforcement. Only comedians can afford to make capital of losing.

A child may have many admirable traits, but if he has no self-respect, he will have little desire to display his admirable qualities or may do so only sporadically. So it is *self-respect* that is the determining factor in character development. Although it is the sum total of a person's morals that determines the qualities of character and conduct a child will have, self-respect gives consistency to the behavior.

Two things are essential to character development: (1) the admirable qualities that formulate character, and (2) a strong sense of self-respect, which will enable a person to control his conduct.

Teaching the Child Right From Wrong

No newborn has the ability to choose between right and wrong, and no child will develop that ability by himself. Instead, every child must be taught these standards through a long, slow process that extends

Building Responsibility

1. All of the time
2. Most of the time
3. Some of the time
4. Infrequently
5. Never

Check your response to the following statements by circling the number on the scale that most closely describes your current efforts with your child.

1 2 3 4 5   1. I give my child responsibilities suitable for his age to show I trust him.

1 2 3 4 5   2. I allow my child the privilege of choice in matters appropriate for his age whenever possible.

1 2 3 4 5   3. I compliment my child on work well done.

1 2 3 4 5   4. I encourage my child's self-respect by giving him responsibilities not usually entrusted to him.

1 2 3 4 5   5. I allow my child to help me do things.

1 2 3 4 5   6. I have not pressed my child beyond his capabilities.

1 2 3 4 5   7. I have been faithful in checking up on jobs assigned to my child.

1 2 3 4 5   8. I pitch in on occasion and help my child finish a job.

1 2 3 4 5   9. I have a positive attitude toward work, thereby modeling positive attitudes for my child.

1 2 3 4 5   10. I have taken advantage of favorable times to teach responsibility.

1 2 3 4 5   11. I have made a real effort to teach responsible work habits by making work fun.

1 2 3 4 5   12. I sometimes work along with my child to encourage him.

1 2 3 4 5   13. If my child grows bored with a job I trade jobs for him.

1 2 3 4 5   14. I have impressed on my child's mind that work is noble and an essential part of developing a healthy mind and body.

Discuss your responses with your partner, a friend, or your parent study group.

from infancy and well into adolescence.

Since a young child is incapable of controlling his own conduct, his behavior must be controlled through restrictions. These restrictions are first imposed by the family and later by the school, church, and society. The first essential in developing character, then, is to learn what the family expects of each member.

Parents should teach a child to love them so that in turn he will learn how to love others. Gradually they should teach a child that by breaking rules he hurts others. The child will learn this first from rules enforced within the family circle. The small child, for instance, will learn not to take something that belongs to someone else. Through penalties for such behavior, a parent gradually guides a child to conform to a standard.

Naturally, parents should not expect a young child to conform to rules in the same way an older child would, but by the time a child reaches school age he must have learned how to obey principles for general living so that he can abide by school rules. He will also need to know how to work and play cooperatively with schoolmates. Before a youngster leaves childhood he is expected to have developed inner controls that will help him make proper choices. As the child grows, the parents should gradually shift away from heavy external controls so that the child can develop internal controls. By the time the youngster reaches adolescence, he should be able to control much of his own conduct. By the time he reaches legal maturity, the transition should be complete.

Developing the Conscience

No child at birth possesses a conscience. And just as a child cannot develop character on his own, so he cannot develop a tender conscience by himself.

What part do parents play in the development of a child's conscience, and how is it accomplished? They have taught their child to love them and others. Next they have gradually taught him that by breaking society's rules he hurts others. When he learns to love and respect the rights and privileges of others, he will feel anxious or guilty when he hurts others. Such feelings mark the beginning of a tender conscience. The young child learns that certain acts are not acceptable because when one does them a sure and certain punishment follows. Anxiety then follows the punishment. In order to reduce anxiety the child learns not to repeat the behavior.

Once the conscience has been developed, it can be used as a guide for conduct. If a child's conduct does not measure up to the standard, he will likely feel guilty or ashamed. Guilt is the negative feeling experienced when one does not live up to the previously taught standard of conformity. When a child feels guilty, he realizes that his behavior has fallen below the standard he has set for himself.

Before a child can experience guilt, however, he must first of all have accepted certain standards of right and wrong. A child must also have the desire to conform to these standards and must be willing to accept blame for not measuring up to them. The child must also have the ability to recognize that he has not conformed to the standard.

It is important during this process that parents not teach their child to fear only the suffering that his improper behavior brings through punishment. Such fear takes away his ability to appreciate the consequences that his actions have on others. Firm but affectionate parents carefully take the time to explain the consequences of behavior, and it is they who ultimtely rear a child with a mature character.

Developing Self-control

Initially, misbehavior and punishment occur in the presence of the parent. Therefore the child learns not to repeat that behavior when Mommy or Daddy is present. But what will the child do when a parent is not around to monitor his behavior? Take, for example, an incident where a child uses bad language. At home the parents would punish the child for such misbehavior. On the playground, with no parent or adult within earshot, the child learns that he will not be punished and may even be rewarded by attention from his peers. The child then learns not to feel anxious about using bad language except when Mommy or Daddy is present.

Obviously, the child's conscience has not yet fully developed. We do not want our children to form right habits only because they fear punishment. Fear or anxiety is not enough. Getting caught is not enough. Guilt is not enough. We want the child to develop internal controls so that when Mommy or Daddy is not present, even when punishment will not be the end result, the child will still choose a proper course of action.

Since it is clearly impossible to punish a child when you are not present, what is the solution? Frequently you will discover a child's misbehavior after it has occurred—from a teacher, or by observing a broken object, or cookie crumbs on the face. At this point any action you would take is "delayed punishment." However, the longer the delay, the greater the possibility the child will not remember or understand why he is being punished.

Self-control will permit the child to choose thoughtfully the act he wishes to accomplish. A multiplicity of rational and irrational choices may surround the child, but if he is being guided by budding inner controls, he will not yield to his own personal interests. He will not act only from impulse but will deliberate and choose wisely.

As parents and teachers we must not expect too much too soon from a child. One foolish act of a child does not make him a criminal. However, unless a child develops self-control, he will be constantly yielding to the wishes of others. Since such a child lacks the ability to decide for himself, his choices will be almost entirely impulsive or dependent on what his peer group urges—an unreliable source indeed!

Rules, Rules, Rules. Aware They're There?

It takes several years before a child has the capability of learning and comprehending the principles of right and wrong.

Therefore, a parent must wait until the child has developed the mental capacity to apply the principles learned in a given situation to other situations. Any attempt to force this kind of learning at an early age simply will not work. At first a child learns how to relate a specific principle to a specific situation. As his ability to comprehend enhances his perception of right and wrong in different but related situations, he will eventually learn to apply the principle learned to a variety of situations. But not so with the preschooler. To the very young child good behavior is obeying Mother or helping others or coming when called. Bad behavior is not doing these things.

According to the noted Swiss behaviorist Piaget, a pioneer in outlining how moral learning occurs, when children 2 to 5 years old play the game of marbles they are hardly aware of rules. Children of this age do not attempt to win. Instead they enjoy rolling and shooting the marbles—often by themselves. As children near the age of 5, however, they become aware of rules by observing and imitating older children.

Are You Training Your Child to Be Obnoxious?

In the following exercise grade yourself on the likelihood that you may be reinforcing obnoxious behaviors. Grade yourself on the scale as listed below:

1. Definitely yes   2. Probably yes   3. Unsure   4. Probably not
5. Definitely. not.

1 2 3 4 5   1. Your child cries for a cookie before supper. When you cannot stand the crying any longer, you say: "All right! But only this one time!"

1 2 3 4 5   2. Your child spontaneously offers to help with the dishes one night after supper. You say: "Thanks for the offer, but I'm in a big hurry tonight and I can do it faster."

1 2 3 4 5   3. You are shopping with your child. He lags behind, so you alternately plead with him to hurry, carry him, and pull him along offering bribes and threats.

1 2 3 4 5   4. Your child dawdles while getting ready for school. You have pleaded with her to hurry so she doesn't miss the school bus. But when she does, you drive her to school.

1 2 3 4 5   5. Your child cries when he is put to bed. When friends visit, you become embarrassed when his screaming gets loud. When you finally cannot stand it any longer, you let him get up for a little while.

1 2 3 4 5   6. Your child has gotten into the habit of sassing you. You continually warn her by saying: "Don't you dare talk to me like that!" But she continues to do so.

1 2 3 4 5   7. Your child comes when you call him only after you have threatened him, gotten angry, and yelled.

See page 238 for scoring instructions.

They are still only barely conscious of rules and do not understand how to play a game cooperatively while bound by rules.

Between the ages of 5 and 10 a different set of attitudes and behavior surfaces toward games. Children become concerned with rules. Their questions are of the variety, "Do people always play like that?" "Why?" "Could the game be played any other way?"

About age 10, children often begin inventing their own rules to games. Why the difference between how a 7-year-old and a 12-year-old play? Younger children regard rules as sacred and untouchable. They think of rules as coming in an unchanging form from their parents, authority figures, or God. Since rules last forever, they must not be questioned or changed. To break one of these sacred rules would make the game unfair, and that would be unthinkable at this stage. Obedience is always right; disobedience is always wrong. They think only in absolutes and ignore intention.

As children mature, their thinking begins to change. No longer do they view rules as sacred and unchangeable. If the players agree, the rules can be changed at will. No longer do they judge right and wrong in accordance with absolute authority, but now right is considered the social thing to do. Children at this stage see laws as coming not so much from parents or God, but from people who agree to carry them out.

How do these changing perspectives relate to character development? The average parent will become much more upset when a child accidentally breaks an expensive, cut-glass goblet than when he breaks a cheap, common tumbler. In most cases, the more expensive the item lost or damaged, the greater the punishment. From this the child likely concludes that it is the *result* of the action that is right or wrong and not his *intention*.

Beyond age 7, however, most children can differentiate between a deliberate lie and a mistake. A young child regards any untrue statement as a lie, whereas the older child evaluates it in terms of whether it was intentional or not. To a 5-year-old, stealing

is always bad. By the time a child turns 8 or 9, he is able to rationalize to a degree. He can realize, for example, that lying is wrong, rather than "It is wrong to lie to Mother." After the age of 10 or so, a child should be able to consider the intent of an action. He will begin to consider the act of a hungry child stealing an apple as a different offense than the mere act of stealing. A child of this age can take into consideration various circumstances that influence the act. At this stage a child is able to look at his problems from different points of view and use more options in solving them.

A child's limited reasoning ability was demonstrated last summer during a visit to my sister's home. One evening I became particularly intrigued as Cyndy, our son Rodney's girl friend, conducted an experiment of her own by using my nephew Brent as a subject. Cyndy placed before this bright 8-year-old two identical jars. Each held equal amounts of water. While Brent watched intently, Cyndy poured the contents of one jar into a plastic bag and then into a tall, thin jar. Amid several giggles and

wiggles Cyndy asked Brent to watch carefully while she took the second jar and poured it into a plastic bag and finally into a short, wide bowl. Cyndy then asked Brent to point to the container that held the most water. Even though he had seen that both jars originally contained equal amounts of water, he pointed to the tall, narrow jar which only *appeared* to have more water.

Cyndy was conducting this experiment as part of a master's degree project. She was demonstrating Piaget's theory that very young children cannot anticipate the results of their behavior. Their minds simply do not have the reasoning ability to make such judgments. Children at early elementary grade levels base their conclusions to the water experiment on their perception that the level of water in the tall, thin jar rises higher than the level in the short, wide jar. The child will make this decision even though he can clearly see that equal amounts are being poured into the jars. The child has the proper information, but his perception of reality leads him to the wrong conclusion.

This is only one example of a child's limited ability to reason from cause to effect. It is through trial and error that a child learns right from wrong. "Oh yes, a *trial*," you say with a knowing smile! Year by year as he matures and experiences the natural consequences of his behavior, he will gradually learn how to make proper choices. Parents sometimes forget the gradual process by which character is formed. Because they have taught a child once, they expect him to remember forever.

The Crowd Versus Character

As previously pointed out, children initially learn right and wrong from parents, brothers and sisters, and other family members. When they get older, their social horizons broaden to include their neighborhood, school, and church friends. Now the child becomes aware that the standards held within the home are not always held by others. For instance, at home mother might praise or reward him for tattling on his brothers and sisters, but within his peer group such behavior would pack an unacceptable wallop.

As the opportunity for a child to interact within a social circle increases, so does peer influence. When home standards conflict with peer standards, peer pressure will almost always win out. At school a child's behavior is controlled by school and classroom rules. Failure to obey these rules brings punishment and disapproval from teachers, although it might bring approval from peers. Even though cheating may always have been condemned at home, among his classmates cheating during tests might be considered the thing to do and bring tremendous approval.

Through social interaction with others, a child learns about the moral codes by which others abide. He also has an opportunity to learn how others perceive his behavior. If his behavior elicits favorable responses, he will be strongly motivated to continue the same behavior. If, however, he receives negative "vibes," he will likely change his standards and accept those standards that will increase his popularity with his peers. A child who is rejected or only tolerated by his peers does not have the opportunity to learn the group's standards. The socially rejected child might be strongly motivated to receive acceptance from the group, but his attempts to gain acceptance might fail repeatedly because he does not understand the code of behavior held by the group among whom he seeks acceptance. What's a parent to do?

Since peer influence strongly affects a child's character development, it is important that the group with which he identifies has moral standards that conform to those taught in the home. When the moral code of peers conforms to that of the home, school, neighborhood, and church, a good foundation is laid for personal and social adjustments in the future. If, by contrast, a child's peer group persistently shoplifts or destroys property, the child who accepts this standard as his moral code might develop into a delinquent. Therefore, the type of friends a child has is much more crucial than the number of friends he enjoys.

How to Give Encouragement

The following situations call for encouragement even though the child's behavior is not yet perfect. In each case reinforce good behavior and future improvement by ignoring any bad behavior and commenting only on what was done correctly. Can you do it?

Situation	Statement That Gives Encouragement
EXAMPLE: Your child's behavior has been good all day except for one fight with a sibling.	"You have made tremendous effort to be helpful and cooperative today, and I appreciate it. Keep up the good work!"
1. Your child spends an hour longer on homework than usual but did play around on several occasions wasting time.	
2. Your child mows the lawn without being asked but leaves the tools out.	
3. Your child runs for a student body office but loses.	
4. Your 11-year-old brings home a report card with 4 A's, 2 B's, and 1 D.	
5. Your child improves in picking up his room, but doesn't always get his bed made.	
6. Your child swims the length of an Olympic-size pool, but his strokes are sloppy.	
7. Your child helps you carry in groceries from the car but drops a bag.	

Check your responses against those of your partner, a friend, or your study group. Could you give encouragement in all seven situations without commenting on bad behavior?

Building Better Habits

Four-year-old Tommie throws a tantrum because Mother refuses to buy him a Popsicle when the ice-cream truck passes by. Is his character ruined? Sneaky Steve fibs when you ask him where he got the baseball glove you found hidden in his closet. Is his character ruined? Sassy Sally tells you to "shut up" when you inform her that she can't go with her friends. Is her character ruined? Richard tattles on his younger brother. Is his character ruined?

One isolated incident does not ruin character. Naturally, such behavior concerns you, but you must realize that it is the *repetition* of a particular behavior pattern that makes a habit and forms character. Every time a child is allowed to misbehave, it establishes a habit pattern that lays a potential hazard to character development. Conversely, every time a child repeats a positive course of action, character is being built. Thoughts form actions. Actions form habits. Habits form character. Sow character and you reap destiny.

How can parents help a child develop consistent growth patterns in a positive direction? The chapter on discipline dealt with proper parental response to a child's defiant behavior, but there are countless situations that do not involve a direct challenge to authority and that parents can use in helping their child develop better habits. How can a parent get a child to brush his teeth regularly, make his bed, or pick up his clothes? How can a parent teach responsibility with money, proper table manners, or courtesy? And what about whining, pouting, sloppiness, or dawdling?

Proper channeling succeeds the best when the child can associate pleasant reactions with what is right and unpleasant reactions with what is wrong. For example, a child will learn to repeat acts for which he is rewarded. It has been reliably established that reward is a powerful determinant of behavior.

If reward can influence a child's behavior, then by controlling reward you can direct him in building better habits and responsible behavior. However, some parents quickly counter, "No bribery for good behavior will be allowed in our home!" The truth is that you are rewarding and punishing certain behaviors in your home whether you realize it or not. A child who receives special attention when he is ill may fake sickness in order to obtain more attention. A child who receives what he wants by screaming for it will increase his screaming in order to get his desires fulfilled.

Unfortunately, some adults ignore the techniques of positive reinforcement because they misconstrue it as bribery, yet our entire society is established on a system of reinforcement. When you hold down a job, you receive a paycheck. If you perform an act of heroism, society might award you with a medal for bravery. After fifty years of service to a company, you might expect a gold watch. Rewards make personal effort worthwhile, yet parents fail to use them where they do the most good—with their child.

The line between bribery and reinforcement is sometimes fine, but it is distinct. Offering a child bigger and better rewards after he has refused to do what you asked is outright bribery and an unwise stratagem at that! If Mother calls, "Come here, Ginger," and Ginger shouts back, "No!" Mother should not offer Ginger a piece of candy if she will obey. A parent should not use rewards when a child has challenged his authority, for that would actually reinforce the child's defiance. However, it is *not* bribery to plan *in advance* an inducement toward good behavior *if the child has not challenged your authority.*

By recognizing the power of holding out incentives and inducements, parents can become more discriminating in which behaviors they allow to succeed and which behaviors will fail.

The Law of Reinforcement

The most effective technique for controlling behavior cooperates with the law of reinforcement: Behavior that achieves desired consequences will recur. Simply stated, if a child likes what happens as a result of his behavior, he will be inclined to repeat it. If Linda tries a new hair style that draws numerous compliments, she will continue to wear her hair that way. At the baseball game if Billy tries a new hitting style and slams a home run, he will continue to utilize the new technique.

Unfortunately, many mothers and fathers unwittingly use the law of reinforcement to train their children to be obnoxious. For instance, while shopping, mother meets a friend and stops to visit. Little Marty asks for something in a quiet voice. Since Mother is busy talking with her friend, she doesn't respond. Marty's voice gets louder and whinier until Mother can't tolerate it a moment longer. Sound familiar? Finally Mother interrupts her conversation and listens to Marty. When Mother does, she reinforces loudness and whining.

Let's look in on a room of 48 first graders. Two teachers are preparing to conduct reading classes in small groups. At the back of the room two college students sit quietly to record for the next six days how often the teachers tell the children to sit down and how many children pop out of their seats every 10 second period for 20 minutes.

During the first six days, about three children are out of their seats every 10 seconds. The teachers said "Sit down" about seven times in a 20 minute period. When the teachers were asked to tell the children to sit down more often, the frequency increased from seven to 27 times every 20 minutes. Strange events ensued. The children stood up more. Now an average of 4.5 children were standing every 10 seconds. This procedure was alternated back and forth. *Standing increased as the teachers said "Sit down" more often!*

Finally, the teachers were asked to stop telling the children to sit down. Instead they were to praise sitting and working. Now less than two children would stand up every 10 seconds. Saying "Sit down" had become a reinforcer for standing up. The teachers assumed that telling the children to sit down worked, because the youngsters did sit down. *But that was only the immediate effect.* The teachers did not notice the long-term effect until they learned what to look for.

This concealed spider's web traps parents too. The more a parent criticizes, scolds, punishes—the worse a child's behavior. Let's learn what behaviors to reward and what behaviors to ignore.

Put Reinforcement in the Winner's Circle

Mother was having great difficulty managing 4-year-old Patrick. Her little darling often kicked objects or people, removed or tore his clothing, spoke rudely to others, traumatized baby sister, made various threats, hit himself, was easily angered, and demanded constant attention. Finally his mother took him to a clinic, where he was diagnosed as being very active, having possible brain damage, and poor verbal skills.

A therapist was asked to observe Patrick's behavior in the home for an hour a day for sixteen days. During an hour, Patrick showed from 25 to 112 behaviors objectionable to his mother. When these behaviors occurred, Mother usually responded by patiently explaining why he should not have done it. Sometimes she

would try to interest him in another activity. Other times she would punish him by taking away a toy or a misused object, but he usually persuaded her to return the item almost immediately. Occasionally she sat him on a chair for punishment. Deafening tantrum behavior usually followed such discipline, while Mother tried to persuade him to stop.

Patrick's behavior was changed by what I call Operation Outsmart. An observer in the home would cue mother by raising one, two, or three fingers. One finger indicated objectionable behavior and meant that Mother should tell Patrick to stop what he was doing—in other words, warn him. If Patrick did not stop, the therapist held up two fingers. This meant that Mother was immediately to place Patrick in his room and shut the door—punish him. He was to stay there until he had remained quiet for a while. If Patrick was playing in a nice way, the observer raised three fingers. This signaled Mother to give Patrick attention or praise, or to show affection physically—reinforcing the desirable behavior.

Patrick's objectionable actions dropped to nearly zero within a few days, and follow-up observations showed a continuing good interaction between Mother and son and an absence of the objectionable behaviors. He was receiving more affection from his mother and was approaching her in more affectionate ways. Patrick's mother learned that by following Patrick's good behavior with attention and affection and by consistently giving a mild punishment for objectionable behavior when a warning failed, she could change Patrick's behavior. You, too, can change your child's behavior by using Operation Outsmart. It puts you and your reinforcers in the winner's circle and your child ultimately in a happier frame of mind!

From Whence Cometh Reinforcers and Punishers?

Research on behavior has convincingly demonstrated that the consequences that *follow* a behavior will strengthen or weaken that behavior. Those that strengthen a particular behavior are called *reinforcers;* those that weaken a behavior are called *punishers.*

Three types of reinforcers are especially important to parents—social, activity, and token. Social reinforcers involve the parent's behavior—the tone of voice, words of praise, attention, smiling, touching, and being near. Some parents use social reinforcers instinctively, but others must learn how to use them.

Several essentials are crucial to the proper use of social reinforcement. When the correct behavior occurs, you: (1) react immediately, (2) react enthusiastically, and (3) repeat the process several hundred times. Notice how Dad uses social reinforcement to teach Steven a new game.

Dad: "The object of the game is to move your man around the board and be the first one home. You must roll a two with the dice before you can begin. What do you have to roll to begin the game?"

Steven: "A two!"

Dad: "Right! Whenever you roll doubles, the same number on both dice, you get another turn. If you roll a six you can move backward and not have to move all around the board. Tell me how you can get two turns in a row."

Steven: "By rolling doubles."

Dad: "All right! You're doing very well at learning this game! You can also send another player back to start by landing on the same square. However, if he is on a blue space he is safe. You can sit beside him on blue. How can you send someone home?"

Steven: "By landing on a blue square."

Dad: "Remember, the blue squares are safety zones. You can send another player back to start only when you bump him off a *white* space. You're paying close attention to learning the rules, and that's important in this game. You're really catching on fast. I'm sure you will be a very sharp player."

Did you notice that Dad took complex rules and broke them into small steps with moves, objectives, numbers, and color? After explaining each step to Steven, he had Steven say it back. Father enthusiastically reinforced each correct response immediately. Steven found this to be a positive learning experience. Even when Steven made an error, Dad did not scold, punish, or put him down. Instead Dad still praised his *efforts*.

In the following examples, the parent labels specific behaviors and reinforcers and then delivers the reinforcers immediately in a variety of social situations.

Mom: "Thanks for setting the table, Mindy. I didn't even have to ask you."

Dad: "Barry, this is one of the finest reports you've ever written. I'm proud of your work."

Mom: "Mindy, your new dress looks lovely on you. I'm so proud of your ability to sew."

Dad: "Thanks for putting the garbage cans out, Barry, I appreciate your doing it without having to be reminded."

In each example Mom and Dad were praising the efforts or behavior rather than the child. A child often does not respond to what the parents consider praise. For instance, if you tell a child that she is "an angel," she may not jump with joy. She may recall all the times she has not behaved like an angel. If the praise does not fit her feelings, she will likely reject it. However, if the child has been working hard on a task and you compliment her efforts, it can much more easily be used as a reinforcer. "Doug, I've been watching you for some time now. You have worked very hard on that arithmetic assignment. I can see that all your answers are correct. Your work is neat and clean. You're doing well, and I'm proud of you." Such praise can be believed. It is usually better to pay attention to a child's behavior, rather than to merely praise the child.

Using social reinforcers may sound simple, but problems do surface. Some children simply cannot accept positive statements about themselves. When you deliver a reinforcer, they neutralize it with a "throw-a-way." Here is what happens.

Mom: "Mindy, your new dress looks lovely on you. I'm so proud of your ability to sew."

Mindy: "It looks awful. I goofed up on this seam, and I'm too fat and . . ." Or:

Dad: "Barry, this is one of the finest reports you've ever written. I'm proud of your work."

Barry: "Ahhhhh, I could've done better."

In these instances, the other person punishes you for being supportive. As a result you will probably become discouraged and give up. One way of getting around such responses is to label them rightly as "throw-a-ways." When anyone in the family uses one verbally, label it as a "throw-a-way" and call it off limits. Recognize also that self-belittling comments indicate low self-esteem, then work on helping that person establish a better self-image.

Another common error is the "double

message"—that is, a reinforcer and a punisher delivered in one breath. Such a package bears a negative ribbon. Those who use "double messages" reinforce a behavior with praise or approval but take it away in the end with a zap. The odd thing about a double message is that the "victim" can't complain because he did receive a reinforcer to begin with. However, the zap took it away, no matter how subtle. Case in point . . .

Mom: "Mike, you have been playing with your cars so quietly. I really appreciate some peace and quiet for a change."

Dad: "Thanks for coming to supper on time, Barry. That was really nice. But how about washing your hands and face before you come next time?"

Mom: "Your report card isn't all that bad, Barry. But you could do better if you would only try harder. Did you see Mindy's report card? She had all A's."

Dad: "Barry, thanks for trying to clean up this workshop. But next time do it right. Look at the mess you left here. I'll have to do it all over again."

Many parents send double messages without thinking. Yet a double message is one of the most devastating hindrances to the entire reinforcement process. For the next few days keep track of your praise comments. Are you sending any double messages with a zap on the end?

Activity Reinforcers

Social reinforcers are the easiest to use of all reinforcers. They are always available, and they require only the spoken word. Activity reinforcers probably rank next in availability. Games, reading aloud, running errands, watching TV, having a party, playing outdoors, making cookies, helping with dinner, telling a joke, going first—all can be used as reinforcers. These activities are powerful motivating tools, yet we frequently do not recognize and appreciate their usefulness.

Our objective is to teach children that good behavior has a better reward than bad behavior. We can do this by constantly providing opportunities to learn this general rule. For example:

Mom: "Jenny, you were the first one to the table tonight, so you can help me serve dessert."

Dad: "Jeff, you completed your homework quickly tonight. How would you like to read a story aloud for family worship this evening?"

When you use an activity reinforcer, always require the less-preferred activity before the more-preferred one. Here's how.

Mom: "Jenny, as soon as you've practiced the piano for 15 minutes, we'll make cookies together. OK?"

Dad: "Jeff, just as soon as you've weeded the flower bed by the front walk, we'll play catch together."

Giving the child a choice also helps reinforcers succeed. Example: It is bedtime for 8-year-old Kenny, and he has just begun to watch a new TV show. Mother is tempted to demand that he go to bed or else. This would likely raise repeated objections from Kenny. Mother would probably continue to nag him, and both would end up frustrated and angry. But notice how this mother handled the situation.

Mom: "Kenny, I'm sorry I didn't catch you before you began watching this show. It's never fun to be interrupted in the middle of a program. I'll tell you what. You put on your pajamas. Then I'll let you decide if you want to continue to watch the rest of the show or if you would rather read us a story from your new book. But whatever you decide, you must be ready for sleep no later than eight-thirty."

By giving Kenny a choice, Mom actually solved two problems at once. Kenny got to watch TV (which is a reinforcer), and Mother got him to bed on time. Allowing a child to make a choice is an important step in making reinforcers work. Decision-making also helps develop character.

And, Then, the Token Reinforcers

Such things as points, stars, stamps, charts, and money fall into the realm of token reinforcers. The child accumulates these tokens and exchanges them for a long-range goal after a stated period of time. By using social reinforcers in concert with token reinforcers, parents can effect the greatest possible change in the least amount of time. What a value for parents who have become discouraged over the slowness with which behavior change comes!

How does it work? Let's say you have a 10-year-old who obeys slowly, neglects tending to home chores, and needs constant reminding to practice the piano. Does this sound familiar? By utilizing token reinforcement with points and a chart system, let's see whether we can change this child's behavior. The following steps are necessary:

1. Draw up a list of responsibilities that need reinforcing. Ten to fifteen responsibilities would be appropriate for most children—fewer for a small child and more for an older child. Include on the list some items

"I coulda gotten 'em all right, but I got a reputation to protect."

MY JOBS	1	2	3	4	5	6	7
1. I brushed my teeth without being told.							
2. I changed my clothes after school.							
3. I made my bed before school without being told.							
4. I fed the dog this morning before breakfast.							
5. I put my toys away before going to bed.							
6. I got up the first time called.							
7. I did my chores cheerfully today.							
DAILY TOTAL							
WEEKLY TOTAL							
THE PAYOFF AFTER 180 STARS: A CAMPING TRIP!							

that the child already does well in order to make it encouraging to earn points. The chart might look much like the one shown here.

2. The child should place stamps, points, stars, or colored check marks beside each item completed satisfactorily by bedtime. Weight the most difficult tasks with the most points. The child should be allowed the privilege of pasting on stamps or stars, of totaling points, or of coloring the dots. An alternative method is to give a small sum of money for each item done properly. You can also deduct points or money for poor or negligent behavior. If the child misses three items in one day, no money or points will be awarded. By using money as a reinforcer, you acquire the added advantage of teaching your youngster lessons in money management. Teach your child to save some, spend some, and give a tenth to God. The portion saved can accumulate in an account or it can be saved to purchase a pay-off—something the child wants very much: a toy, an article of clothing, a baseball glove. You might ask your child to draw or paste a picture of the pay-off on the chart to help him visualize the goal.

3. At the end of each week add up the points or stars or money so the child can see his progress.

4. The list of behaviors should not change for four to six weeks, since it generally takes that amount of time to establish a new habit.

Set aside the chart system after using it for the four to six-week period. Later you can use it again to produce excellent results. Charts must be adapted to the age of the child, but they are effective for children as young as 3 right through the teen years. (The next chapter points out how to develop a chart system for teen-agers.)

If you find that your son or daughter still has difficulty performing any of the tasks listed on the chart you may need to increase the reinforcer. For instance, double the points or money. The system will work if the immediate reinforcer and the long-range goal are used correctly and if they are strong enough. One mother told me that the chart system had failed in her home. She had used money as the reinforcer, and in her words, "It just didn't work." Upon inquiry I learned that her 9-year-old son was an active member of 4-H. He raised cattle and sold them each year. By the time he turned 9 he already had $1,000 in a savings account. Money was the wrong reinforcer for this child! We discussed the possible use of a weekend camping trip as a pay-off. That worked beautifully.

Enter Mother and Stephanie.

Mother: "Stephanie, you're getting to be such a big girl now. Mommy wants you to learn how to share your things with others. Every time I see you sharing something in a nice way with others I'm going to give you a point. When you get three points, you can have a surprise from this surprise bag." (Mother shows her the bag.)

Stephanie: "Can I have something now?"

Mother: "No, you must earn three points first. Now tell me how you might get a surprise."

Stephanie: "When I share some of my toys with others."

Mother: "Yes, when you share your toys three times with others, you can have a surprise."

Another variation to the point program is the grab bag. You will need to purchase inexpensive objects from the toy store, and fill a bag with them. When a child performs the appropriate behavior, first reward him with a social reinforcer, then allow him to reach into the bag and take out one object. This method is particularly effective when you want to potty train your child.

Parents often report to us that the week following our lesson on reinforcers is the most peaceful week they can ever remember! Why? Because the pressure to perform daily tasks and to behave in a responsible manner now rests on the child's shoulders, where it belongs. Yet there remain a host of parents who take the responsibility for delivering papers on their child's paper route, for getting their child's homework in on time, for calling their child umpteen times so he will not be late for school or work, or for driving the child to school because he dawdled and missed the school

bus when it arrived in the morning.

When and how can such parents understand that responsible behavior is not elicited by protecting a child but by allowing him to feel the full weight of responsibility and the consequences of his actions? When he fails to pull his share, Mom and Dad must refuse to protect him by playing the role of the "good" parent. Parents must allow natural consequences to take over. In addition to suffering natural consequences, your youngster may ' need a powerful motivator to help him do what is right and to avoid wrong and irresponsibility. Try it. You'll like the results.

Ignore Negative Behavior

As you work to improve your child's behavior, pay little or no attention to what the child does that you do not want him to do. Our son Mark wrote an English 10 paper that he entitled "Two Men on Everest." The teacher gave him an A +. In the lefthand margin the teacher wrote: "Mark, I think this is the best—probably *the* best—paper you have done. You express yourself clearly and logically. Your paper is neat, well-organized, and attractive. I believe you have a special talent in writing and am very pleased with what you have done." The teacher, however, made five corrections in red on the first page and seven corrections on the second. Interestingly enough, she said nothing about the corrections. In her note she only praised his good behavior and ignored his mistakes. This teacher understood the value of reinforcing good behavior and overlooking the bad.

On another occasion, this same teacher sent us a "Teacher's Report of Unsatisfactory Progress" for a typing class. Once again she wrote no negative comments, only a positive one. "Mark is making tremendous improvement. I'm proud of him!" Crossing off the *un* on unsatisfactory, she had transformed it into a satisfactory work report—an encouragement to the parents as well as to the student!

You can learn how to do this too. Ignore the behavior you wish to extinguish. Nega-

tive comments about it may only reinforce it! Learn to reward positive behavior, and the unreinforced behavior will eventually disappear.

A Word With Mom and Dad

Teaching your child new habits while trying to get rid of bad ones can be a long and difficult process even under the best of circumstances. Naturally both parents should participate in the program in order for the process to move rapidly. Both parents should discuss the type of reinforcement program used, and they should agree ahead of time concerning what reinforcers and punishers will work best. Otherwise one parent might be shaping one behavior while the other parent is trying to shape a behavior diametrically opposed to it. (Single parents won't have this problem, at least!) So begin your reinforcement program by discussing the tactics you will use. It might sound like this:

Dad: "Barry's behavior has been getting worse, and I think it's time to do something about it, don't you?"

Mom: "I have been doing something about it. When I get mad enough, he obeys."

Dad: "That's what you *have* been doing, but it hasn't been too successful. I've heard a lot of yelling and screaming, and I can't stand it. If we could reinforce his good behavior, rather than his bad behavior, I think we could get faster results."

Mom: "I just don't think parents should have to hand out points, stars, and kisses just because their kids do what they were supposed to do in the first place. The real world just isn't like that. When was the last time someone paid you for getting to work on time?"

Dad: "Be reasonable, Honey. He'll learn faster if we reward him each time for good behavior rather than scream at him for being bad. Let's develop a chart for him and agree on a pay-off that he won't be able to resist. The whole program will save you many hassles after he starts doing what he is supposed to do."

Mom: "I know I sound pretty negative. I'm really discouraged over his behavior. It's worth a try. Let's give it our best for the next four weeks."

A good motto for parents might be: *Catch your child being good, and reward him for it.* Stop acting as though you were trying to catch your youngster doing something wrong so you can bawl him out. Instead, look for good behavior that you can reinforce with positive comments.

When you get all the principles outlined in this chapter down pat, you will find that your child will move more rapidly toward developing a positive self-image and responsible behavior. All this will be a real advantage in achieving your ultimate goal—assisting your child in his overall development.

Your Chance to Sparkle: Making Work Fun

The assumption of responsibility should be pleasurable, for it produces a feeling of satisfaction and fulfillment. It makes a person feel important and useful. These good feelings are a reward in themselves, and they provide a solid foundation for developing self-respect. A child can enjoy doing necessary tasks and doing them well if, when he is between the ages of 2 and 7, he learns to accept work as a part of living. But you should make work fun for him.

Two-year-olds can pick up their own toys. Three-year-olds can empty trash containers and can even dry pots and pans. Four-year-olds can help set the table and hang up their own clothes (if the hooks are low enough). Five-year-olds can watch younger brothers and sisters, care for pets, and even help with dusting. The important thing with a preschooler is not the elaborateness of the job but his faithfulness in doing it.

A grade-school-age child can make his own bed, go to the store, water the lawn, cut the grass, take care of pets, wash the car, have a paper route, set the table, wash dishes, iron flatwork, dust and sweep, wash

some of his own clothing, and learn to cook simple recipes.

If a child shows signs of boredom, give him a new task that offers a challenge. Eleven-year-old Ellen was enthusiastic over her job of setting the table for Sunday morning breakfast, but in a few weeks she began to lose interest and became careless. Mother wisely gave her more to do. Now instead of just setting the table, Ellen also prepares breakfast on Sunday. She plans and cooks the whole meal but does not have to help clean up afterward. She finds this much more interesting than just setting the table.

A child works better if someone works along with him. We often get so busy that we lose opportunities of working side by side with our child. The family can go outside and work together in the yard or the garden, each one having a different task but all working together. This can be a real togetherness time, an opportunity for communicating, teaching, sharing, and playing. The same technique can be used for cleaning the garage, the basement, or just

A Plan for Making Work Fun

DIRECTIONS: Below are several suggestions for building responsible work habits in a child. This can be done by *making work fun.*

1. Make a list of jobs, each on a separate piece of paper, and drop them all in a paper bag. Have each child draw a job from inside the bag. "You draw your job and you take your chances!"

2. Put a record on that plays music your child enjoys. You may also whistle or sing while you work.

3. Play "Beat the Clock" by racing against time. You can set the buzzer on your oven for this game.

general housecleaning. Add a song, a game, or whistling, and your child will learn that work can be fun.

A child works more happily and willingly if his parents are willing and happy workers. This cannot be overstated. On the other hand, negative comments from parents— "Oh, no, not dishes again!" or "I'm so sick of cleaning this house day in and day out!" or "I hate yardwork!"—are not conducive to a happy, matter-of-fact attitude toward work on the part of their child.

A child also should be allowed to express his preference and dislikes for household chores. One mother, in assigning work to her four youngsters, lets them list three "likes" and one "pet peeve" each. The plan works pretty well, except that there are some jobs that all the children like and a few that they all dislike. So the pet peeves are rotated so that no one escapes them completely, yet no one is saddled.

Another method is to make a list of all the jobs to be done that day and to let the children take turns choosing which jobs they prefer. This method encourages willingness and cooperation among the children, for, after all, they have *chosen* the job.

It is wise to check up on a child's work so that unsatisfactory work can be redone immediately by the child. Parents should not accept slipshod work or redo it themselves, for then they deprive the youngster of learning how to work cooperatively and of achieving the sense of satisfaction that comes from a job well done.

When a heavy load of homework burdens a child or some unexpected social event materializes, then parents have the opportunity to pitch in and help or even take over the household jobs entirely. In this way the child learns the importance of helping others and respecting the rights of every family member.

Work is the best discipline a child can have, but it should not be used as a punishment. Parents should impress on their child's mind that work is noble and an essential part of developing a healthy mind and body. If the active minds and hands of youth are not directed to useful tasks, they will find mischief to do which may permanently injure character development.

Television: Potential Assault and Battery on Character

Any activity that absorbs a large portion

of a child's time will influence his character. Since the average child watches nearly three hours of television daily, it exerts a major influence on his character. The subject of TV pulls most parents in two directions, because they appreciate its baby-sitting qualities. But also the content of programs concerns them. One study concludes that in recent years the number of crime-programming hours has increased by 90 percent. Some researchers actually feel that television is a "school of violence" which teaches young people that crime is not reprehensible, but a great adventure. Researchers have also found that much of what a child sees on the screen he will carry over into his day by day play. A young child is particularly susceptible to such influences because he cannot differentiate between fantasy and reality as well as older children and adults can.

A majority of parents consider cartoons relatively innocuous, but closer examination reveals that cartoons often deceptively portray violent elements as fun. One researcher measured the frequency and duration of violent episodes in children's cartoons shown by two major networks during a one-week period. (Violence was defined as any attempt in which one character inflicted pain or bodily harm or rendered unconscious, forcibly restrained, killed, or destroyed another individual, either to prevent him from engaging in an act or out of malice.) He found that cartoons of the "Bugs Bunny" and "Tom and Jerry" type frequently depicted a much greater degree of violence and aggression than those of the "monster" or horror variety.

It seems safe to say that portrayals of crime and violence arouse an appetite for violence, reinforce it when it is present, show how it is carried out, and blur a child's consciousness that it is wrong. Continued viewing of violence may retard a child's awareness of the consequences of violence in real life and may teach a greater acceptance of aggression as a proper solution to conflicts.

Television also frequently advocates mediocre (and in some cases less than mediocre) values. Many shows that are considered good family entertainment depict dishonesty, illicit sex, divorce, juvenile delinquency, and homosexuality. Every time a child views such things, it makes an impression on his mind which, when repeated, will determine a habit, and habits determine character.

In addition to teaching mediocre values, TV can cut family communication, offer a child a convenient crutch so that he can withdraw from family interaction, produce callousness toward human suffering, and consume a large share of leisure time, thus reducing play activity.

Yet, in view of all the questionable information available on television and its effect on character and personality, most parents make little effort to supervise their child's viewing. Research indicates that less than half the mothers exercise any control on their child's TV viewing, and those who do, feel more concerned with the amount of viewing time than with program content. More highly educated parents regulate their child's viewing to a greater degree, but they appear to do so mainly to avoid disrupting family routines rather than to shield their child from the adverse effects of programming. Only a few mothers forbid the viewing of specific programs.

Regardless of how you feel about television, it is unconsciously shaping your child's character (as well as yours). We need not organize a crusade to banish all mass media, but we do need to develop self-control and parental control so that TV programs do not constitute a steady daily diet.

The most effective way a concerned parent can curb a child's television viewing is to have the child participate in "Project Television." Project Television involves the child in the decision-making process to analyze programming. Estimate how much time your child spends in front of the tube. Then set up a log in which the child, if he is old enough, enters the date, the name of the program, and how long he watched the program. Keep this log for one week.

During the week take notes on program content, which means you will have to monitor all programs watched during that

the contract in sight during its duration. This will help facilitate its enforcement.

Other forms of entertainment are just as destined as television to destroy elements of character within a child. These things include various movies, books, magazines, forms of music, and places of amusement. The solution lies not in mere banishment of these items but in providing adequate substitutes. "Don't prohibit without providing" is the way one pastor put it, and the biggest thing parents must share with their child is themselves.

Spiritual Training in the Home

Attitudes which a child learns during the first five to seven years of his life become almost permanent. When the opportunities of these early years are missed, they are gone forever. If parents want a child to be obedient, kind, honest, faithful, unselfish, patient, and God-fearing, they should make these characteristics the conscious objective of their early teaching. Heredity does not equip a child with character, and parents cannot expect character to appear magically unless they have done their homework early.

1. *Make an early beginning.* After a young duckling hatches from its shell, it imprints itself to the first object it sees moving. Ordinarily, of course, the duckling would attach itself to its mother, but if the mother is removed, it will settle for any moving object. In fact, the duckling, researchers tell us, will become imprinted most easily to a blue football bladder dragged in front of it on a string. A week after this process is begun it will fall in line behind the bladder whenever it scoots by. However, time is the crucial factor. The duckling is susceptible to imprinting for only a few seconds after hatching from the shell. If that opportunity for imprinting is lost, it cannot be regained later.

Similarly, between 1 and 7 years of age, a youngster is most susceptible to religious training. His concept of right and wrong is formed during this time, and his ideas of God take shape. As with the duckling, the opportunity of that time period must be

time span. Elicit the baby-sitter's cooperation as well, if necessary. When compiling your data, look for patterns. Is your child watching only cartoons? Only situation comedies? Only science fiction? Which shows would you rate positively? Negatively? For what reasons? What values are these programs teaching? What kind of language is the child hearing? How much violence is being depicted?

At the end of the week, with your child, go over the results recorded in the log. Check to see how accurately you estimated the time he spends watching TV. Next have the child rank the programs he wishes to watch from his most favorite to his least favorite. If the most objectionable program is your child's most favorite, you might have to become arbitrary. In some cases, you may want to work out an agreement that would limit viewing to a specific number of hours a week. A written contract signed and dated by both of you (the more official-looking the better) is very effective. Keep seized when the child is ready, not when the parent is ready.

Unfortunately, the opposite is also true. Depriving a child of spiritual training or subjecting him to the misapplication of it, severely limits his capacity to ever reach spiritual maturity. When parents say that they will wait until their child is old enough to decide for himself if he wants religion, they have almost guaranteed that he will decide against it. An adolescent resents being told exactly what to believe, but if the parents have done their early homework, he will have an inner mainstay to steady him.

2. *Live out consistent Christian behavior.* Your child's everyday experiences of life will influence his religious experience. Parents who give religious instruction must not overlook this fact. If you wish your child to incorporate spiritual values into his life, you must first exemplify them in your own life. A child's visual image of God may include a blend of information from pictures he has seen and stories he has heard. His concept of God may change from a compassionate Being to a vengeful one. His understanding of God as a Father will be influenced by the relationship he has with his earthly father. The child's idea of sin will be shaped by his own experiences of guilt and remorse—when after hurting others he has to face the resultant feelings of regret that follow punishment. His ideas of forgiveness will be affected by his parents' ability to forgive him. A young mind finds it very difficult to grasp forgiveness if the parents do not forgive him. To a great extent parents stand in the place of God to a child.

You do not have to be perfect in order to maintain the respect of your partner or your child. But your family will lose respect for you if you are pious at church or in front of friends but the opposite when no one but family members are present. Such behavior forfeits respect of the watchful child. One minister noted after years of observation that the church's best young people came from either consecrated Christian homes or non-Christian homes. Homes in the mediocre category just don't produce dedicated

Christian young people because of the inconsistency present. Youngsters can pick at words, but they have a hard time disputing an example of good living. A few minutes a day spent in reading the Bible and meditating on spiritual themes will help you live a consistent Christian life.

3. *Teach without preaching.* A child asks questions from his earliest years, and as long as parents obey the laws of communication they will have every opportunity to teach, to instruct, and to fill their child's mind with the very best character-building material available.

How? Through stories, for children particularly love stories. Reading character-building stories to a child has two advantages. First, when you answer your child's questions from good books, you are teaching without preaching. Second, you have given him time and companionship. Nothing spells love to a child more than your personal, patient interest in his thoughts and questions.

During early childhood and elementary school years, many religious teachings may hold little meaning for a child. That is why parents must learn how to translate religious concepts into terms that their youngsters can understand. For example, children may wonder about "Jesus' twelve bicycles" (disciples) or be puzzled by "the consecrated cross-eyed bear" ("the consecrated cross I bear"). Too often our children understand Jesus from the pictures they have seen—a little baby whose mother put him in a straw bed in a barn and to whom odd-looking men in striped bathrobes brought presents that no baby would want! All this fascinates but also confuses a child. We must do better than this!

Substantial research has shown that until a youngster turns 8 or 9, he is most interested in stories about the birth of Jesus and about the childhood of Biblical characters such as Moses, Samuel, Joseph, and David. From 9 to 13 or 14 years of age, historical portions of the Old Testament hold the greatest appeal. From then until age 20 (the upper age limit of the study), an individual shows increased interest in the Gospels. At all age levels children express

The Plastic Years

They pass so quickly, the days of youth,
And the children change so fast,
And soon they harden in the mold,
And the plastic years are past.

Then shape their lives while they are young,
This be our prayer, our aim,
That every child we meet shall bear
The imprint of His name.

—*Author Unknown*

more interest in persons than in other aspects of the Bible.

Where can you find such books that meet the need?

Three particular sets of books supply superior reading material for children. The first is *The Bible Story,* authored by Arthur S. Maxwell.* This ten-volume set portrays the Bible stories in modern language, and the artwork makes the stories come alive for young minds. The second set, *The Bedtime Stories,* consists of twenty volumes of character-building stories which are categorized and indexed according to subject material.* The third set, *Tiny Tots Library,* contains three volumes entitled *Bible ABC's, Bible Firsts,* and *Boys and Girls of the Bible.** The last three books are designed particularly for the very young child.

4. *Family worship.* The family who comes together for worship already knows its value and benefits. "But we don't have time!" is a familiar cry. However, it is simply a matter of priorities. "There's just no time when we're all together." The problem here is scheduling. The average person wants a comfortable and convenient religion, but Christianity has a price. Take away the price, and you have nothing left. "Our family doesn't need it. We go to

*Available through the publisher of this book.

church once a week. That's enough!" This is locking Christianity in one small compartment for use one day a week.

A person makes time for that which means the most to him. Think it through. Does God take top priority in your life? Then, and only then, will your youngster give Him first place in his life.

Set up a regular time for family devotions and make no exceptions unless absolutely necessary. Decide upon a time, either morning or evening or both, and create the habit regardless of who is in your home. Read a passage of Scripture. Make the Bible interesting to your child. Be brief but not rushed. There is also a place for music during family worship. Some children hum the tunes of hymns before they can speak. Have prayer together, allowing each child to join in. Even a small child can repeat a few words after you in his first attempts. Kneeling together is best, and some families join hands in a prayer circle.

Most Christian parents begin early to teach their children to pray, but in so doing they encounter many pitfalls. Parents often thoughtlessly teach their youngsters to approach God as though He were an absentminded magician who will perform a miracle to grant anything asked of Him. Children readily accept the idea of praying to a Higher Power. Frequently, however, their prayers include such expressions as "please give," which probably means "I wish" or "If only I had——" The please-give-me type of prayer is the easiest to pray, but it is also difficult for the child to understand why God does not always—or usually—send what he asked for. Parents must lead their youngster to recognize that prayer is not so much for the granting of wishes or fleeting desires as for confession, repentance, thanksgiving, and praise. You can say things and share burdens through prayer that you would not be able to share with your family on any other level. But when all is said and done, remember that it isn't the number of prayers you pray that makes the difference. A child must see in his parents' lives that there is power for living in order to know that such power is available.

5. *Regular church attendance.* The church exists to help people grow as Christians by giving them opportunities to study the Bible, by encouraging them to read it and pray daily, and by giving them opportunities to serve and help other people. Each couple should give careful thought to what they want to give and receive from their church.

Many years ago, Richard Baxter, pastor of a very wealthy and sophisticated parish in England, preached for three years with all the fervor in his being, yet with no visible response. In mental agony one day he threw himself onto the floor of his study and cried out, "God, You must do something with these people, or I'll die!" And it was almost as if God answered him audibly, for the words came back to him, "Baxter, you're working in the wrong place. You're expecting revival to come through the church. Try the home!" Richard Baxter began visiting his church members in their homes, often spending an entire evening helping them set up family worship. He moved from home to home until finally the Spirit swept through the homes and into the church.

Charles J. Crawford once wrote: "We wouldn't think of building a stone fireplace without stones or of baking an apple pie without apples. Why then are so many people trying to build Christian homes without Christ? They try to maintain 'Christian' principles, establish a 'Christian' home, and even use 'Christian' terminology; but without the presence of Christ there cannot be a Christian home. The great and holy God must be living in that home; He must be living in the hearts of those who call that house 'home.'"

The Greeks had it right: Character is an engraving. What kind of permanent inscription is now being deeply etched into the very heart and soul of your child? We must never forget that character is all we will take with us to heaven.

Further reading you will enjoy . . .

Becker, Wesley C. *PARENTS ARE TEACHERS.*

Dinkmeyer, Don and Gary McKay. *RAISING A RESPONSIBLE CHILD.*

Dobson, James. *DARE TO DISCIPLINE,* chapters 1, 2.

Dodson, Fitzhugh. *HOW TO PARENT,* chapters 8, 9.

Kuzma, Kay and Jan. *BUILDING CHARACTER.*

Leman, Kevin. *PARENTHOOD WITHOUT HASSLES.*

Van Pelt, Nancy. *TO HAVE AND TO HOLD,* chapter 11.

Chapter at a Glance

Chapter 6

Between Parent and Teen—Relationships That Count

Webster's Third New International Dictionary contains 2,662 pages and was originally produced at a cost of $3½ million. It defines teens as "the years 13 to 19 in a lifetime." Not very enlightening! The origin of the word *teen* sheds a little more light. Derived from the Old English word *teona,* it means injury, anger, and grief. Yes, the teen years can be painful for both teen-ager and parent.

Although a teen-ager has not yet earned the freedom of adulthood, he has lost the privileges of childhood. As a result, for seven years he finds himself suspended in time, so to speak. The average 15-year-old feels as though everything that he finds appealing is prohibited. He can't drink, drive, marry, borrow money on his own, make his own decisions, vote, or enlist. But he *must* go to school whether or not he wants to. All these *don'ts* put a strain on relationships between adults and teen-agers that usually lasts as long as a teen-ager is financially dependent on his parents.

Radio, television, and other media overflow with statistics on juvenile crime, delinquency, pregnancy out of wedlock, and drug abuse. Are the teen-agers of today worse than we were when we were kids? Not *worse,* maybe, but it is safe to say that the teen-ager of today definitely differs from

VII. **How to Motivate Teen-agers**
  A. Choose motivators important to them
  B. Formalize an agreement
  C. Provide immediate rewards

VIII. **Relations With Teen-agers**
  A. Respect their privacy
  B. Make home attractive
  C. Supervise subtly
  D. Respect their cry for independence
  E. Maintain a sense of humor
  F. Discuss forthcoming changes
  G. Enlist sibling understanding
  H. Listen
  I. Provide security, love, acceptance

IX. **Parents Have the Right** —
  A. to question unsavory friendships
  B. to refuse use of the car
  C. to control phone calls
  D. to withhold unearned privileges
  E. to expect good grades
  F. to set standards of appearance
  G. to monitor music
  H. to regulate dating

X. **Help for Discouraged Parents**
  A. Even teens of perfect parents rebel
  B. A good foundation pays off
  C. Appreciate your own worth
  D. Rely on a Higher Power

the teen-ager of twenty or thirty years ago. Although adolescents today do very much the same things you did, they do them at an earlier age than ever before. Sociologists have confirmed that children do grow up faster these days. They date earlier and are introduced to all facets of life at an earlier age. Teen-agers have more money, more modes of transportation available, more leisure time, and less supervision than ever before. They also mature sexually three years earlier than the past generation.

And the problems of the adult world only compound the difficulty. Divorce, inflation, energy crises, and political corruption are not pretty pictures. Adults who cannot handle their own difficulties are hardly equipped to cope with the problems erupting inside a teen-aged member of the family. Through this difficult time of growth, a teen-ager needs parents who can recognize that he is changing into an adult, parents who will patiently understand rather than overreact to the attitudes and behaviors of the teen-ager.

Until the teen years, your youngster has more or less accepted your guidance, at least with a little persuasion. Now, however, you may notice that your teen-ager wants every sentence verified. The child who once seemed so content in your care now seems troubled, restless, and easily upset.

The methods of discipline you previously used no longer seem effective. Your teen-ager's self-esteem takes a nose dive. Responsibility becomes a thing of the past. The closeness you dreamed of maintaining with your teen-ager seems unattainable. The active listening you've been saving to use isn't working like you thought it would. He never wants to stay at home with the family anymore. When he is, his mind wanders elsewhere. He acts as though it is a crime to be seen in your presence. His emotional highs and lows, bursts of temper, and periods of sluggishness confuse you.

You wonder whether you are losing your knack for parenting—losing touch with your child. You flounder about as you seek help in understanding yourself and your teen-ager. You try to remember what it was like when you were young. But the span of years blurs your memory. The scary stories that your friends relate about how they failed to cope during this difficult time add to your confusion. Fortified with little hope of success, you bravely turn your face into the storm only to discover that the current deluge is over but a new one is brewing.

If this even partially describes your home, relax. It's normal! You need not feel as though you are failing as a parent because you find yourself embroiled by emotional struggles with your emerging adolescent. You are experiencing the early process of rebellion.

The Pros and Cons of Rebellion

When we conduct seminars for parents of teen-agers, we frequently ask whether they perceive rebellion as a negative or a positive experience in life. Parents overwhelmingly tack a minus sign onto rebellion. By definition, rebellion refers to resistance or rejection of authority or control. But think a moment. What would happen if your child never resisted or rejected your control? He would remain under your authority (and perhaps roof) forever.

During the teen years the emerging adult begins to extricate himself from his parents' values, ideas, and controls—and attempts to establish his own. So in this sense, it is a positive process—the process of establishing one's own individuality, code of ethics, values, ideas, and beliefs. For some youngsters this process occurs early in the teen years; for some it occurs later. For some it will be a difficult transition; for others it will be easy. Parents of the latter group stand around scratching their heads in bewilderment as they listen to the wild stories of parents who feel that they have been to hell and back with their teen-agers.

For all teen-agers the process of establishing one's own identity is a very necessary procedure. If it does not transpire during the teen years when it is supposed to, it will likely occur at some future time. For instance, during mid-life. Many mid-life crisis situations might actually be termed latent periods of rebellion. How much healthier when the experience occurs during the time frame set aside for it.

Through rebellion the teen-ager cries out for recognition of his individuality. He no longer wants you to consider him your property, but nonetheless he remains your responsibility. He is attempting to find out who he is, what he believes, and what he stands for. Both his identity and self-respect are on the line. In his search to find these answers he may react more strongly to your authority than he previously did. You must

be wise enough at this time to recognize that his reaction is not something personal against you but something normal developing within him.

Normal rebellion will lead the adolescent to a mature life. This constructive time period will assist the teen-ager in shedding childish ways and developing independence. You may find it difficult to keep the lines of communication open at times, but even through periods of difficulty both parent and teen-ager should remain open to exploring persistent problems. Remem-

"So much for family planning!"

ber that the teen-ager remains a novice in coping with his own feelings as well as in coping with your feelings and reactions.

Your teen-ager's vast mood swings may frustrate you. Sometimes he behaves as though he is "king of the mountain," from where he obtains an eagle's view of life and all its dazzling splendor. Before you adjust to that mood, he may plummet into the abyss of despair and hopeless despondency. All facets of life seem to appear greatly magnified or exaggerated. Everything is either great or awful, the coldest or the hottest, the most wonderful or the most detestable. The maturity of your actions and reactions will help him recognize that life is 10 percent what happens to a person and 90 percent how he reacts to it.

Although he scrutinizes everything, he does not pause long to look in any given direction. One day he may walk a block out of his way to see Julie. In a few weeks he may walk two blocks out of his way to avoid her. At one point he cannot get his fill of pizza. Later he cannot understand all the excitement over it.

During the normal phases of rebellion you may expect your teen-ager to challenge your authority in a number of areas: He may talk back to you, argue with you, test rules and curfews, question religion, and reject long-established family values. He will also clearly demonstrate the same challenge to authority through the clothes he wears and the music he listens to. Many teen-agers will experiment with alcohol, drugs, and sex.

Whether your teen-ager's period of rebellion will remain within the confines of "normal" or whether it becomes abnormal in its intensity and direction depends to a great extent on your reaction to it. If you redouble your efforts to dictate and control, the seeds of insurrection may take root deep inside your child. You may be able to control him for a time, but he will likely vow that someday, someway he will get even with you. However, if you can show patience while your child is finding himself, you will not work yourself out of a relationship. And that's of utmost importance, isn't it?

Abnormal Rebellion

Perhaps you are saying, "If all this is normal, what on earth is abnormal?" Abnormal rebellion bogs down the family in constant battles over the car, dates, friends, curfews, rules, or money. A cold war rages in the home where family members fear to speak lest they escalate rebellion. Abnormal rebellion takes a youngster out of the mainstream of life. It forces him into a narrow detour that can lead to a life seething with bitterness and hate.

Abnormal rebellion can often be measured in terms of degree and frequency. In one neighborhood some youngsters drove their sports cars across lawns, uprooted shrubs, broke windows, smeared walls with paint, smashed plaster and lights with sledgehammers, and hacked wall paneling with hatchets. One of the fathers of these bored, frustrated, rich kids said, "They were only letting off steam." Some steam—$400,000 worth!

The hushed up American scandal is the billion-dollar dilemma of shoplifting. More than half the shoplifters today are teen-agers—most of them white, middle-class girls. They steal not from need but for the thrill of it. It's called "beat the system." A couple of girls in Beverly Hills tried to steal several expensive blouses. They sobbed to the police that they would put the stuff back if they would only set them free. Their caper was just another way of rebelliously declaring, "I'm not going to obey the rules." Often these youngsters are desperately trying to tell their parents, "Now maybe I can get you to pay some attention to me."

Rebellion becomes abnormal when a teen-ager refuses to abide by reasonable household rules; ignores curfews; habitually experiments with alcohol, drugs, and/or sex; has repeated brushes with the law; or appears in bizarre fashions. In short, abnormal rebellion involves a total refusal to cooperate in family or social responsibilities. The younger the teen-ager when he enters this abnormal rebellious stage, the more difficult it will be for the family—particularly if younger children in the family will witness and perhaps emulate the behavior.

It can set a precedent that younger siblings may follow. At times you will puzzle over how far you should or should not go with the child.

Perhaps you will never have to face abnormal rebellion. However, if you have two or more children, your chances of having to deal with it are greatly increased—regardless of what you have said through the years about other people's teen-agers. "When my kids get to be teen-agers, they won't act like that! I won't permit it!" It is difficult for the parent of a small child to visualize what might lie ahead in the years to come. This parent can tell his child to sit on a chair till he returns and expects that the child will be there when he gets back. Not necessarily so with a teen-ager. The teen-ager has a mind, an individuality, of his own. And try as we may, this mind and individuality cannot always be controlled. I, too, was inclined to point the finger of blame at parents and their faulty methods of discipline until we experienced abnormal rebellion from one of the three children to whom I dedicated this book.

As a young mother I was the close friend of a mother with four children. I speculated that if anyone could produce perfect children this mother could. She and her husband were devout Christians, and the entire family regularly participated in home worship. No double standards were practiced in the home. Family time together held a high priority. Yet they had severe difficulty with one of their children during the teen years.

This distressed mother wrote to me at one point: "Things are somewhat better as far as Tim is concerned. He attends church regularly and has broken off with a girl I thoroughly disapproved of. He's working afternoons and attending school mornings. In his spare time he works on his '55 Chevy. He has a long way to go yet, but things are looking up.

"This has been a very hard experience for me, but good has come out of it too. I have at last been able to separate what I am responsible for—and what Tim's responsibilities are. Somehow, I had the mistaken idea that if we raised our children according to the Book, they would automatically turn out all right. I forgot about the human will. We can do only so much, and the child must decide whether to follow our example and teaching. P.S. I pray that your 'day' will never come as far as your children are concerned."

My friend mentioned several important points. To begin with, the time comes when we parents can no longer feel responsible for the irresponsible decisions our teen-agers make. If they choose to make irresponsible choices regardless of our warnings, then they must also reap the consequences of those decisions. Second, children do not automatically turn out all right just because we read the Bible, have home worship, and "do our best." Whereas the Bible, family worship, Christian schools, regular church attendance, parental example, and consistency are essential and helpful in rearing children, *these do not guarantee that our children will turn out well.* No parent can or should attempt to control his teen-ager's destiny to such a degree. Just as God leaves us free to make certain choices, so we should allow our teen-agers freedom to make some decisions.

God always welcomes us back after we

Rights vs. Privileges

Teen-agers frequently demand *privileges* interpreting them as *rights.* Consequently parents have become very confused about what is a "right" and what is a "privilege." And what about parental rights? Are we clear on this issue? Let's find out. Read each of the following statements and score yourself according to the scale of 1-5 as shown.

1. Definitely yes   2. Probably yes   3. Unsure   4. Probably not
5. Definitely not.

1 2 3 4 5   1. I feel I have a right to restrict my teen-ager from associating with questionable peers.

1 2 3 4 5   2. I feel I have the right to refuse my teen-ager the use of the family car when my needs supersede his or for any other logical reason.

1 2 3 4 5   3. I feel I have the right to deprive my teen-ager of privileges he has not earned.

1 2 3 4 5   4. I feel I have the right to set standards concerning my teen-ager's appearance particularly when moral issues are involved.

Please turn to page 238 for scoring instructions.

repent and ask forgiveness. Likewise we should always be willing to welcome back the erring child. Our son Mark has manifested the greatest degree of rebellion in our home. During these years he tested his religious values by attempting to reject ours. He would sit with us during family worship, but he made sure we understood that he did not wish to be there. Friday night was our "family night." We would read inspiring stories, lift our voices in song, and in the wintertime sit around the crackling, warm fire. It was a time to pull our family together after a stressful week. At the close of this enjoyable evening, we would kneel in a circle and put our arms around each other as we prayed. It symbolized our unity and closeness as a family.

During the week we may have engaged in many struggles with Mark, heated words, or a bad scene, but on Friday evenings we would always embrace him. We wanted him to know that we loved him and that he belonged in our family despite the disagree-

ments we might have had. For a period of time during these years he would permit us to encircle him with our arms, but he remained like a wooden soldier, arms straight at his side. His silent message was crystal clear: "I'll show you. If you won't let me have my way around here, I'll get even with you!" Never did we make mention that he did not return our love. We just kept loving him. Our unconditional message of love must have reached him during a difficult time, because one Friday night his arms encircled us once again, and he's been returning our love ever since.

God never withdraws His love from us. And since we parents stand in the place of God to our children, we must be able to demonstrate this kind of unconditional, indestructible love to a rebellious teen-ager, no matter how difficult it may be.

Several broad principles may help you as you guide your teen-ager through this demanding period. The first principle: Learn to communicate. Set aside the endless verbal battles that tend to leave you exhausted and discouraged. Shouting only weakens your authority and provides a strategic advantage for your teen-ager. Look for a better way. If your 14-year-old is getting more difficult to handle by the minute—breaking rules left and right—and if his defiance is reaching epidemic proportions, and if he seems bent on living by his own code of ethics, it is imperative that you do something quickly or you will lose control and possibly might lose your son or daughter.

Such a situation calls for a serious conference with your teen-ager. You might want to conduct the conversation in a public place such as a restaurant where control must be exercised. During your talk you will want to convey, without blaming or judging, the seriousness of the situation. Explain that what has been occurring is natural and normal even though not necessarily pleasant. It is part of the process of establishing one's own identity and values. However, just because he desires more freedom, you cannot set him free to do whatever he wishes. As a parent you have a God-given responsibility to guide and protect him even though he is a teen-ager. You cannot neglect this responsibility since God holds you accountable for each child you bring into the world.

You may wish to apologize for not always reacting in a positive manner. Sincere parental apology can go a long way with a teen-ager. It can actually build your child's respect for you and restore the bond between you. You may have lost your cool, overreacted, or not acted in wisdom. State your intentions to correct such behavior and to be more understanding in the future.

Next, set limits. Let your teen-ager know that even though he is growing up and will soon be on his own, this does not now mean he can be on his own in your home. All must abide by certain general rules for family living in order for peace and harmony to abound. Enumerate the rules on which you will not compromise. Then calmly let your teen-ager know that if he chooses to deliberately disobey you from this point on, you will have to resort to drastic measures. (You do not have to enumerate them at this point.)

Convey your entire message in love. Reassure your child of your concern and deep love. Tell him that you want a happy home during your few remaining years left together as a family and that these years can either be shared in war or peace. Ask for his cooperation in contributing to family harmony and in shouldering his responsibilities around the home. If you respect him, his respect for himself and for you may be fostered or at least facilitated.

If you do all this and your teen-ager remains hostile and defiantly disobeys your every expectation, you might have to resort to "tough love." In fact, the organization ToughLove is an international network of support groups of parents who draw a tough line for problem kids. Members of ToughLove tell their kids to straighten up or else—even if the "else" means banishment from the home. The founders of Tough-Love, family counselors David and Phyllis York, declare: "You have to say to your young person, 'You have to choose between living in our family as a decent human being or you have to leave.' To make that decision is awfully hard." (The Fresno *Bee*, September 24, 1982.) Parents then give their youngsters the choice of living with friends, relatives, or other ToughLove parents. (You can obtain information about ToughLove by contacting ToughLove Community Service Foundation, 118 N. Main Street, Sellersville, PA 18960. Phone [215] 257-0421.)

I regard ToughLove as the last resort for parents who have been unable to handle problems such as drug and alcohol dependency, sexual permissiveness, shoplifting, stealing, and other serious problems. It is a radical but effective step. It works.

Protecting, Preaching, or Inoculating?

How can parents help a teen-ager move more smoothly toward independence? The most common method used by Christian parents involves completely controlling the teen-ager's environment. The parents make the decisions when it comes to choice of entertainment, friends, clothes, music, reading material, television shows, and movies. These parents will likely place the teen-ager in a Christian school in an attempt to shield him from wrong influences and reinforce Christian principles.

However, trying to control a teen-ager's environment simply will not work. You cannot shield your youngster from worldly influences. The same problems that exist in the public school system can also be found in Christian schools to a lesser degree. Attempting to isolate a teen-ager from worldly influences is a most ineffective method of control. Since such a teen-ager must eventually leave the structured environment, he or she may be the least prepared of all young people to deal with the realities of life.

Another common mistake is parental overreaction to negative influences. These parents hope that by overreacting with negative remarks regarding non-Christian standards and activity, their teen-ager will avoid such folly in the future. For instance, in an effort to deter his teen-ager from listening to rock music, Dad constantly makes belittling remarks about such music.

This technique often backfires by producing the opposite effect. Under such a regime many teens simply tune out their overreacting parents. They may listen respectfully if not indifferently when at home, but outside the home they pursue what their parents have "preached" against. Unknown to the parents, the youngsters may also carry out clandestine activities inside the home, having become clever at secluding their behavior from their parents. When at last the parents discover the truth, they become fraught with guilt and grief. The overriding question is never far from mind: How could my child follow the ways of the world when we have so adamantly taught against them?

The most effective method of teaching values and standards to a teen-ager has been labeled the "inoculation approach." Just as parents provide the opportunity for their child to receive small dosages of infectious agents in order to gain immunity from disease, so the parent prepares his child during the early years. Rather than preaching against negative influences or isolating the child from them, this parent teaches values through example and open, direct discussion in the face of exposure to what is questionable.

When an issue arises both the pros and cons are discussed in an open way. The young person is talked *with* (not *to)* and gently guided. The parent, as frequently as possible, allows the young person to make his own choices early in the selection process—*even if the decision is poor.* How much better that the youngster learn early how to avoid poor choices than later on when decisions with greater consequences are at stake. Few parents can tolerate such an atmosphere of openness, yet it is by far the most effective approach. Most parents feel compelled to make decisions in all matters for their teen-agers. When their teen-ager makes a poor choice, the parent feels tremendous guilt and failure. However, wise decision making is an acquired ability. Like a muscle, it must be used repeatedly to develop.

Informed parents who wish to complement the inoculation method will involve their teen-ager in setting standards for the home in advance of the event. Certain crucial areas such as driving, dating, and sexual behavior can be successfully addressed in such a manner. Prior to the time a teen-ager is allowed the privilege of dating or driving, he or she should be encouraged to suggest guidelines to follow when using the car or dating later on. Parents, too, can have input into the agreement, which can then be drawn up.

This method is very effective because when a young person formulates and agrees to abide by a rule, he will tend to follow through much more consistently than if it has been demanded by the parents. It is important that you get as much input from your teen-ager to begin with and offer as little parental input as possible.

Such an approach takes time, effort, and patience, but rich dividends are the handsome payoff. A teen-ager who has been allowed and encouraged to make choices is likely to cooperate with family policies and to develop a healthy independence and positive self-respect—two indispensable characteristics.

Everybody's Doing It

A common trap parents get caught in is the argument that "everybody's doing it." Parents caught in this bind should explain that everyone does not do things alike; therefore they do not need to know what other parents are doing. Parents should make every effort to be as lenient as possible and, within reason, give their teen-ager the freedom he desires. However, it is very important that Christian parents establish early in their child's life that they do things differently as a whole than non-Christian parents because their value system is different.

With this thought in mind, it is often a mistake to say "No" immediately when your teen-ager asks for permissions. Parents always feel that they are on safe ground by thinking it over. So they begin by saying, "No," then listening to the arguments in favor of "Yes," and frequently changing the "No" to a "Yes." This teaches young people that it pays to argue and that "No" really means "Maybe; . . . I'll think it over." A wiser plan might be to suggest, "Give me the facts, and then I'll make a decision." When he has presented them, say, "I really haven't made a decision yet. Give me some time to think it over. I want to talk with your dad [or mom], and I'll let you know what we decide." Then make as rational a decision as possible, and once you make it, *stick with it* at all costs.

Punishment for Teen-agers

As you will recall, parents should never spank or whip a teen-ager. An adolescent considers himself an adult and views spankings as "baby stuff." His self-esteem must not be sacrificed on the altar of resentment.

This does not imply that you should abandon control. On the contrary. A teen-ager needs firm and consistent super-

vision. Indeed, his sense of security depends upon it. But you should not need to mete out specific punishments as often as you did during his younger years. Talking things over within a matrix of reasoning and concern can adequately handle many infractions. If this process fails, you may decide to withhold privileges—an evening with friends, a trip, the use of the car, and so forth. Withholding allowance may help control some types of misbehavior, but do not use it to improve failing grades. Poor grades point to problems that may lie beyond the teen-ager's control.

Disciplinary measures work most effectively for teen-agers when they have had a hand in setting the rules and consequences for infractions. While parents regard such negotiations as a calculated attempt to influence behavior, teens regard it as a fresh breeze on the scene. Hence it aids both sides of the encounter. One mother used this method when her son came in one night fourteen minutes after the established curfew. She simply said, "Let's hear you

needs to learn about life and how to live it. Therefore, wise parents will make their homes a test laboratory where each teen-ager can practice the art of living and homemaking. Every teen-ager should learn to cook, care for the laundry, clean house, make household repairs, buy groceries, balance a budget, care for the yard, and plan social events. Adolescent daughters can and should assist with the preparation of food, occasionally preparing an entire meal; sew some clothes for themselves; and help with the housecleaning. Older boys can take down storm windows, assist with yard work, tend the garden, help in car repairs, and fix broken items around the home.

It is especially important that older teen-agers have some household duties that seem important to them and are in keeping with their greater maturity. A 16-year-old boy, for instance, not only should have to wash the car, but also should be permitted to express his opinions about buying a new car or having the present one overhauled. Not only should a teen-age girl have to wash windows and vacuum; she should also have a voice in deciding on fabric and room colors at redecorating time.

Although teen-agers should keep busy with home chores, parents must also allow them time for outside activities. If John has basketball practice on Tuesday nights, it isn't fair to keep him from practice because it is his night to do the dishes. Better scheduling is called for. If Mother or Dad would pitch in and help John with the dishes, he would more quickly learn to help others when they are in need. Parents should be considerate of a teen-ager's outside interests—if, of course, the teen-ager remembers his home obligations.

Parents should especially give priority to a teen-ager with a part-time job. Home chores should not stand in the way unless the situation at home desperately requires it. Part-time work to a teen-ager offers a sense of prestige and a source of income and may help him choose a career. Gradually a teen-ager should be allowed to give more of his time to a job and less time to home chores if he so chooses.

give yourself the lecture you deserve right now."

"You stupid jerk," he readily began. "You do that again and you'll lose your license, and you wouldn't want that." Grinning, he continued fluently with a mildly dramatic and beautifully detailed recital of the parental scolding ritual. He even included reasons and his "resolve" henceforth to return home on the early side of the deadline. His performance kept Mother from foolishly flaring up at an hour when she was too tired to do it justice. Furthermore, she enjoyed watching the boy express his own growing responsibility. P.S. Since that night the boy has been early, never late!

Work Responsibilities for the Teen-ager

Before an astronaut steps aboard a space capsule, he receives careful instruction on how to operate it. The more he learns and trains, the better astronaut he's going to be. And before a teen-ager can assume the responsibilities of adulthood, he

Self-Test on Handling Teen-agers

Circle how it is you feel about each of the following statements according to the scale at the left.
1. Strongly agree   2. Mildly agree   3. Not sure   4. Mildly disagree
5. Strongly disagree.

1 2 3 4 5   1. I believe teen-agers today are worse than the teen-agers of my generation.

1 2 3 4 5   2. I view rebellion and the entire process of breaking away from parental values and establishing one's own individuality as negative.

1 2 3 4 5   3. During normal phases of rebellion, I expect my teen-ager to challenge my authority, talk back, test rules and curfews, and question religion and long-established family values.

1 2 3 4 5   4. Sometimes I feel tremendous guilt and failure when my teen-ager makes a poor choice—as if I were personally responsible.

1 2 3 4 5   5. If my teen-ager's defiance should reach epidemic proportions, I would ask him to straighten up or leave.

1 2 3 4 5   6. When an issue arises, I discuss the pros and cons in an open way, gently guiding my teen-ager toward right choices.

1 2 3 4 5   7. I can allow my teen-ager to make his own choices—even when the choice is a poor one or diametrically opposed to family standards and values.

1 2 3 4 5   8. I have encouraged my teen-ager to participate in formulating guidelines for behavior in crucial areas such as driving and dating.

1 2 3 4 5   9. Even though my teen-ager may at times be hostile, bitter, rebellious, sullen, or unresponsive, I feel I am able to keep the doors of acceptance, love, and communication open.

1 2 3 4 5   10. I am able to see my teen-ager as a person of worth even though he may choose different values than I would have him choose.

Discuss your responses with your partner, a friend, or a parent study group.

mischief, and builds integrity, feelings of confidence, and self-respect. It also helps calm the passionate energies which surge through vital young bodies by providing a healthy escape valve for them.

How to Motivate a Teen-ager

Perhaps you have done your best to teach your teen-ager responsibility, but it is still difficult to get him on his feet and moving in the right direction. Since this is a very self-centered time of life when rewards appeal to young people, the principles of reinforcement are particularly useful. If you feel that your teen-ager needs motivating, the following information will be helpful:

1 *Choose a motivator which is important to him.* A couple of hours with the car some night could prove a marvelous incentive to a young man. Another youngster might want a special article of clothing. Offering a teen-ager a means of obtaining luxuries is a happy alternative to the whining, crying, begging, complaining, and pestering that might occur otherwise. You might say, "Yes, you may have the sweater you want, but you will have to earn it." Once the incentive or motivator is agreed upon, the second step is in order.

During teen years, "timing" continues to be important in the teaching of responsibility. And again the most favorable time to teach responsibility is when the young person shows a heightened interest in some activity. Sonny came home from school full of enthusiasm over learning to make an electric eye during his "shop" class. He figured he could make one that would open the garage door. Sonny's dad encouraged this new interest, and together they purchased the necessary materials and began work in the garage during spare time. Since the electric eye was a success, they planned new projects with the use of Dad's power tools, and Sonny, who was never very interested in planning for the future, began considering a career as an electrician.

A recent study among teen-agers indicated that almost 88 percent of those who had been in trouble with the law had answered, "Nothing," when asked this question: "What do you do in your spare time?" Housework, particularly active scrubbing of walls and floors, is good for the figures of girls and will build muscles in young men. Cooking, baking, and sewing will prepare a young girl for homemaking. Yard work, mechanics, and building teach essential masculine skills. Work is the best discipline a teen-ager can have. It teaches the virtues of industry and patience. It teaches trades from which to choose a life occupation in years to come. It occupies time which could be spent in idleness or

2 *Formalize the agreement.* An excellent way of accomplishing this objective is through a written contract that both teenager and parents sign. Harry and I drew up a contract for Mark just prior to the time he turned 15 and could apply for a learner's permit to drive. Yes, he could obtain a learner's permit and drive our car in our presence, but he would have to *earn* the privilege by behaving responsibly. Driving a car calls for accountability, and if Mark could demonstrate responsibility in other areas of life, he would be allowed to drive.

We insisted that Mark earn 25,000 points within a six-week period or the contract would become null and void.

Mark also understood from the inception of the contract that he could lose points for disagreeable and unreasonable behavior. (See chart below.)

Along with the removal of points for poor behavior, you may wish to include bonus points for commendable behavior not enumerated in the contract.

3

Establish a method of providing immediate rewards. Most of us need something tangible to sustain our interest as we move toward a goal. In Mark's case we adapted the chart system for the subsequent contract. Points were accurately recorded nightly, and a weekly score was totaled. The first week he earned only 750 points. He could easily see that he would never reach the required 25,000 in six weeks at that rate. Interestingly enough, he earned 7,500 points the second week.

The contract system can be adapted to multiple situations. The principle is effective, but you may need to vary the method.

It is important that the teen-ager not receive the end product that served as the motivator if he has not earned it. Likewise, parents should not delay or deny the reward once their youngster has earned it.

Homework for Parents

Parents can help their adolescent when they—

1. *Respect his privacy.* A teen-ager needs privacy, and parents need not feel rejected because a bedroom door is closed to them. The need for privacy should also include personal letters, diaries, and phone calls. Parents who search through a teen-ager's room or personal effects seeking evidence of clandestine activity are violating their youngster's right to privacy. If you suspect that your youngster may be taking drugs, search and seizure is in order, but confiscating diaries and mail, or routine prying through pockets, purses, and drawers, is not a parental prerogative.

2. *Make the home attractive.* Small considerations such as a neat personal

---

Contract for Driver's Permit

Schedule of Points

100 pts	for each half-hour of work beyond chores without being asked
50	for every school paper with an A on it
50	for getting up first time called
50	for saying "I'd be happy to" when asked to do something
50	for making bed and straightening room before leaving for school
50	for leaving bathroom spotless
100	for each half-hour spent listening to classical music
150	for every six verses memorized from the Bible
100	for each day of studying Bible lesson
50	for completing assigned tasks quickly
200	for each hour of study at home
100	for each half hour of outside reading

May Lose Points for Each of the Following:

100	for loss of temper (name-calling, door slamming, disrespect, et cetera)
50	for tardies at school
50	for being late for appointments
100	for citations from school
50	for arguing

Teen-agers and Discipline

Circle the proper disciplinary response in each of the following situations:

1. A 14-year-old gives forth with an emotional outburst of anger, upset, and despair.
   a. natural consequences
   b. ignore it
   c. active listening
   d. I-statement
   e. temporary isolation

2. A 16-year-old wants to stay up and watch the late show every night.
   a. restrict privileges
   b. natural consequences
   c. active listening
   d. reason with him
   e. forbid it

3. A 17-year-old who chooses companions of questionable character.
   a. active listening
   b. lecture
   c. restrict privileges
   d. forbid the association
   e. invite questionable friends to your home

4. A 16-year-old abuses the guidelines set up regarding the use of the family car.
   a. lecture
   b. withhold use of car
   c. active listening
   d. reason with him
   e. temporary isolation

5. A 16-year-old receives poor grades and has multiple behavior problems at school.
   a. lecture
   b. ground him
   c. seek professional help
   d. active listening
   e. try a "contract" to motivate him

6. A 14-year-old spends hours on the phone each evening.
   a. draw up an agreement for phone use
   b. lecture
   c. restrict phone privileges
   d. active listening
   e. natural consequences

7. A 17-year-old follows every dress fad with great enthusiasm.
   a. nag
   b. send an I-statement
   c. forbid it
   d. accept it as inevitable and try not to make a major issue over it
   e. restrict privileges

8. A 15-year-old fails to accept responsibility for cleaning his room or handling his share of household tasks.
   a. try a "contract" to motivate him
   b. natural consequences
   c. lecture
   d. one hard whipping
   e. restrict privileges

9. A 17-year-old listens to music of which you do not approve.
   a. forbid it
   b. accept it as normal
   c. restrict privileges
   d. discuss a compromise
   e. take stereo away

Most effective answers found on page 239.

appearance, made beds, and a clean kitchen can save a teen-ager embarrassment when friends visit. A teen-ager is keenly sensitive to his peers' reaction toward his parents—even though he might need a comb himself.

And never stop doing things together as a family. Many a youngster has splendid persons for parents, but he has never discovered it because the only time he sees his parents is when they are correcting him, criticizing him, or telling him what or what not to do. One of the greatest influences on the happiness of the family is the feeling of companionship and understanding which comes from play together. Because so many of the parental contacts with youngsters are, of necessity, for routine and regulation, it is important that some contacts with parents be less serious and aimed at mutual enjoyment. Family games, camping trips, vacations, hikes through the woods, building projects, and friendly debates create an atmosphere in which young people naturally want to share.

3. *Supervise subtly.* A teen-ager does not respond to a parade of don'ts, yet inwardly he craves guidance. He is seemingly caught between opposing forces. On the one hand he resents spineless parents, but on the other hand he rebels at the infraction on his freedom, especially when his parents become arbitrary over things which he feels he can handle himself. This is when a teen-ager may cry out, "Give me liberty, or I will leave home!"

However, discipline by no means stops or tapers off during teen years. A teen-ager needs the anchor of parental discipline to hold him during this time of life. And, as always, discipline should be fair and never divided. No youngster should be allowed to play one parent against the other, and where a decision must be reached, the father, as leader of the family unit, should assume this responsibility.

4. *Respect his cry for independence.* A teen-ager needs bonds but not bondage, and parents must distinguish between the two. Everything parents do from infancy on works toward making a teen-ager more dependent or independent—until they work themselves out of a job, not out of a relationship. Often parents fear to grant independence to an adolescent because they fear the youngster is not old enough to handle it, but the young person who longs for independence and who is clearly not ready for it is not made wiser by being reminded of this fact in sanctimonious tones.

When your teen-ager indicates he wants more freedom, step back a little and allow him to make his own decisions and also to bear the responsibility for them. Usually if he isn't ready for his newfound freedom, he will come back to you and ask for further guidance.

5. *Maintain a sense of humor.* Managing a teen-ager successfully means balancing love and discipline on a scale of good humor. A teen-ager, or an adult for that matter, will do almost anything within reason when a request or a suggestion is made with a light touch. A sense of humor is an antidote for taking the teen years too seriously. Parents should remember that even though their teen-ager may relegate them to the second century BC, in a few years they'll be recognized as back in the twentieth century. Laughter in the home creates an atmosphere of acceptance and joy, and a teen-ager needs to learn to enjoy family living and laugh with others and at himself.

6. *Discuss changes that may take place.* Casually discuss with your teen-ager the changes that take place in adolescence, the changes in any house rules, and the pressures he may face in the future. It is years too late to begin sex education, but sex education should continue through the teen years. Of course, you already have prepared him for the many changes taking place in his body, but now is a good time to review these things and open communication lines on the subject of sexuality.

7. *Enlist sibling understanding.* It may help to promote better understanding of siblings if you talk privately with younger members of the family concerning areas of conflict where understanding is needed or where they might help lessen trouble. By taking them into partnership on this matter,

parents can help them better understand adolescence when they reach this stage themselves.

8. *Listen to him.* Many parents don't really listen to their teen-ager—at least not with an open mind. Many parents couldn't care less about the thoughts and feelings of their teen-ager: "After all, he's only a kid. We'll listen to him when he learns what he's talking about!"

A survey among adolescents asked, "When you establish a home of your own, do you want it to be just like your present home, or do you plan to make some changes? If so, what?" A vast majority replied that the change they would make would be to take time to listen to their kids. One answered, "If I go to my mother with a personal problem, she acts horrified with what I say and tells me to get that silly notion out of my head! If I go to Dad, I get a sixty-minute lecture."

Today's youth are a new generation, and they must feel that we really do care and that we can listen to them without getting angry, without blaming and judging them, and without name-calling. Active listening becomes increasingly important during teen years in attempting to close the generation gap.

9. *Provide security, love, and acceptance.* A teen-ager needs security in a relationship that doesn't change with circumstances. He needs to know that even through misunderstandings and differences, his relationship with his parents is never broken—no matter what happens.

Mature love for a teen-ager means that Mother and Father are ready to share in the life and growth of their child and to release that growing person into an ever-enlarging sphere of existence. Parents should give a small child large quantities of physical affection, and the teen-ager who has been comforted for all his bumps and bruises when a small child will not be embarrassed by affection and will not be as apt to look for a premature sexual relationship to make up for something missed now that there is the added incentive of erotic satisfaction.

10. *Provide a model of a happy marriage.* Teen-agers need to see their parents express their love for each other—daily. According to careful studies, a marriage relationship can sink to its lowest ebb when a couple's children are in their teens. One of the contributing factors is the tension engendered from dealing with adolescents. Other problems have little to do with the child but arise from unmet needs between husband and wife.

During the early years of a child's life, the mother can meet his needs for security on her own, but during the tumultuous years of adolescence, a youngster needs the attention of both a mother and a father. If husband and wife could resolve the problems that keep them from fully enjoying their own marital relationship, many of their teen-ager's problems might vanish also. A teen-ager's security is greatly enhanced by the security evidenced in his family.

Parental Rights Versus Teen-age Privileges

The needs and privileges of children have received so much attention recently that the basic needs and rights of parents are often ignored. Consequently, parents have become confused over the distinction between rights and privileges in the family. Teen-agers often demand privileges, interpreting them as their rights. The following partial list includes some issues that need clarification in most families.

1. *Parents have the right to dissuade their teen-ager from association with questionable friends.* The choice of friends poses a common problem. Many parents have thought that some boy was unsuitable to associate with their daughter or that certain companions were leading their child astray. A typical parental reaction is to forbid the relationship. Resentment, bitterness, and misunderstanding usually follow—making the forbidden friends appear even more desirable. Disapproval will only drive your teen-ager to hide his associations from you. Why not encourage your teen-ager to bring his friends home? It is here within the bonds of acceptance that the teen-ager is able to make comparisons. An adolescent must feel free to select his own friends. However,

it is a parental prerogative to interfere in extreme cases. Sometimes a move to another city can adequately solve intensely complicated problems.

2. *Parents have the right to refuse their teen-ager the use of the family car when parental needs supersede his, or for any other logical reason.* Your teen-ager will have unlimited rights to a car only when he purchases his own. Teen-age use of a family car is a privilege with certain associated responsibilities. In our family, each child was held responsible for a portion of the increase in our insurance rates as he or she became eligible to drive. Along with this we used "The Driving Agreement" previously mentioned. In addition to paying the increase in insurance costs, parents and child should agree concerning what portion of the deductible he or she should pay in the case of an accident. The privilege of using the family automobile is a powerful motivator for inducing good behavior, and the withholding of this privilege is equally effective. But be fair.

3. *Parents have the right to control all incoming and outgoing phone calls from all telephones installed and maintained at their expense.* Someone has quipped that turmoil is living in a home with three teen-agers and one telephone! Possibly more disagreements between parents and teen-agers begin over the use of the telephone than over any other potential issue. Therefore families need to clearly establish and consistently enforce ground rules concerning the use of the phone. First of all, limit the length of all phone calls to a reasonable time period. This limit will apply to phone conversations with girl and boyfriends. If the teen-agers can't say it in 20 minutes, it probably isn't worth saying. Second, limit the number of calls per evening. Under most circumstances two calls each evening will be enough. However, you will need to bend a little if your teen-ager is involved in a school or church function. Count incoming calls as part of the two calls unless the call terminates within five minutes. Require a 15-minute moratorium between calls.

4. *Parents have the right to deprive their teen-ager of privileges he has not earned.* A teen-ager is too old and too large to spank, yet punishment is often necessary. But parents can find an effective tool in the withdrawal of privileges. Does your teen-ager keep his promise about returning home at a certain hour or else phone you? Does he do his chores without your having to nag or remind him? Does he get acceptable grades? A teen-ager who goofs off should not receive or expect privileges.

5. *Parents have the right to expect their teen-ager to do his best in school and also to insist that he graduate from high school.* Are your expectations for your teen-ager's grades fair? Remember that knowledge in itself is not as important as learning how to process and use that knowledge in getting along with others as well as adjusting to one's environment. Not only should parents encourage their youngster to finish high school, but if he is college material they should encourage him to continue his education.

Eight weeks before graduation Mark informed us that he wanted to drop out of high school. Rather than overreact to his

announcement, we cautiously suggested that he list on a sheet of paper the pros and cons of such a decision. After much deliberation Mark decided to finish the year. When he subsequently received a four-year scholarship to college, our expectations ran high. Disappointment struck when he flunked out after one quarter and refused to give college another try. After drifting from job to job for three years, he once again enrolled in college. Just yesterday we received a letter that stated in part: "I'm totally and thoroughly enjoying myself here at college. Why just the other day, by accident and an oversight on my part, I missed a class. And I was mad at myself . . . I feel that the reasons for my happiness are these: this time around I want to be here and once again I have some meaning and a goal in life. I really was getting tired of roaming around, not accomplishing anything or ever getting ahead. I just want to say a big thank you for helping me have another chance. This time I'm going to make it."

Had we overreacted several years ago he might never be where he is now.

6. *Parents have the right to set standards concerning their teen-ager's appearance.* Mom and Dad must realize, however, that any campaign designed to thwart the teen-ager who is bent on looking like everyone else is most assuredly doomed. Parents of a teen-ager must understand that an adolescent changes the way he looks and dresses in order to differ from his parents, to be conspicuous, and then to fade into the crowd of his peers.

If your patience is being tried by a teen-ager who embraces every new fad with equal enthusiasm, exercise caution. The more you oppose each craze, the more he'll pursue each one as it comes along. As much as is humanly possible, allow your teen-ager to select his clothes. He needs to wear what is important to him so he can feel accepted by his group. If his clothing is too bizarre, group pressure from his peers may quickly accomplish what you never could.

However, if there is an important issue involved—such as suggestive dress or a lack of underclothing—take a firm stand. Never

be lax about standing against those things that you consider morally objectionable. It is extremely difficult to explain to young teen-age girls why they should not wear certain clothing. They do not yet have the knowledge and wisdom to understand how their clothing affects males. Since they are not stimulated by the appearance of men, they cannot fathom how men are affected. They will need subtle guidance during these years. But do not allow the values you have arbitrarily arrived at from your own upbringing stand between you and your teen-ager, who is growing up in a different world. In other words, if the issue at hand involves nothing more than a fashion whim, let your teen-ager dress like the others.

A teen-ager expends feverish energy in conforming to peer standards, which could be modified if he felt accepted at home. In seeking acceptance, a teen-ager sometimes adopts clothes, hairstyles, and manners that his parents abhor. If they refuse to provide the acceptance he so desperately needs from family members, they will drive him to imitate his peers even more closely and to take up with even more outlandish styles.

7. *Parents have a right to monitor the type of music being played in the home.* Notice the word *monitor.* If you try to restrict a teen-ager entirely from listening to the music of his age, he'll break loose. In one parenting seminar, a discussion of rock music came up. The father of a young child cut in and said, "Why discuss rock music? We're all Christians here. All you do is forbid it!" Parents of a small child sometimes find it difficult to comprehend that some day they must allow their child the freedom to make certain choices for himself. Naturally parents should try to screen the music and affirm the principles that define appropriate types of music.

Even if you could control what your teen listens to at home, you cannot control what he will listen to outside the home. Certain things are beyond parental control, and this is one. You must trust that you have instilled proper values during the early years and that these will carry your teen-ager through this difficult time period when peer pressure remains heavy. Few teen-agers

will be strong enough to reject entirely the music of their age. Once again you will need to offer subtle guidance without sounding totally arbitrary. Naturally, a teen-ager's taste in music does not need to be forced on other members of the family, and controls can be put on volume.

8. *Parents have the right to set up rules regarding dating.* Parents should grant the privilege of dating only after they have examined such factors as age, dependability, willingness to accept responsibility, and mature behavior.

During the early-teen years it is better for teen-agers not to pair off or date singly. Parents can easily circumvent early single dating by making their homes a warm and welcome place for teen-agers to visit. Families of this age group can engage in activities together thus giving the opportunity for young people to establish healthy friendships without moving into single dating. Families can get together at one another's homes, plan a trip to the mountains, set out on a picnic, go skating together, or foster any number of activities that allow young people to mix under controlled circumstances. Church-and-school activities can supplement the activities planned by parents.

At some point during the middle-teen years most young people begin single dating. Girls usually believe themselves ready for single dating at 13 or 14. But wise parents encourage their daughters to hold off until they turn 15 or 16. Statistical studies indicate that the earlier youngsters

begin the dating game, the greater their chances for early marriage. Likewise, the earlier they marry, the higher the odds for divorce.

Going steady—the stage when each pledges not to date anyone else (or that's the way it is suppose to be!)—should be discouraged until the junior or senior year of high school. I must hasten to add, however, that you can probably prevent your 13- or 14-year-old from going steady, but it is much different with a 17- or 18-year-old. Wise parents do not try to forbid a high school senior from having a steady relationship. It is better not to forbid such a relationship but rather to dissuade or discourage it. Keep the channels of communication open. Both you and your teen-ager should recognize that steady relationships provide perfect hideouts for the insecure. The more insecure your teen-ager feels, the more he or she is likely to seek a steady relationship in an effort to solve the problems they encounter in relating to their peer group. Help your youngster solve the root problem. That is much more effective than trying to deal with the symptom of early steady dating.

Curfews, where to go and what to do on dates, and whom a teen-ager dates, are questions of grave concern to parents. Interracial and interfaith dating pose problems particularly in devout homes. Young people from devout and happy homes will usually prefer to follow the teaching and example of their parents when choosing dates. However, much grief could be averted if parents were equipped with a few management skills during this crucial period of time.

Dating and Sexual Behavior

Perhaps parents have less input into these two areas than any other during the teen years. Unknowingly they set up roadblocks of unacceptance so that their teen-agers find these two important areas the most difficult of all to discuss with their parents. Dating and sexual behavior are two subjects of great popularity among young adults, but only a few parents are aware of their own adolescent's behavior or standards.

And for good reason. Parents are well-equipped with great intentions but faulty methods! By refusing to talk about the topic, they hope to discourage early dating. Later, when they can no longer ignore the subject, they become dictatorial and domineering regarding curfews and activities that may or may not be engaged in. In addition to overreacting, they frequently make wisecracks about their child's love relationships so that the kids wish to hide as much as possible in order to spare themselves from ridicule.

There is a better way. Even during the early-teen years dating standards should be a frequent topic at family worship and family conferences. Young people should feel free to make any statement and ask any question as shocking or adverse as they might be. The parents should avoid responding with lectures, put-downs, or any form of retribution. Wouldn't you prefer that your teen-ager obtain information from you rather than just from his peers? Remember also that during these sessions your child is learning and growing. Your perspectives may differ. He may overstate his views in an effort to meet your objections or break loose from your values.

An overreaction from you at this point may well insure that he will some day attempt the very things you more or less forced him into defending. Under patient and consistent guidance and open acceptance, his values will gradually emerge.

After having paved the way through such discussion, you may wish to utilize a dating agreement. In a dating agreement issues such as initial dating age, number of dates permitted per week, curfews, purpose of dating, blind dates, and so on, are negotiated *before the teen-ager enters the dating game.* You will want to solicit as many suggestions as possible from your teen-ager as you draw up the agreement. Discussion and negotiation then have a solid footing.

Perhaps even more difficult to discuss but just as necessary is the topic of sexual behavior. Parents often close the door to discussion by being arbitrary. Overreaction only forces the teen-ager to defend his or her beliefs—or to "go underground."

Dr. Norman Wright has designed a sexual behavior exercise that I have adapted for use with young people. It assists them in classifying their sexual values and can be found in *The Compleat Parent Workbook,* Unit 5. This exercise includes a list of physical intimacies. An accompanying chart depicts the seven stages of dating as it leads to marriage. The young person identifies which sexual behavior he believes to be appropriate for each stage. The completed exercise provides a quick but graphic picture which clearly illustrates that if a couple uses all methods of affection during courtship, they will have nothing new for expressing their love in marriage.

Many parents will be shocked at how free young people are today when it comes to expressing physical affection. Brace yourself for some startling revelations, and be prepared to give information in a nonjudgmental manner that will help your teen-ager formulate personal standards.

Letting Go

A college student, carrying his umbilical cord in his hand, entered his professor's office. "Prof," he asked, "where do I plug this thing in?" We smile at the humor. However, probably the most difficult parental duty during the teen years is "letting go." Christian parents have a more difficult time with this, in most instances, than do non-Christian parents. Parents with deep religious convictions find it overwhelmingly difficult to think of their teen-ager functioning independently in today's world. These parents are critically aware of the dangers ahead—premarital intercourse, marriage to a nonbeliever, and rejection of spiritual values. Therefore many parents become overzealous and try to *force* their teen-ager to make "right" decisions.

Harry and I stand guilty as charged. We tried frantically to hold onto our oldest child. One day in desperation, and unable to communicate verbally, she penned the following letter to Harry:

Dear Daddy,   July 6, 76

I'm sorry about the argument tonite - I didn't want to have an argument. I tryed not to.

I guess what I want to say is that I am a person - not just your daughter. I am your 20 year old daughter, agreed. But I am also a person... A thinking acting person. One capable of anything. But I have to be given a chance. I have to be treated as an adult. I'm sorry but I am not a 12 year old brat who is hiding things behind your back (any way not anymore than is necessary for your sanity!) I am a person who has accepted responsibility for my life. For the things I do - even if I don't get the house clean or any food fixed - wouldn't it be more imbarassing for me - than you? My guest know moms in bed. they know I am the house cleaner. Who are you trying to shelter? me - or you? Please just for a little while - let me be me! You might even get to like me - sure I goof - but I'm also learning. Please let me!

143

"Please let me!" Try as we would, we could no longer force-feed Carlene. That day was long past. We had to face the fact that we had either done our "homework" or we had neglected it. We could not go back now and try to redo things. We had stirred up feelings of resentment and rebellion. It was time to let go.

We have only eighteen to twenty years with a child to instill proper values. Then comes the time when we must maintain a hands-off policy regardless of how difficult it might be to watch our own flesh-and-blood make mistakes that will affect their future and even their salvation. We know. We've been there. But we can trust in divine power to influence the outcome. Your child's chances for making right decisions are better when he doesn't have to fight you in order to maintain his adulthood and independence.

A Word for Discouraged Parents

Feelings of inadequacy are widespread among parents of teen-agers. Questions such as, "Did I handle this situation correctly?" haunt them. Have you ever felt like this? If you continue to ask such searching questions, then rest assured that you are functioning as you should. Things may appear hopeless, but they are probably better than you imagine.

During the years you have teen-agers at home, the resulting tension and disagreements may confuse and distress you. Disagreements may not be pleasant, but they do indicate that the channels of communication are open. Such open conflict is better than a cold-war atmosphere in which family members retreat to silent hostility or indifference.

Regardless of how difficult your teen-agers may be, keep open the doors of acceptance, love, and communication. Be firm, yet loving. Your teen-ager may be hostile, bitter, rebellious, sullen, and unresponsive. You may have reached your wit's end and wish to withdraw, fight back, or ask him to leave. However, always remember that the more difficult the child, the more he needs your love and concern. He may reject every effort you put forth, but never reject him. You are the mature one; this difficult child is the immature one. You can choose to act maturely during times of stress even when he cannot. Acting in a firm but loving manner no matter how traumatic the circumstances will pay rich dividends someday since he will emulate your behavior in the years to come. You want to behave in such a manner that you will work yourself out of a child but not out of a relationship.

Guilt over what has or has not been done only makes matters worse. Our fear of failure often clouds our thinking so that we can no longer distinguish between valid guilt and irrational guilt. Each new problem encountered presents new fears of inadequacy until the oppressing guilt we feel paralyzes us. If we cannot deal with guilt feelings openly and honestly, they will corrupt all our relationships—with our mate, other children in the family, in-laws, and fellow workers. Guilt is a thief. It robs us of joyful living.

Recent studies in child development indicate that a child's temperament has more to do with his development than we had previously understood. (See "The Difficult Child," page 88.) The overwhelming power of the parent and the helplessness of the child have been taught repeatedly. We all recognize the profound influence of a parent, but *we have underestimated the child's involvement in the process of development.* Parents should distinguish between influence and control. Both can be exercised during the early years, but parents should ease up on control when a child becomes a teen-ager. Even with younger children the parents will avoid exercising too rigid control. Every child is a unique individual and has a will of his own and the power to make decisions.

The Bible shows us that God values persons in spite of their failures. Your worth and identity are not dependent on what you have or have not accomplished as a parent. *Appreciate your own worth!* Only then will you be able to deal with your guilt and help your child through those traumatic teen years. Your child is a person of worth, even though he may have chosen different values than you would have him choose. He must be allowed to develop his own values and live his life as he sees fit. The older he gets, the less we are able to control and the more we can only influence a youngster.

Parents need to remember that there is a person of worth behind objectionable behavior. How Harry and I wish we had always been able to have seen beyond behavior to our children's attitudes! Behavior is only a symptom of a troubled teen who is unable to cope with the pressures of life. What would happen to us if our relationships to God depended on our behavior? One day we might enjoy God's love and favor, and the next we might experience rejection. God does not ignore our behavior, but He also does not reject us based on our behavior. His example of unconditional love provides a model for us when dealing with wayward teen-agers.

Times may come when you will hurt, and nothing will make the pain go away. Only our own children can hurt us in such a manner. What should a parent do at this point? What happened to the promise in Proverbs 22:6 that if we do a good job with our kids when they are young, they will turn out all right when older? You lapse into tremendous periods of guilt. You wait. You pray. You hope. But for how long?

Although not set in concrete forever, circumstances are the way they are. You can't make the pain disappear. But you can choose to focus on hope for the future. Resist dwelling on the negative side of life or your teen-ager. Cling to hope for the future. Hold fast. Oh, how difficult this is in the middle of the night when you do not know where your teen-ager is!

In addition, remember that your maturing teen-ager has the right to make certain decisions regarding his future. Make him responsible for his decisions, his behavior, and the resulting consequences.

Finally, rest in the Lord. Psalm 37 may help you survive when you think you are drowning. You will find great comfort during the trying periods of your children's adolescence if you can lean on a higher Power. But never forget that it isn't the number of prayers that makes the difference to a youth, rather it is the difference that praying makes in our own lives which will speak to his heart. God loves your teen-ager with an everlasting love. His Son died to save your son, your daughter. Can your young person see that God is loving him through you?

The impact is eternal.

Further reading you will enjoy . . .

Campbell, Ross.	*HOW TO REALLY LOVE YOUR TEENAGER.*
Dobson, James.	*THE STRONG-WILLED CHILD*, pages 189-230.
Dobson, James.	*PREPARING FOR ADOLESCENCE.*
Dobson, James.	*PREPARING FOR ADOLESCENCE GROWTH GUIDE.*
Dobson, James.	*PREPARING FOR ADOLESCENCE TAPES.*
Ginott, Haim G.	*BETWEEN PARENT AND TEEN-AGER.*
Stoop, Dave and Jan.	*THE TOTAL(ED) PARENT.*
Van Pelt, Nancy.	*THE COMPLEAT COURTSHIP.*
Wright, H. Norman and Rex Johnson.	*COMMUNICATION—KEY TO YOUR TEENS.*

Chapter at a Glance

I. **Drug Use Is All-pervasive**
   A. It crops up in the best of homes and neighborhoods
   B. "Good" kids can be on drugs

II. **Why Teen-agers Turn to Drugs**
   A. Parental example
     1. Drug use is learned
     2. Parental attitudes can contribute to drug abuse
       a. Many parents drink
       b. Many parents smoke
       c. Many parents gulp pills
   B. The need for acceptance

1. Many teens use drugs to ease emotional problems
   a. Some teens feel unloved
   b. Some teens feel lonely
   c. Some teens feel anxiety-ridden
2. Teens need reassurance and approval
3. People especially susceptible to drug abuse are—
   a. those who feel inadequate
   b. those who feel insecure
   c. those who feel rejected
C. Peer pressure
   1. Peer pressure often overwhelms parental influence
   2. Yielding to peer pressure can be learned at home

Chapter 7

Parental Intervention in Drug Prevention

"Mrs. Potter? This is Sergeant Quigley from the Hillcrest precinct, and we are holding your two daughters here at the station on drug charges."

"I'm sorry, Sergeant. There must be some kind of mistake," Mrs. Potter gasped. "My daughters are right here at home in their rooms asleep!"

But were they?

The policeman continued his story without hesitation and in a serious voice. Both 16-year-old Susan and 14-year-old Jan had been arrested along with a group of others. Yet the situation seemed impossible to Mrs. Potter. The officer must have some other girls in custody named Potter. Other young people used drugs. She knew that. But she and her husband lived in the best part of town. They were well educated. They attended church regularly. And she spent most of her time with the family.

Her husband, Bob, reacted in much the same way. Where had they gone wrong? Susan and Jan were both popular at school, well behaved at home, and pretty girls. They did not have excessive allowances, and the parents thought they had carefully supervised their girls' activities. Susan on heroin! And Jan had been smoking marijuana for about five months!

Perhaps you, too, find this story hard to believe. Perhaps you have pictured in your

---

D. Boredom
E. Family breakdown
   1. Self-centered parents often ignore their children
   2. Divorce often leaves no strong male figure at home
F. Rock music

III. **What Parents Can Do**
   A. Both parents and children need drug education
      1. Many parents don't recognize when a child is stoned
      2. Signs of drug use
   B. How to make home rewarding
      1. Encourage your child to have positive goals
      2. Encourage your child to choose wholesome friends
      3. Encourage your child to take up good leisure activities

"I've warned her about drugs."

mind the type of homes that drug addicts come from—homes like those in the ghetto. But times have changed. Now with its many arms, drug abuse reaches into all types of homes, neighborhoods, schoolrooms, and businesses. Just because this nightmare has never touched your family is no assurance that it won't—especially if you refuse to admit that a problem of this nature could exist in your home.

What kind of kids get trapped by drugs? You probably incorrectly picture some juvenile delinquent. However, two recent studies support the fact that 78 percent of the boys on drugs are quiet, likable, conservative, and well-mannered but are also easily influenced and desirous of pleasing others. They have few, if any, close friendships, and their interests are frequently more feminine than masculine. Often the addicts are soft-spoken and gentle.

If 78 percent of the fellows on drugs are quiet, likable, conservative, and well-mannered, what causes them to turn to drugs? This is the problem we seek to explore here—not a cure for addicts but how parents can prevent drug dependency from getting a foothold in their homes.

Parental Example

In exploring the first reason why kids turn to drugs, we shall focus on parental example. A staff psychiatrist at Highland General Hospital in Oakland, California, James. W. Hawkins, points out that drug abuse is an attitude the child learns from his parents. "All children copy their parents," Dr. Hawkins says. "If parents portray the behavior which they desire in their children, they will more likely get it from their children.

"However, if a child sees his mother or father swallowing pills every morning to get going and every night to get to sleep, or if he sees that his parents need a drink whenever they're under stress, then the child will probably copy this type of behavior."

Students at Long Island, New York, high schools conducted a five-month survey on the use of drugs in their schools. The students themselves conceived, designed, and administered the survey. Teachers and other adults had nothing directly to do with it. The students were surprised that only 42 percent at that time had tried marijuana. Everyone believed the statistic would be at least 70 and possibly 90 percent.

The major influence on whether a student might use drugs, the survey discovered, was parental habits. Not that parental habits necessarily cause drug abuse, but they certainly "significantly affect drug use." Certain questions in the survey were designed to determine how frequently parents used alcohol, smoked cigarettes, took drugs such as sleeping or pep pills, and argued in front of their children. Parental habits which showed the greatest effect were drinking habits, "specifically how many drinks the parents have when they drink and how often they get drunk," the survey concluded. Those who said their mothers had ever been drunk had a significantly greater tendency to use drugs.

Advertising for patent medicines has encouraged the public to develop a "take something" syndrome, suggests John E. Ingersoll, director of the Bureau of Narcotics and Dangerous Drugs. "From sunrise to closing benediction in the late evening, the American public is bombarded on radio and television by catchy little jingles, cute sketches, and somber warnings, offering drugs and medicines to cure most little symptoms of real or imagined illness—or to provide escape from reality," he says. "The average medicine cabinet gives testimony to the success of this mass-media campaign," concludes Ingersoll.

Former mayor John Lindsay of New York suggested that children from the age of 2 have been conditioned by what they see on the TV screen "to expect to wake up, slow down, be happy, or relieve tension with pills."

Each year, medicine manufacturers spend some hundreds of millions of dollars on television advertising which implants the idea that there should be a chemical solution for all of life's problems, including pain, boredom, and anxiety.

How do you, as a parent, handle your anxieties and frustrations? Is each new situation a crisis for which you need a crutch? Are you forever running to the medicine cabinet? Have you taught your child that there is a pill for every problem? We can respect the medications which aid us through difficulties, but we must not develop a panicky dependency on them for every problem. Your own attitude toward medications is vitally important, because parents form a "major portion" of the drug problem rather than just the "spectator portion," as they have thought of themselves in the past.

The Need for Acceptance

A second reason why kids turn to drugs is in an effort to ease emotional problems. "Teen-agers who take drugs usually have severe emotional problems that have reached the crippling stage. Their greatest need is to solve the problem," observes district court psychologist James W. Vander Weele of Denver.

This specialist tells of one girl hooked on

drugs who pleaded, "This is the first time I found friends who love me. Please don't take them away." Psychologist Vander Weele explains, "This girl had never really had friends until she became part of a group. The only thing other group members required of her in exchange for their friendship was that she use drugs with them. She didn't care about drugs, but she did care about friends; so she participated."

Dr. Vander Weele has found that many teen-agers on drugs are "unsuccessful children who are desperately lonely. They haven't found acceptance anywhere. They haven't succeeded academically, athletically, socially. . . . They find their places only by joining others who have similar problems."

Most people use drugs to relieve their anxieties, for they have found that they hurt less when on drugs. One heroin addict told a reporter, "You don't even know what I'm talking about; you feel OK all the time. Me, it costs me $100 a day just to stop hurting so much."

It is hardly surprising, then, why drugs appeal to adolescents. They need reassurance and approval, and they are easily swayed by those who convince them that an almost unbelievably wonderful world is waiting for them in drugs.

In his book *Parents on Trial,* David Wilkerson tells of Nicky Cruz, a child of the streets, who makes him aware of the many homes without love. When Nicky was four years old, he overheard a group of women chatting with his mother at tea, and his mother said something that permanently scarred his heart: "We did not really want Nicky. I wish he had never been born."

Since Nicky felt unloved, he ran away from home in later years and lived like an animal until David Wilkerson found him through Teen Challenge. Now Nicky is an associate of Wilkerson.

People with neurotic tendencies, feelings of inadequacy, insecurity, or rejection are more susceptible than others to involvement with narcotics, yet if the drug user has any latent neurosis, drugs may bring it out.

Is there anything in the world which can help young people with emotional problems, those who feel alienated? Is there anything which can help them cope with their day-by-day difficulties? Is there any society other than the drug-oriented one in which they can find acceptance and feel a part of the group?

The potential teen-age drug addict is seeking what another youngster already has—a home in which he feels approval and acceptance. An emotionally secure teen-ager may be on his own much of the time, but his heart feels assured of his parents' love. They have given him part of themselves as well as their possessions, and he knows that they care for him and that if he needs them they are always there.

Peer Pressure

Peer pressure is a third reason teen-agers first experiment with drugs. Particularly during adolescence, peer pressure begins to influence young people, and it can be as great, if not greater, than your own. And yielding to peer pressure, like dependency on drugs, can be taught—for example, by the mother who rushes off to get a new outfit just because her best friend got a new outfit or by the father who buys four-wheel drive just because his friend has a vehicle with four-wheel drive.

When society becomes the parents' answer to everything and when what others say or think or do becomes their conscience, the child learns that his peers should dictate his actions and attitudes too.

Boredom

A fourth cause for drug use is boredom. The recent Canadian LeDain inquiry into the nonmedical use of drugs concluded that many people turn on with drugs because they are bored. Unlike the drug user who needs drugs as an umbrella against stimulation, this group apparently wants to strip off a mental insulation and let in the outside world.

Dr. James Hawkins concurs with this theory. "Many young people get into drugs because they are bored. If parents show an interest in what their children are doing and

Self-Test on Drug Prevention

Parental example is the strongest major influence on whether a child will use drugs. Circle your response to each of the following.

T or F   1. My life is free of any crutches seen as solutions to life's problems such as:
  a. alcohol
  b. cigarettes
  c. sleeping pills
  d. pep pills
  e. pain pills

T or F   2. My child feels approval, acceptance, love, and security in my home.

T or F   3. I have not allowed society and/or peers to become conscience for my attitudes and actions and have consistently modeled the same for my child.

T or F   4. I show an interest in my child's activities and have guided him into constructive after-school interests and hobbies.

T or F   5. Our home has been untouched by divorce and there is a strong authority (preferably male) figure present.

T or F   6. My child is not being influenced by music that glorifies the drug culture.

Please turn to page 239 for scoring instructions.

try to make sure that their children are busy with constructive activities, this certainly helps combat drug abuse.

"For instance: The child is interested in music, and he practices, and gets into the school band, but if mother and father never attend a band concert, the child may drop out. If he quits band, he has more time on his hands; he will probably seek company of other uninvolved individuals, which could very easily lead to trying drugs. Children want their parents to be interested in what they're doing. They're disappointed when the parents don't think their interests are important."

Family Breakdown

Dr. Hawkins also believes that a fifth aspect of the drug problem is related to the breakdown of the family structure. Often mother and father are interested only in what they themselves are doing to the exclusion of what others in the family may be doing. They could easily involve the children.

153

The alarming rise in current divorce statistics means broken homes, and this usually means homes without fathers. And sociologists and psychologists insist that if only there were a strong male figure, the juvenile crime rate would plummet. In many cases addicted boys come from homes where a woman was the only or the strongest influence. The boys lacked that essential male leadership, and they soon identified with their mothers, grandmothers, or sisters. This identification brought feelings of inadequacy, which led to confusion in relationship to their parents and their role in life.

Rock Music

A sixth influencing factor on drug usage is reflected in the current popular music. I do not mean to suggest that rock music has created the drug-abuse crisis, but few parents understand the subculture jargon described through the words of hard rock and punk rock.

In some instances the reference to drugs is clear and unmistakable. In other cases the lyrics are ambiguous or perhaps only suggestive, but many teen-agers and even younger children assume that these lyrics are related in some way to drugs and their use. "Aquarius" from the American Tribal Love-Rock musical *Hair* obviously alludes to drug use, with a naive idea about its ability to deliver Utopia, to liberate the mind, and to inspire the user with golden visions. Parents will have to make up their own minds as to whether these songs which glorify the drug culture are affecting their young people's decisions.

What Can Parents Do?

Are you convinced that you don't want your children or others to partake in the nonmedical use of drugs? Are you wondering what you personally can do? Drug education for both parents and children is another step to drug prevention and a good place to begin.

An enormous number of young people admit to bring "stoned" in front of their parents, who didn't even realize it. Parents should be alert for the clear and unmistakable warning signs of drug use. Generally speaking, persons addicted to narcotics might display the following symptoms: needle marks on arms or legs; red, watery eyes; small pupils in the eyes; furtive glances; chronic drowsiness; marked restlessness with body spasms and a tendency to walk fast; easily upset stomach; ulcerous sores on arms, legs, and body; uncontrollable giddiness; a strong body odor; habitual scratching or rubbing of nose; frequent dizziness; obvious mental and physical deterioration; depression and despondency; persecution complex; chronic sleepiness; loss of interest in school; inability to concentrate on studies; lack of interest in athletics or any other forms of exercise; irritability; telling of stupid lies; refusal to talk because of preoccupation with self.

A good drug-education program should also be presented in the schools to the children themselves. The Washington, D.C., school board has approved a drug-abuse education program that will become part of the curriculum from kindergarten through grade twelve. In kindergarten through grade three, the course will emphasize nutrition, note the dangers of medications normally found in the home, as well as explain the common childhood misuse of such things as coffee, teas, and soft drinks. Smoking cigarettes, sniffing glue, and the use of alcohol and narcotics will be discussed in grades four through six, and in junior high schools the classes will review the sociological effects of drugs, emphasizing contemporary issues. Senior-high students will find the antidrug curriculum integrated into such subjects as home economics, English, and sociology.

The most effective weapon in keeping a young person from drug addiction is the security of a well-adjusted, rewarding homelife with family ties made strong by love. The following three suggestions are the most important preventive steps that parents can take:

1. *Encourage your youngster to have positive goals in life.* Give your child an intelligent appreciation for the dignity of labor so that he is prepared to make an honest living. Teach him that life is a sacred trust and that we must all answer for ourselves in the day of judgment. When a young person is taught Biblical goals, he will be less inclined to find the time or place to become involved with narcotics, alcohol, or other temptations.

2. *Encourage your child to choose wholesome companions.* Encourage him to bring his friends home for supervised activities. Guide him to the kinds of places where he will meet the sort of friends he would be proud to bring home with him.

3. *Guide your youngster into the proper choice of free-time activities.* Young people who are interested in school and who keep busy with extracurricular activities seldom get involved with the kind of people who might drag them into addiction.

Encourage your child to participate in music, athletics, and club activities offered through your church or school or community. When he is old enough, an after school job will keep him occupied; provide money for future schooling, clothes, and for social life; and make him feel worthwhile, which will greatly add to his self-esteem. Since much experimentation takes place during the afternoons and long weekend vacations, David Wilkerson urges, "It is a parental duty to see to it that children have little time for unplanned or unchaperoned social activities, particularly at these times."

In the final analysis, then, the answer to the common drug problem lies within a strong family relationship where family members respect and love each other. Mutual respect gives new meaning to the home situation and offers an atmosphere which will help the child mature in a healthy environment. In addition, parents must set examples for their child in harmony with the standards they hold up as the ideal, thus offering their child something more than platitudes and poor examples. In short, drug prevention begins with the parents themselves.

Further reading you will enjoy . . .

Dobson, James.   *DARE TO DISCIPLINE*, chapter 6.
Wilkerson, David.   *PARENTS ON TRIAL.*

Chapter at a Glance

I. Sibling Rivalry Is Common
  A. It takes many forms
    1. Fighting
    2. Competing
    3. Grabbing
    4. Teasing
    5. Tattling
    6. Arguing
  B. It is universal

II. Each Child Vies With the Others
  A. Each craves parental love
  B. Each craves parental attention

III. Sharing Must Be Learned
  A. The intrusion of other children does not diminish parental love
  B. Even an only child cannot always be the center of attention
  C. The way siblings learn to respond to each other determines largely how well they will get along with others
  D. Sibling jealousies should be handled carefully

IV. How to Handle Sibling Rivalry
  A. Allow the children to have eye-to-eye confrontation
  B. Ask the disputants for a written account of their differences

Chapter 8

Sibling Rivalry Versus Sibling Harmony

Through the ages, loving and sharing, fighting and competing, grabbing and teasing, tattling and keeping secrets, agreeing and disagreeing, playing and hiding from one another, have existed between brothers and sisters. The Bible, mythology, fairy tales, songs, dances, and dramas all illustrate the universality of the harmony, rivalries, and tensions that exist between siblings.

Each child in the family wants to be sure of his parents' love and attention regardless of how many other children there might be in the family. It is difficult for a child to understand that the intrusion of another child will not lessen his parents' love for him. However, sharing his parents' love and attention is more difficult for some children than others, and even an only child learns that he must share his mother with his father, and his father with his mother.

Psychologists recognize that the way brothers and sisters learn to weather growing up together largely determines how well they can get along with other people throughout their lives. Although jealousy and guilt feelings about it constitute a natural part of growing up together in a family, when these jealousies and rivalries between siblings are handled clumsily by parents early in the training process, it is often difficult to reverse the destructive

---

C. Insist ahead of time that they take turns (sometimes "tickets" can help)

D. Put the children to work

E. Put all the participants in the same boat

F. Whenever possible, allow them to settle by themselves their disputes
  1. Parents sometimes make matters worse by intervening
  2. Parents often do not know who is guilty and who is not
  3. Quarrels require two participants
  4. It teaches children how to arbitrate differences
  5. It teaches children how to resolve conflicts

V. **Other Simple Methods of Smoothing Troubled Waters**
  A. Use active listening
  B. Provide distracting amusements
    1. Read them a story
    2. They can assemble a puzzle
    3. They can use modeling clay

patterns that develop.

Jealousy is a fact of life. The question here is, How are you, as a parent, responding to rivalries now? How do you feel about your child's bickering, fighting, and competing? Parents often get tired of it, fall under strain, get upset, and then cannot consistently satisfy their child's needs. Yet children often depend on their parents to tell them when they have had enough, for children need help in controlling themselves. A limit must be set on sibling rivalry.

Eye-to-eye Confrontation

Eye-to-eye confrontation is superior to any other method for permanently reducing rivalry. Peter and Leland had been scrapping and fighting all day, and nothing Mother had said made any lasting effect. She had threatened them, she had sent them to separate rooms, and she had screamed. Although she had become exhausted and discouraged, the boys were still devil-ridden and ready for more hassling.

As Mother stood in the kitchen contemplating the penalty for double murder, a tiny spark of rationality shone through the darkness. "Make them confront each other," it suggested. Grabbing two dining-room chairs, she insisted, "Peter, you sit here. Leland, here. Now, you just sit there and look at each other. You may not move or speak. Just sit and look at each other. When you start doing it, I'll set the timer for five minutes. [With 2- and 3-year-olds, half that time works well.] OK? Start."

Peter was 9, and he argued. Leland, less than four years old, tried to climb down from his chair, but Mother forcibly held him in. Then he tried to push the chair back, but finally both boys settled into the chairs after some wiggling, a kick or two, and a loud "Ouch!" Mother stopped the scuffling, ignored all protests, and reset the timer for five minutes.

After the boys completed five minutes of what might be considered slightly better than hopeless confrontation, Mother let them go. Still unsure the method would

work in the end, she vowed she would continue it with more love and purpose.

From that day on, "OK, boys, in the chairs," became a familiar call. Mother learned not to wait until their scraps reached the stage of total mayhem, but ordered Peter and Leland into chairs at the first indication of trouble. They protested, of course, and sometimes even fought over who would sit in which chair. She never yielded to pleas such as, "He started it" or "I didn't do anything." When the "innocent victim" tried to convince her that he was blameless, she might ask, "What part did you play in this trouble?" or "What could you have done to prevent it?" There was always an answer.

Many days Mother felt like giving up, because she doubted that her method would ever work. At last, however, she realized that the trips to the chairs were becoming less frequent while the household was becoming more peaceful. She was teaching the boys that it takes two to make a fight because it is impossible for one person to pick a fight by himself. Gradually the boys began to take more and more responsibility for their own actions, and this helped them outside of the home as well.

One day Mother left the boys alone while she took a quick trip to the grocery store. When she returned, Peter and Leland were sitting in the chairs—with two minutes left on the timer. Mother said nothing. When the bell rang, they got up and sauntered out to play. Mother never asked what led to the self-discipline. They had taken the right action, and that's all that mattered. Mother's *consistency* had guaranteed the effectiveness.

The breakdown in this system seems to appear in the lack of consistency in which a parent carries out the plan. The lessons will not be learned by dragging out the chairs once a week when patience is at a low ebb. The rivalry will be lessened for that time, but not on a permanent basis as could be accomplished through consistent use of this method. Parents with small children from 2-and-a-half years up may find it works well if the time limits are cut in half. Have you tried this method?

Written Accounts

A written account can also help settle a dispute by ridding the children of hostile feelings through the avenue of creative writing. We used this method in our home when our boys, 10 and 12 years of age, were having a heated battle. I brought them upstairs, put them in separate rooms with pen and paper, and told them to tell me about it *on paper.* Ten-year-old Mark, who has always been more emotional and expressive, took a full forty-five minutes to describe the scuffle and get all his feelings down on paper:

Rod, the older boy, is much more stable, quiet by nature, and more unemotional, and he wrote out his account in five to ten minutes:

Roddey and I were playing floor hockey when I accidently hit him with my stick. He got mad and started swinging at my feet so I jumped up and started to run just as I got to the door Rod hit me on the heel with his stick. I turned around and through my stick at him and it cracked. So he got up went to the room pulled out one of my cars and went out to the corner of the basement were were we keep all are tools and stuff and through it so that it would hit the ground and then hit the wall. So just as he through it. I kicked him. Then he went back to the family room and I went and got the car. I looked at it and set it down and ran in to the family room and I kicked him and then I started to hit him then I quit took the car and came to you. The reason why I kicked and hit him was cause I did'nt think that he should have done that.

Rodney V.P

I smashed marks car because he kept hitting me with my drumstick so I hit him back. In rage he attempted to hit me by throwing the drumstick at me cracking the drumstick in half so then I smashed his car

THE
END

Sibling Rivalry

Take the following *True or False* test to measure your knowledge on how to control sibling rivalry.

T or F   1. Whenever possible, parents should allow children to settle their own disputes.

T or F   2. It is frequently difficult to establish in a quarrel who is guilty and who is innocent.

T or F   3. When one tattles on the other, the parent should handle the problem by saying he/she is confident the child can handle it.

T or F   4. A positive method of dealing with sibling rivalry when you cannot determine the guilty party is to put them all in the same boat (punish the innocent with the guilty).

T or F   5. A parent should avoid acting like a referee in the game of "he started it."

T or F   6. Many young siblings deliberately provoke older siblings in order to win the parent over to their own side.

T or F   7. Parents should never, even unintentionally, pit one sibling against the other by comparing good performance in one with poor performance in another.

Scoring instructions on page 239.

Reserved Seats

Another method appeared in the "Hints From Heloise" column of the newspaper.

"Dear Heloise: Now that our six children are growing up, whenever we go for a drive in our station wagon there's always an argument about who will sit next to which door, or who will sit up front with Mother and Dad. So my husband came up with this idea.

"Each time we head for the car, he passes out 'reserved seat tickets.' Each ticket has two numbers on it, one for going and one for coming, and each seat number is listed on a little chart in the car. The child automatically knows where he will sit both going and coming home. No more squabbling.

"You draws your number and you takes your chances."

Put Them to Work!

Another valuable escape valve when feelings are running high and you haven't the time or the patience to arbitrate is to put the children to work. They can shovel snow, weed the garden, mow the lawn, wash the car or windows or walls, sweep the walk, or do an endless array of useful tasks which will help reduce the emotional turmoil constructively.

Stay Out of It

Whenever possible, allow children to settle their disputes themselves. Parents often make matters worse when they try to solve the quarrel. It is often difficult to establish in a quarrel who is guilty and who is innocent. The quarrel most often is a result of combined effort. The obviously good child may have egged on, pushed, or dared to provoke the bad child. Thus, when the first child comes running to you, you might say, "I'm sorry you are having trouble, but I'm sure you can work things out between you." Turn the problem-solving over to the children, where it belongs, and refuse to get involved in it. At times it may be necessary to send them to another room to solve the problem.

Often it is extremely difficult for parents to understand why they should not arbitrate. They feel it is their duty to teach their children not to fight, and this is true. But arbitration does not accomplish this purpose. It may solve the immediate situation, but it does not teach children how to avoid future conflicts. If parental interference satisfies them, why should they stop fighting?

Put Them All in the Same Boat

When someone in the family misbehaves, defaces property, or provokes a fight, and you cannot determine who the guilty party is, put them all in the same boat. If discord arises at the table, ask all the children to leave until harmony is restored. Don't worry about punishing the innocent with the guilty, and ignore any protests from them on this point. By putting them all in the same boat, they will come to understand their interdependence and take care of one another.

Other simple methods of smoothing troubled waters involve the art of active listening. Talking things over is a helpful measure, especially since children have difficulty separating fact from fantasy. Bad thoughts to them often seem just as bad as actions. "Ted, I understand how you feel. We all have mean feelings sometimes," a mom might begin.

If quarreling always seems to break out in the hour just before supper when the children are tired or hungry, Mom might get an early start on supper and then read a story aloud. A cut-and-paste routine or a puzzle might work. Other fun-type projects such as modeling with clay, dress-up times, and puppetry allow children to act out their feelings. Channeling feelings of rivalry into constructive outlets takes time, effort, and imagination, but it has its rewards in promoting good home relations.

Further reading you will enjoy . . .

Dinkmeyer, Don. *RAISING A RESPONSIBLE CHILD*, pages 166-168.
Dobson, James. *THE STRONG-WILLED CHILD*, pages 125-144.
Ilg, Frances L., and Louise Bates Ames. *CHILD BEHAVIOR*.
Ostrovsky, Everett. *SIBLING RIVALRY*.

Chapter at a Glance

I. **Problem Behavior and Nutritional Status**

   A. Symptoms
      1. Personality fluctuation
      2. Misbehavior
      3. Hyperactivity
      4. Depression

   B. Factors Behind the Symptoms
      1. Heredity
      2. Environment
      3. Nutritional status

II. **The Importance of an Adequate Diet**

   A. Many behavior problems are diet problems

B. Malabsorption of nutrients

C. Diet and juvenile delinquency

III. **The Adequate Diet**

   A. God appointed food for Adam and Eve
      1. Grains
      2. Fruits
      3. Nuts
      4. Vegetables

   B. Appetite is not a safe guide

   C. A good breakfast is vital
      1. It should include—
         a. fruit juice
         b. whole-grains
         c. dairy products

Chapter 9

The Kitchen Scene—Keeping Your Family Happy and Healthy

"I just had a conference with my son's teacher. She says he is inattentive in class and uncooperative. She insists that he isn't stupid and could do the work if he wanted to. Some days he will and other times he won't. What's the problem with my child?" Nutritional factors could explain this boy's behavior.

"For us a simple thing like going to church can be the worst experience of the week. All morning long the kids drag their feet, and we are pushing and shoving as we struggle to get them out the door. The sermon is probably on showing kindness and being loving toward one another, but we miss it all because of our constant shushing and the children's misbehavior. We go home with splitting headaches and feelings of frustration and discouragement." Lack of an adequate breakfast could be the explanation for these children's misbehavior.

"My 2-year-old is unbelievable. She cruises around the house and fingers, smashes, or knocks over everything in sight. She has frequent temper tantrums. I've tried behavior modification techniques, but these scenes can go on for an hour. I think she's hyperactive, although the doctor can't find anything wrong with her. I'm ready to give up motherhood for another occupation!" A close look at this girl's diet

---

2. It should provide one-fourth of the daily dietary needs
3. It can improve a child's school achievement

D. Recent studies show the adequacy of vegetarianism
   1. Diets high in animal flesh contribute to—
      a. heart disease
      b. strokes
      c. cancer
   2. Vegetarians are stronger and have more go-power

E. A vegetarian diet costs less

IV. **The Junk Food Junkie**
   A. The average American eats 1,200 empty calories daily
   B. Eating between meals is harmful
   C. Refined foods lack nutrients
   D. Natural nutrition is best

V. **Making Meals a Positive Experience**
   A. Have a simple and light supper
   B. Pleasant conversation aids digestion
      1. Avoid TV during meals
      2. Avoid constant correcting

could uncover the true cause of her behavior.

Pediatricians, counselors, and grandparents might respond to each of these cases with: "You've got to be more strict." "Get control of this child before it is too late." "There must be home problems underlying this child's behavior." Or "Try rewarding his good behavior and ignoring bad behavior, and things will get better."

How much of a child's behavior is related to environmental factors such as the home, school, church, and society? How much may be related to diet, heredity, and other factors? One thing is certain: the more irritable the child, the more the personality fluctuation, the more depressed or violent he gets, then the more an analysis of his body chemistry, his diet, and his environment is in order.

Until now you may have been taught or assumed that your child's problems were the result of bad parenting—the seeming absence of the ability to accept, nurture, communicate, discipline, reward, or punish correctly. This has probably produced guilt complexes and depression for you but little improvement in your child's behavior. The truth is that your child may have behavioral problems because he lacks certain nutrients. *Many a diet problem has been misdiagnosed as a behavior problem.* Treating the misbehavior as an entity in itself without considering possible underlying nutritional causes would be like treating the symptom without concern for the cause. Is it any wonder parents confront some instances of misbehavior with a sense of futility and frustration?

Furthermore, what is put into the body is not always what the system absorbs. If you know that your child is eating properly but still manifests hyperactivity and irritability, it would be advisable to have medical tests run to determine the child's digestive enzyme level. A lack of certain digestive enzymes allows food to pass through the body without being absorbed. Hence the child does not benefit from the nutrients you are providing him. This is a more common problem than most people realize.

It is now common knowledge that there is a direct and astounding link between delinquency and poor nutrition. Problems of running away, defying authority (at home or at school), vandalizing property, setting fires, stealing, truancy, and the tendency to break as many rules as possible may well be the undeniable results of a poor diet, low self-respect, and a chronically unsupportive home life. Any authority who deals with delinquents is aware of the almost universal statistics: 75 percent of criminals were hyperactive as children; more than half have abnormal glucose tolerance tests; 50 to 75 percent of criminals have severe reading problems; and 50 percent of crime is related to alcohol ingestion.[1]

It is possible to lower such statistics by (1) helping such individuals find some type of work that will increase their feelings of worth and (2) by reducing or even banning the use of sugar and white flour products by such persons. Dr. Lendon Smith, an authority on children's nutrition, states forcefully: "If school authorities want to stop discipline problems and vandalism in the classroom, they must do away with sugar and junk foods in the halls and close the candy stores within two miles of the school."[2]

A nourishing diet of nuts, cheese, vegetables, fruits, grains, as well as high-protein snacks and legumes can help children with a history of poor self-image, periods of depression, headaches and stomachaches, severe acne, hyperactivity, allergies, and delinquency.

Sugartime

Grains, fruits, nuts, and vegetables constitute the diet our Creator chose for us. These foods, prepared in as simple and natural a manner as possible, are the most healthful and nourishing.

The appetites of most people have become so perverted that they are no longer a safe guide. We have been trained to enjoy sweets, and children particularly prefer sweets to all other foods. Two and one-half billion dollars are spent on three and a quarter million pounds of candy eaten annually in the United States alone. The average sugar consumption is well over 120 pounds a person for a year, which means that the average person eats 33 to 35 teaspoons of sugar every day. By age two, one out of every two babies already has a decayed tooth.

It seems as though soda pop has replaced water, milk, and fruit juices in the diet. Over 5 billion dollars a year are spent on pop. Adults drink about 290 bottles of soft drinks a year, and teen-agers drink over 500 bottles a year. Soft drinks harm the teeth as the acids erode the enamel of the tooth, and these sweetened beverages have contributed to North America's greatest nutritional fault—obesity.

When the family raids the refrigerator for a refreshing beverage, offer fruit juices. They are delicious as well as nutritious. And never forget that the most satisfying between-meal drink for young and old alike is a glass of cool water. Six to eight glasses of water are needed every day for good health.

"You've never tasted it—how do you know you don't like it?"

Since the free use of sweets is often the cause of sour stomachs, one wonders how many family quarrels could be traced to poor food combinations. One way to obtain a sweeter disposition is to eat fewer sweets. It is possible that what your child eats at this moment will determine his behavior in only a matter of minutes—the time it takes some sugars to be absorbed into the bloodstream. The tremendous rise in sugar intake may be one explanation for the apparent increase in the incidence of hyperactivity. It is suspected that hyperactivity is related to a defective sugar metabolism. The key to handling many previously diagnosed "problem" children, then, may well lie with a consistently natural, unrefined diet!

Our Creator has given us delicious, refreshing, healthful fruits, which not only taste sweet but also contain nutrients essential to building body tissue. Sugar lacks these nutrients essential to health, and it becomes even more deadly when taken between meals at all hours of the day. Most of us need to reeducate our tastes so that we can enjoy the wonderful desserts produced by the garden and the orchard.

The Wake-up Meal

Good nutrition begins with a good breakfast consisting of fruit juice, whole-grain cereals and breads, and milk. Children who eat inadequate breakfasts become tired and inattentive to their schoolwork by the latter part of the morning.

"No teacher should be required to teach a child who did not bring his brain to school; she cannot teach the animal limbic system. Every morning each pupil should report what his breakfast contained. If he had no protein and ate mainly carbohydrates, he should be sent home," Dr. Lendon Smith insists. Sugary refined carbohydrates and classroom concentration don't mix. The Norwegian government has solved this problem by providing fish and cheese to school children shortly after they get to school. The famous "Iowa Breakfast Studies" have shown that a good breakfast can improve a child's school achievement and

energy levels substantially.

Avoid the highly refined sugar-coated cereals commonly found on the supermarket shelves. The cereal my family prefers above all others is granola—for taste, nutrition, and power to hold them over the midmorning slump. See page 171.

A nourishing breakfast will supply at least one fourth of the daily dietary needs. Sufficient protein in the form of dairy products, nuts, and grains should be included along with carbohydrates for energy. Protein foods tend to maintain the blood sugar above the fasting level for a longer period of time than do carbohydrates.

Meals Without Meat

In recent years there has been a phenomenal upsurge of interest in obtaining protein from plant sources rather than from animal sources. An increasing number of people, young and old, want to return to a simpler way of life, and they are exploring healthful living through a vegetable diet. Even Yale students are requesting meals featuring soybean patties, freshly cooked vegetables, and whole-grain products.

Recent scientific evidence has proved not only that a basically meatless diet is adequate for children, teen-agers, adults, and the elderly, but that it may actually be superior. Diets high in animal flesh are major contributors to the high death rate from heart disease and stroke which are the big disease killers in North America today. The United States alone claims one million heart attacks resulting in 600,000 deaths annually. A commission organized to control this disease suggests that to keep serum cholesterol at proper levels, people should derive less than 10 percent of their total calories from saturated fats. The average fat intake approaches 40 to 50 percent! The commission recommends the use of grains, fruits, vegetables, and legumes, and specifically suggests avoiding egg yolk, bacon, lard, and suet.

Yet some mothers continue to feel that their families must have meat in order to be strong and physically fit. A number of tests and surveys have conclusively proved that vegetarians are stronger, have more go-power, greater vitality, and recover more rapidly after fatigue.

One such test,[3] recently and widely publicized in medical and nutrition journals, centered on an endurance test on bicycles given to nine athletes after they had been on a specific diet for three days. One diet was high in meat or protein; one was a normal mixed diet; and one was high in vegetables and grains and carbohydrates. The tests were done on the same athletes so the differences in endurance can be accounted for only through diet. First, the athletes were placed on the high meat-and-protein diet and put on the ergocycle where they pedaled for 57 minutes. When placed on the normal mixed diet after a period of several days of rest, they averaged 114 minutes of pedaling. The high carbo-hydrate diet of vegetables and grains,

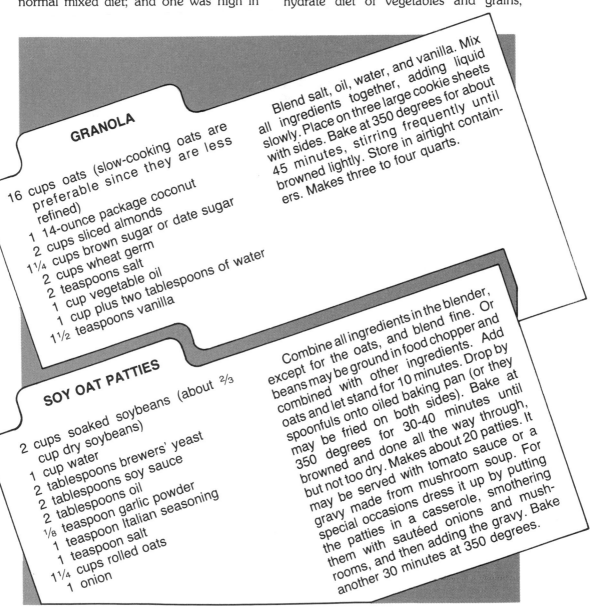

GRANOLA

16 cups oats (slow-cooking oats are preferable since they are less refined)
1 14-ounce package coconut
2 cups sliced almonds
1¼ cups brown sugar or date sugar
2 cups wheat germ
2 teaspoons salt
1 cup vegetable oil
1 cup plus two tablespoons of water
1½ teaspoons vanilla

Blend salt, oil, water, and vanilla. Mix all ingredients together, adding liquid slowly. Place on three large cookie sheets with sides. Bake at 350 degrees for about 45 minutes, stirring frequently until browned lightly. Store in airtight containers. Makes three to four quarts.

SOY OAT PATTIES

2 cups soaked soybeans (about ²/₃ cup dry soybeans)
1 cup water
2 tablespoons brewers' yeast
2 tablespoons soy sauce
2 tablespoons oil
2 teaspoon garlic powder
⅛ teaspoon Italian seasoning
1 teaspoon salt
1¼ cups rolled oats
1 onion

Combine all ingredients in the blender, except for the oats, and blend fine. Or beans may be ground in food chopper and combined with other ingredients. Add oats and let stand for 10 minutes. Drop by spoonfuls onto oiled baking pan (or they may be fried on both sides). Bake at 350 degrees for 30-40 minutes until browned and done all the way through, but not too dry. Makes about 20 patties. It may be served with tomato sauce or a gravy made from mushroom soup. For special occasions dress it up by putting the patties in a casserole, smothering them with sautéed onions and mush-rooms, and then adding the gravy. Bake another 30 minutes at 350 degrees.

excluding meat, provided almost three times as much energy as the high meat and protein diet—167 minutes of pedal power.

Other recent scientific evidence links meat-eating and cancer—the second major killer in the United States (even of children). In a little over two pounds of charcoal-broiled steak, there is as much benzopyrene (a cancer-stimulating agent) as there is in the smoke from 600 cigarettes. When mice are fed benzopyrene, they develop stomach tumors and leukemia. Methylcholanthrene is another cancer-stimulating agent, and when the fat of meat is heated to a high temperature, as is frequently done when cooking meat, methylcholanthrene forms. When it is given in large quantities to small animals, they also develop cancers. Researchers gave methylcholanthrene to mice in a single dose too small to cause cancer itself, but when these animals ingested a second cancer stimulating agent also in amounts too small to produce cancer alone, the mice *did* get cancer.[4] In other words, in a single small dose, methylcholanthrene sensitizes animals to other cancer-producing agents, making them more likely to develop cancer.

Parents who are interested in cutting food costs but also obtaining all the nutrients essential for health, should consider lowering the family intake of meat and substituting vegetable protein dishes and legumes (dried beans, peas, lentils) several times a week. Legumes, which contain concentrated sources of protein, can be cooked simply and seasoned or made into tasty dishes when combined with other foods. Combining grains and legumes in the same dish enhances their nutrient value. A six-ounce steak will provide 700 calories and only about 30 grams of usable protein. But 1½ cups of cooked beans will provide an equal amount of calories and yet yield 50 percent more usable protein! Furthermore, beans are low in fat and virtually cholesterol free.

Among legumes, the soybean has the highest quality and quantity of protein, and many soy products are available today. Spun soy protein is used as a filler or as a meat extender. To get you started using the soybean, which nowadays can be found in large bins near the vegetable section of many supermarkets, I would like to include my favorite recipe for using them (p. 171).

All protein needs may be met by the following foods: milk, preferably skim milk, low-fat milk, or soy milk fortified with vitamin B^{12} (2 cups for adults and 3-5 cups for children and teen-agers); two or more servings of legumes, nuts, cottage cheese, or meat alternates; and four or more servings of whole-grain cereals.

The Snack-break Generation

We live in the age of the snack and the coffee break. Eating is almost a nonstop activity for some. The average North American eats approximately twelve hundred empty calories as snack foods every day. Overloading the diet with empty-calorie foods is one of the chief reasons why so many people, including children, are overweight. Eating between meals delays digestion and interferes with the digestive process of the duodenum. Because the food is assimilated more slowly, the general nutritive processes of the body are slower, and vigor and vitality decline.

Eating candy or sugary snacks between meals can cause more damage than eating the same foods at mealtime. Carbohydrates that are sticky adhere to the teeth and promote the growth of bacteria. Crisp, juicy, fresh fruits and vegetables help prevent tooth decay since they act as tooth cleansers.

Supermarket shelves overflow with processed and highly refined foods, many of which contain chemicals in the form of preservatives. Unfortunately, the refining process removes many of the vitamins and minerals. As a result, the food industry often tries to add back the necessary vitamins and minerals.

What chances does a child, who is a junk-food junkie, have of growing into a healthy vibrant adult? A building without a foundation will inevitably collapse under the storms of life. Are you willing to let the junk food advertisers have the upper hand in influencing your child's daily food consumption, to the downfall of his behavior and total future health status?

Getting your vitamins and minerals naturally from foods has several advantages over having them added back or buying them in bottles. First of all, it costs less that way—much less. Second, getting your vitamins and minerals directly from foods also ensures that they come in suitable concentrations that do not overwhelm the system with surpluses that cause the excretory organs to work harder to throw them off.

To assure nutritional health balance of all the necessary foods, choose them from a wide variety of whole and unrefined sources and prepare them in a simple, tasty way. When you do this you can be sure you are following a sound program that will result in good health. And remember, healthier families are happier families.

A word of caution: Resist the temptation to change all your family's eating habits overnight or you will meet loud cries of opposition. For instance, if you announce to your teen-ager that he can't have any more junk food because you want him to get better grades, he'll likely fight you all the way. He will better understand incentives such as fewer pimples, less weight gain, and more stamina for sports. The best plans for

changing a family's eating habits are to make a few subtle changes at a time in the diet, while allowing everyone's body chemistry to adjust. At first, you might allow one junk-food night per week in order to prevent withdrawal symptoms such as depression, anger, or irritability.

Remember, too, that all meals should be a positive experience. Particularly is this true of the last meal for the day. The evening meal ideally should be simple and light. Heavier meals, as much as possible, should be eaten earlier in the day when energy is needed and used most. Suppertime should be a time of family togetherness where *every* member of the family has an opportunity to contribute to the conversation and made to feel important. A recent survey of Detroit families indicates that only three meals out of a possible twenty-one weekly meals are shared by the family unit!

Avoid constant correcting of table manners and grammar at mealtime. *And keep the television OFF during meals!* Everything that mealtimes should stand for is destroyed by the intrusion of television. Pleasant conversation and even laughter during meals aids digestion; bickering slows the digestive process.

Make meals a happy, treasured time. They really are the last frontier when it comes to family togetherness.

Further reading you will enjoy . . .

McEntire, Patricia. *MOMMY, I'M HUNGRY.*
Smith, Lendon. *FEED YOUR KIDS RIGHT.*
Smith, Lendon. *IMPROVING YOUR CHILD'S BEHAVIOR CHEMISTRY.*

Chapter at a Glance

I. Sex Education Is a Live Issue
  A. Parents do not want to be narrow

  B. Parents want their child to adjust

  C. Parents often don't know what to say

II. The Essentials of Sex Education
  A. Facts of reproduction

  B. Moral values

III. The Goals of Sex Education
  A. The ultimate goal: the most pleasure and the least hurt

  B. Basic goals

    1. Ability to give and receive love

    2. Satisfaction with the sex role

    3. Respect for one's body

    4. Acceptance of physical changes

    5. Knowledge of how life begins

    6. Living by sound standards

IV. Handling Questions About Sex
  A. A child is naturally curious

  B. Overmodesty is harmful

  C. How to relate to questions

    1. Answer clearly

    2. Answer frankly

    3. Tell the truth

    4. Don't overanswer

  D. How you say it is often more important than what you say

Chapter 10

Positive Sexuality

The topic of sex education has become an extremely popular subject among parent-education groups because Christian parents do not wish to appear narrow-minded or behind-the-times, but neither do they wish to condone the permissiveness of a society which ignores the teaching of the Scriptures. They want to help their child develop healthy sexual adjustment and understanding, but how does one go about it? How do parents prepare themselves for the questions kids ask? What kind of answers can they give? How should parents present the basic facts of sex? How do parents talk with the older child about sex without feeling uncomfortable? How can they help their child gain both accurate information and the ability to view sex from a Christian perspective?

Parents are confused partly because they are unsure of what to tell their child and partly because of the films, newspaper stories, magazine articles, books, and TV shows that distort their child's views about sex and sexual love. In recent years advertisers and publishers have learned that exploitation of sex produces considerable profit. Consequently never before in history have young people had so much misinformation on sex available to them, while the importance of sexual

---

V. **The Child Who Doesn't Ask About Sex**
   A. Why a child may remain silent
   B. This child needs the same information as does a curious child

VI. **Experimentation**
   A. Sex play is common
   B. Parent overreaction causes harm
   C. Every child should have his own bed
   D. Discourage overnight visits

VII. **Masturbation**
   A. Much misinformation abounds
   B. Masturbation is normal
   C. Masturbation can cause problems
   D. Dealing with masturbation

VIII. **Pornography**
   A. How to react if your child reads it
      1. Don't make a scene
      2. Discuss the one-sidedness of pornography
   B. The child who receives a good sex education is less likely to read pornography

morality, honesty, and integrity have been downgraded subtly. And although the Biblical standards of morality have not changed, its guidelines are being ridiculed throughout our society.

In the face of glaring immorality, many families are endeavoring to teach their children moral values based on Biblical principles. When you teach your child about sex, always keep in mind two facets: basic anatomy and moral values. The child should always be taught basic anatomy. Help him identify each body part by its proper name. Thoroughly explain its purpose and function in terms your child can understand.

"Where's Gloria's baby?" a 4-year-old innocently queried one day after his parents told him that his older stepsister was going to have a baby.

"It's in her stomach," Mommy answered absentmindedly.

"Did she eat the baby?" the 4-year-old wanted to know.

At this point the mother realized what she had said and attempted to correct her error. "The baby is not really in her stomach but in her uterus."

"What's the uterus?"

"It's an organ mommies have that daddies don't have."

"Well," the enlightened child continued, "Gloria doesn't have an organ. She has a piano!"

Try as we may to teach correctly, problems may be encountered during the process of interpretation.

The second factor that must be included when teaching a child about sex is the relationship of sex to moral values. It isn't enough to teach a child the facts about reproduction and sexual functioning. The child needs to be able to relate the information received to his developing moral code. Sex education and moral values must always go hand in hand.

While attending a sex education seminar at a university, I witnessed a teacher pleading with her fellow teachers to teach sex education with a book in one hand and a pill in the other! Such teaching clearly lacks the essentials of responsibility,

attitudes, and morals involved in educating a child to make moral judgments on his own when the time comes. Are you willing to relinquish your sacred right to guide properly your child in this area and allow him to absorb the secular values that he may learn in public school?

Sex education, then, means building *attitudes* concerning the whole subject of sexuality, rather than just teaching physiological facts. Sex education involves exposure to all the facts, to the understanding of the reasons behind the facts, and to the formulation of attitudes toward sex based firmly upon these facts. Sex education should encompass the psychological, sociological, economic, and social factors that affect the personality and behavior as well as the physiological facts of human reproduction.

The ultimate goal of sex education is that the child might arrive at attitudes that will bring him the greatest amount of happiness and subject him to the least amount of hurt. And this is not easy, for today's parents have the difficult task of teaching "sex can be wonderful" and yet "sex can be dangerous" all in the same breath.

Basic Goals in Sex Education

The following six suggestions list a few goals which parents may hope to accomplish:

1. *That he might learn to give and receive love.* Sex education should help the child to be both loving and lovable, to be able to give love as well as to receive it. A baby thrives on the love of his parents and family, and he learns to trust them and to give love in return. When a child begins school, his circle of love expands as he makes friends and meets teachers. In preteen years he develops friends of his own age and sex. Then in adolescence he transfers his devotion to certain members of the opposite sex. Wise parents will help their child progress steadily from one step to the next in this pattern of giving and receiving love.

2. *That he may be satisfied with his sex*

role. One of the most important aspects of sex education is that of teaching healthy masculine and feminine identification. Sexuality involves the name given at birth, the toys played with, the clothes worn, the friends played with, the choice of courses in school, the way the roles and responsibilities in the home are viewed, and last, the way in which sexual needs and urges are satisfied by responsible and committed human beings. Obviously, sexual identity forms an important part of developing a healthy self-image and affects every aspect of life.

Parents must teach their boy to be glad he is a boy and their girl to be pleased she is a girl. Such satisfaction develops through a girl's admiration for her mother and a boy's respect for his father. During the transitional ages, particularly in early adolescence, a child may have trouble accepting his or her sexual identity. Some girls feel no pride in being feminine and actually fear being a woman. Many boys, especially if they are smaller in build than others, fear that they may not be able to be a real man. The respect and love which parents show each other help teach that both men and women have a worthy place in life. Parents can also reassure their child that they love and appreciate him for what he is.

3. *That he may respect his own body.* A child should respect his body and feel that each part of it is good and has a good purpose. The way the child feels about himself will largely reflect his parents' attitudes toward his body.

4. *That he will understand and accept bodily changes.* A closely related goal is that the child should be prepared for the bodily changes that come as he grows out of childhood into adolescence. He should learn to accept such changes as a normal part of development. Both boys and girls need also to understand the changes occurring in the other sex.

5. *That he will know and appreciate how life began.* Children have a great curiosity about how life begins, how the baby develops, and how he is born. This gives Christian parents the opportunity to teach the true story of birth, which is so full of dignity and wonder that it encourages an attitude of respect.

6. *That he may eventually live by sound standards of sexual conduct.* One of the chief aims of sex education is to help a child develop standards of sexual conduct. Parents can best teach their child morality through a healthy parent-child relationship during the early years. He can be taught to respect what his parents believe and accept what they recommend for him. A child should also learn loyalty to God, who is not only a God of love, but also a God of wrath. If we choose to defy His laws, there are consequences which we must suffer. The youngster who understands this truth is likely to live a moral life in the midst of an immoral society.

Can Information Be Dangerous?

Knowing the truth is less disturbing than not knowing the facts and wondering what they are. Indeed, sex experimentation comes most frequently from the child who is uninformed, for experimentation is one

"Son, I'd like, ah, to talk to you, er, about sex."
"Sure, Dad. Whatcha wanna know?"

way of getting information. Several research studies have shown that the typical sex offender usually comes from a home where he has received little or no sex education.

When Should Sex Education Begin?

A concerned mother recently asked her physician, "Do you know of any good books about sex for my boy? He is almost thirteen, and I think it is time he learned the facts of life." Sadly, this mother had closed her own eyes to the facts of life. A child's sex education begins the day he is born. When mother loves him, cares for him, and plays with him, she is indirectly involved in sex education.

A child is taught how he should feel about his body much earlier than we might imagine. Suppose little Johnny, age 14 months, is being given a bath. He sits in the warm water delightfully exploring his body. He touches his toes, and Mother exclaims, "Toes, see Baby's toes." He plays some more and feels around his navel. Mother might say, "Belly button, that's Johnny's belly button." Then suddenly he discovers his penis and starts to play with it. Not many mothers would say, "Penis, that's Johnny's penis." Instead most might try to distract him or do something to indicate that what he was doing was not nice. Some mothers might even slap his hand and tell him, "No! No!"

When a mother handles the situation this way, she is teaching her child that his toes are nice, his belly button is nice and all right to play with, but there is something bad and nasty about that other part of his body. Yet to Johnny his penis is just as interesting as his toes, but Mother causes him to be morbidly interested in his sex organs by making him feel that they are a taboo part of his body.

What should parents do when their child discovers his sex organs? They should teach him the names for his sex organs and organs of elimination the same as they teach him the names for the other parts of his body. The right names may seem more difficult for the parent to say, but not so for the child, who will learn penis, testicle, buttocks, anus, vulva, and vagina just as easily as elbow, nose, eye, and ear. The words are not hard to say, and they should be used with accuracy when speaking with a child about his body. Good opportunities for teaching also arise when words such as urinating or menstruating are used.

One word of caution. It is better to teach a young child that with the possible exception of going to the bathroom, toilet words and really personal words should be used only in his own home or with his own parents. Part of his personality development involves learning what words are socially acceptable and what are not.

Modesty

A child learns modesty both by instruction and by example. It is not something that is entirely instinctive. Small children must be told what is proper and what is not. Without conveying a sense of shame, parents can help their child understand that certain things one does not do in public. Tell him why he must not go to the bathroom out-of-doors. Tell him why he must not undress in front of the windows. Tell a little girl why she must learn to keep her dress down and a little boy why he must keep his pants zipped up.

Occasionally a child will burst into a room and find Mother or Father not fully dressed. A calm, poised manner at this time means more than anything else you can say or do. Naturalness and poise will let the child know that the human body which God has created is wholesome and worthy of dignity. A parent might say, "You forgot to knock" or "I didn't close the door. Please hand me my robe." It is important that the parent not overreact with shouts or threats. Parents who feel ill at ease will teach the child to feel embarrassed about his body as well.

However, it is important for a child to learn a healthy respect for privacy. It is not good for a child to be constantly exposed to adults who are not fully dressed. Seeing a naked body too frequently may arouse feelings and emotions too strong for a young child to cope with. Parents often fail on this point, feeling that their child is too young to be sexually aroused, but even a young child has sexual feelings, and he is often stimulated through parental ignorance of this fact.

But it does little good for parents to preach modesty if they do not practice it. A small boy was eating supper with a baby-sitter when his mother came to kiss him goodbye before going out for the evening. She was dressed in a low-cut evening dress.

"Where are you going, Mommy?" he asked.

"To a concert, dear," she replied.

"But somebody might see you," the boy retorted.

Questions, Questions, Questions!

Children want to know about everything from stars to bugs. They are as wholesomely curious about sex as they are about cars, animals, and electricity. Toileting, bathing, and dressing are normal times to see and learn.

A teacher reported to Jimmy's parents that he seemed overly interested in little.girls in school. Several times he had even peeked into the rest rooms, trying to get one of them to show him how girls looked without panties on. The shocked and embarrassed parents rushed to their physician with the problem. The doctor discovered that the mother locked Jimmy out of the room every time she changed the new baby's diapers! This was no solution. If Jimmy could have naturally and normally seen baby sister, his curiosity would have been satisfied. It is unwise for parents to make too much of modesty. Parents who overemphasize modesty can cause their child to gain peculiar and false attitudes about himself and others. There must be a happy medium.

When a child asks questions about his body or a little girl's, parents should answer these questions clearly so that he knows he is made the way he should be. You might say, "Boys and girls are made differently. God planned it that way. All boys have a penis. Girls do not. You are made just the way God wants you to be."

When a child wonders where a baby comes from, he should not be told that it comes from the stork, the supermarket, or the hospital. He should be told that the baby grows inside a special place in the mother's body. He should not be told that the baby grows inside the mother's stomach, which is physiologically incorrect. It depends on further questions at this time and on the age of the child whether the place should be identified as the uterus and whether any more information should be given. Parents must forgo the temptation to give too much information too soon.

A new preacher arrived to deliver his first sermon to a country church, but only one cowhand showed up. The preacher asked him if he wanted to hear the sermon alone. The man replied that he was just a cowhand, but if he went out to feed his cows, and only one showed up, he would feed her anyway. The preacher began his hour-long sermon. When he finished, he asked the cowhand if he had liked it. The cowhand answered that he was just a cowhand, and he didn't know much about preaching, but if he went to feed his cows and only one showed up, he wouldn't dump the whole load!

A child can ask questions about abortion, adoption, adultery, artificial insemination, contraception, circumcision, exhibitionism, fornication, homosexuality, masturbation, menopause, menstruation, pornography, prostitution, and intercourse. And there is no reason why parents should not answer his questions frankly, but he does not need a course in obstetrics.

Often it is not so important what you say as how you say it. When you go into as many or as few details as you wish in a calm, unanxious voice, the child will feel calm and unanxious. But if you speak in a worried or anxious manner, the child will assume that there is something worrisome and anxiety-provoking about sex.

About the Child Who Doesn't Ask

There are a number of reasons why a child may remain silent on the subject of sex. His interest may not have been stimulated through natural family living. He may be an only child or a last child who is not alerted by the new baby. A child may try "to be good," but somewhere he has picked up the impression that certain questions might be "bad." Another child who has already gotten his information outside the family circle may have been embarrassed or ridiculed and therefore may not feel free to raise any more questions.

But regardless of the reason, a child who does not ask needs help just as much as one who does. There are many positive ways of teaching sex education from everyday life that don't involve sitting down with a book and delving into a question-and-answer period. The first way we have already discussed—learning from brothers and sisters. If there isn't a new baby in the family, take him to visit a friend who has one and just let him see the baby. Nothing special needs to be said.

Another method of learning is from nature. The child who sees animals mating gives parents an excellent opportunity to point that children have mothers and fathers just like animals. Parents can also point out that when people mate it is different than when animals mate, because mothers and fathers love each other—that is why they get married and live together, to have a child they love.

Often parents feel they have done their duty when they merely announce to their child, "If you have any questions about sex, just come and ask us." Yet this child never asks his parents. It isn't enough just to tell your child that he may come to you with questions. A good teacher will not see his task merely in terms of sitting by and waiting until questions are asked. He will try to stimulate wonder and curiosity so that questions will be asked. He wants to do more than just impart information. He wants to help each child become a learning, growing person who eagerly explores the wonderful world in which he lives. And a good teacher knows that learning occurs gradually.

Parents who say nothing are neglecting their responsibility to bring up the subject. Christian parents are most anxious, for instance, to share their Christianity with a child during his early years. They point out all the things in nature God has made, how God loves us and cares for us, and how we can talk with God. Few Christian parents sit back and refuse to discuss God and the Bible or wait for their child to take the initiative in asking. On the contrary, most

Christian parents talk over the all-important concepts of God, faith, and salvation with their child. Why, then, should they lock up sex in a separate compartment marked, "Don't investigate"? Bring sex out in the open. If you find it difficult at first, read a book about sex, attend a class, or somehow educate yourself so that you can discuss the subject with ease. And every time you do discuss it, it will make it easier for the next time.

About Experimentation

Mothers and fathers sometimes get shocked and upset when a group of neighborhood children are discovered

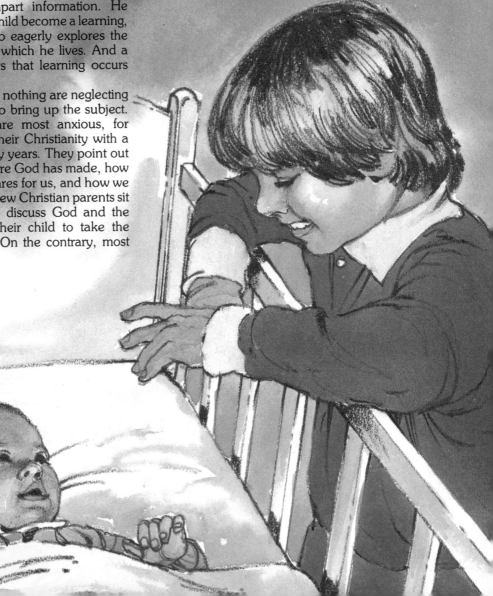

Thinking Back: How It Was for Me

Our ease and ability to discuss sexual topics with our children is very much influenced by the attitudes, thoughts, and feelings carried over from our own childhood. The more positive the instruction from our early years, the more likely we will be able to pass on healthy attitudes to our own children. In each of the following statements circle the number that most closely matches your recollections.

1. Not true   2. Somewhat true   3. Largely true   4. True

1 2 3 4 5   1. During my own childhood my parents allowed and encouraged me to ask questions about sex.

1 2 3 4 5   2. My parents never made me feel guilty for exhibiting curiosity about my sex organs.

1 2 3 4 5   3. My parents, not my peers, were my first and primary source of sex information.

1 2 3 4 5   4. In reviewing what I was taught in my childhood, I feel I grew up with healthy, comfortable attitudes toward sex and reproduction.

1 2 3 4 5   5. Both of my parents participated in giving me information about sex over the years.

1 2 3 4 5   6. (For males) One or both of my parents talked with me about nocturnal emissions or "wet dreams" prior to the first time I had one.
(For females) One or both of my parents prepared me for the onset of menstruation prior to the time I had my first menstrual period.

1 2 3 4 5   7. My parents were free in expressing appropriate demonstrations of affection for one another in front of me.

1 2 3 4 5   8. I do/did feel comfortable and free to express appropriate demonstrations of affection for my spouse in front of my children.

Total the point value of the numbers circled. Turn to page 239 for scoring instructions. Discuss the results with your partner, friend, or parent study group. If changes need to be made: (1) What are they? (2) How will you go about making these changes? and (3) When will you begin?

involved in sex play. Sex play and experimentation are not uncommon among children between the ages of four and ten. They want to compare, so behind closed doors they show each other their genitals. They experiment with different ways to urinate. Girls stand up; boys sit down. They giggle about bathroom words. They play doctor and nurse.

Sometimes parents become so upset that they forbid their child to ever play with that group of children again. Such an overemphasis makes the incident stand out in the child's memory as a dirty and terrible experience, and wholesome attitudes are not built on feelings of guilt and shame.

The best thing a parent can do is to talk quietly with the child about the matter, answering his questions and giving explanations. Wise parents will minimize the whole affair and, without causing a scene, lead their child to other activities.

On Sharing Beds

Every child should have his own bed. A child who regularly shares a bed cannot avoid physical contacts that invite sex play. A significant number of adults with sex problems trace them to times when they slept with brothers or sisters, relatives or friends. Many parents might be very surprised to know the amount of sex play and masturbation that takes place between children who are forced to sleep together. In addition, brothers and sisters should have separate bedrooms after the age of five or six. If this is impossible, arrange the furniture to give them as much privacy as possible.

Some parents innocently allow their child to spend the night with a friend or allow a friend to come and spend the night at their home. Another common practice is the so-called slumber party for young girls. This is not to say that a child should *never* have a friend stay overnight or should *never* sleep over at a friend's home. But a child is exposed to experimentation when he is permitted these privileges, and it is far easier to prevent an evil than to cure it afterward.

Masturbation

For generations, the very word *masturbation* has brought fear and shame to thousands. Just a few years ago masturbation was said to cause insanity, deafness, blindness, epilepsy, baldness, weight loss, weakness, and sterility. Often a child caught "in the act" was beaten and sternly warned that he would go to hell because of it. A special chastity belt for boys was patented in this century and could be purchased. Another method of controlling this most dreadful of all habits was aluminum mitts into which the hands of a child could be locked at night. Some parents used handcuffs. Even a buzzer device was invented to ring in the parents' bedroom indicating that the boy had had an erection, whereupon the father could rush in and save the boy from himself! Occasionally parents resorted to such extremes as cutting out a girl's clitoris or suturing the labia in an effort to stop masturbation. Operations were also performed on boys.

Nowadays medical authorities insist that masturbation is a normal part of growing up. Almost all boys and at least 75 percent of girls practice self-manipulation at some time or another during adolescence, for they have discovered the pleasant sensations that come from pressing against, rubbing, or handling the genital organs. Many times masturbation merely reflects the child's search for knowledge about his own body, but some children resort to masturbation in an effort to compensate for a lack of love and attention.

It is unlikely that masturbation causes many of the feared diseases for which it has been credited during the centuries, but it can destroy self-respect, character, and morals. Self-manipulation may result in melancholy, irritability, and jealousy. The child may suffer keenly from feelings of remorse and may feel degraded in his own eyes. Continual masturbation can destroy the energy of the entire system and thus trigger depression. By his focus on self, the masturbator can lose sight of spiritual things.

When parents discover their child masturbating, they should not threaten punish-

feels new urges, moods, and physical sensations as his sexual responses and capacities awaken.

The most serious damage resulting from masturbation is the guilt connected with it. There are known cases of young people who have committed suicide because they felt too weak and evil to go on living. Young people need to understand that as they grow into manhood and womanhood their sexual concepts can become more meaningful. They must learn that genuine sexual satisfaction comes from the deeper need to give than to receive. They need to grasp the concept that real fulfillment can be found only in a love relationship that involves another person and not in solitary physical pleasure. This is why God made man and woman.

Parents should realize that the adolescent is deeply concerned about the subject of masturbation, yet it is one of the most difficult areas to discuss. Who can understand? Parents can help their teen-ager by assuring him that there is nothing wrong with what is happening in his body. They must not burden him with feelings of guilt, self-hatred, or degradation. At the same time they should emphasize guidance and control of sex.

A child who masturbates a great deal is usually a troubled and unhappy child. He may have few friends and may not enjoy a normal amount of childhood fun. Masturbation in such a child is not the cause of the problem but a symptom that everything in this child's life is not right. Parents should make an effort to create good play situations and see that he enjoys active playtime. They should provide him with worthwhile tasks at home and compliment him on tasks well done and effort expended toward doing it. They should include him more in family fun and projects. If he does not respond after all these things, it would be wise to seek professional guidance.

A child must be taught to control his sexual drives. If he does not learn self-control, he will grow up to be a cruel, selfish, greedy, undisciplined adult. The great danger is that some parents, in a desperate attempt to help a child control his sexual

ment or condemn or embarrass him. They should check his play life. Does he have enough physical exercise? Does he have enough playtime? Does he have appropriate playthings that he can build, push, pull, and handle in his own way? If he is older, does he have a hobby or an interest in sports, music, and a variety of Christian services? Does he feel accepted, loved, and appreciated? Do his clothes fit properly? Is his body clean? Does he have a skin irritation?

During teen years, masturbation takes on a different meaning for the most part. No longer a matter of curiosity or simple childish pleasure, it has a deeper sexual meaning. The teen-ager has lived with his body for over a dozen years, but now he urges, go either to the extreme of overcontrol or to the opposite extreme of not teaching enough control.

Pornography

Another frequent question that crops up, particularly among parents of teenagers, is what they should do when they find obscene pictures or reading matter in the possession of their youngster. The book *Books and the Teen-Age Reader,* by G. Robert Carlsen, offers this advice to parents who encounter this problem: "When you discover a copy of a lurid book, a girly magazine, a dirty joke book concealed in your teen-ager's room or notebook, do not act with emotion or embarrassment. He is not some strange monster, nor are his interests unnatural. He is fascinated by this material because he has heard about it from friends. He wants to find out for himself. Making a scene, destroying the material, accusing him of shameful desires, will not necessarily decrease his interest. It may only make him more clever in hiding it from you and plant the notion in his mind that he somehow is twisted and perverted."

In discussing pornography with a teenager, point out how it depicts genital contact only. It is not a relationship containing affection, love, or commitment between two human beings. Sex for the sake of sex becomes boring. Producers of pornography realize this fact, and that is why they inject a variety of strange, often bizarre scenes.

Someone has said that pornography is material "to be read or seen with one hand," or in other words this implies that one would masturbate with the other. For Christians of any age, the use of such materials to stimulate erotic fantasies would fly in the face of all the Bible says sex can and should be.

The child who receives a good sex education and who can openly discuss sex with his parents is far less likely to turn to pornographic materials. When natural curiosity is not satisfied in an intelligent manner, however, a young person may turn to pornography to answer his questions. Unfortunately such material offers wrong answers, misleading information, and an unwholesome view of sex by separating it from love and marriage.

The sex education of the child is a privilege as well as a responsibility and must be rooted in Biblical principles and not in human arguments that change with the times and leave young people with nothing to hang on to. It is a parental privilege to give to the world boys and girls with healthy attitudes toward sex and morals who can grow up to establish loving, happy, and unselfish families.

Further reading you will enjoy . . .

Lerrigo, Marion and Cassidy. *A DOCTOR TALKS TO 9-12 YEAR OLDS.*
Levinson, F. and G. L. Kelly. *WHAT TEENAGERS WANT TO KNOW.*
Meilach, Dona A. *A DOCTOR TALKS TO 5-8 YEAR OLDS.*
Scanzoni, Letha. *SEX IS A PARENT AFFAIR.*
Van Pelt, Nancy *THE COMPLEAT COURTSHIP.*
Wood, Barry. *QUESTIONS TEENAGERS ASK ABOUT DATING AND SEX.*

Chapter at a Glance

Chapter 11

The Role of the Father and Mother—Blest Be the Tie That Binds

A woman and her teen-age daughter were lunching in a restaurant that had its share of young mothers and their restless offspring. Four of the mothers were very noticeably pregnant. For fifteen minutes the teen-ager had listened to the mothers' harping at their preschoolers. Finally, she turned to her mother and asked perceptively, "Mom, if they hate their kids so much, why are they having more?"

Did the girl's question strike a responsive chord in your mind? Most of us grew up playing house, and we indulged in marvelous fantasies of marrying a handsome prince or beautiful princess. The ads we heard and saw told us that all we needed to do was to use a certain toothpaste. *Voilà!* The right person would instantly appear on the scene, and we would fall madly in love. Soon we would have perfect, charming babies. We would feed them brand Eat-um-Up baby food, which is so fantastically fortified they will never get sick, cranky, or daffy. No one ever suggested that life would get complicated. We had the least realistic preparation for the most demanding job of all.

Here's the beautiful young princess who knew she could handle marriage. She felt certain that she knew what marriage and raising a family were like. She's seen it a million times on television. Every romance novel told the story—you get married and live happily ever after. But soon after the dream began, a nightmare was brewing on the horizon. Something wasn't working as it should. By the time Baby Number One arrived, their relationship with each other was deteriorating. Married life began with such high hopes and with a tender song in their hearts! So now, how could the Bib Question loom so high in their path: Why is our marital satisfaction continuing to sink throughout the child-rearing years?

Has that question ever risen from your disappointed heart?

Let's look at the facts. Notice in the accompanying diagram that the level of marital satisfaction dips to the halfway point

by the time children enter the home. Happiness continues to decline for families with children and reaches its lowest ebb when the children are in their teen years.

Most persons assume that the highest level of marital satisfaction will be achieved during the latter portion of life. This assumption reflects the thought that the longer a couple live together, the greater will be their desire to increase the happiness of one another. But this holds true *only* for couples who were happy in the first place. It is very unlikely that a couple who has never experienced a high level of marital happiness will suddenly find bliss just because the children have left the home. Although this diagram portrays

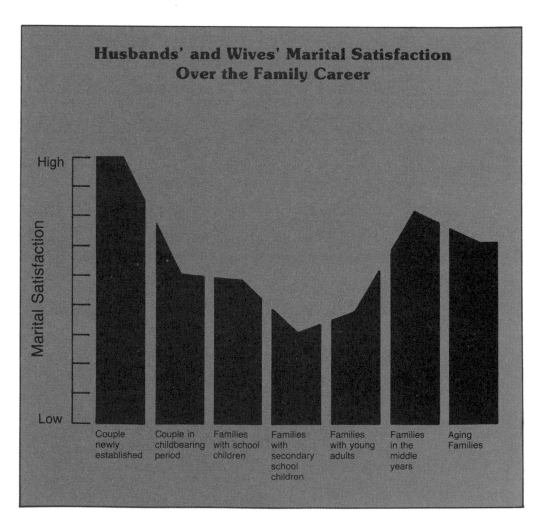

the results of numerous studies, not every couple will fall into the same pattern. However, most couples will tend to reflect these trends unless they spend as much time and effort in preparing for marriage and parental roles as they do for their lifework. So it is important that couples be able to identify and understand the stress and disruption of the marital relationship at each stage.

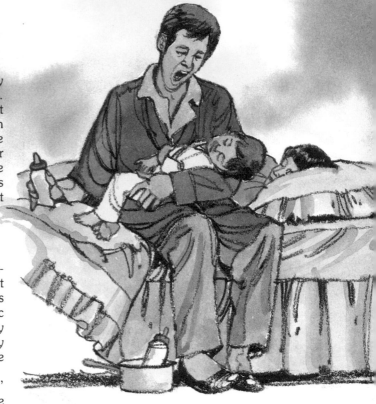

As the Dream Fades

Why the sudden drop in marital satisfaction immediately after marriage? Most couples are ill-prepared for the adjustments married life requires. Often romantic dreams have blinded them to the many realities that newlyweds must face. But why does the presence of children also decrease marital satisfaction?

Children are a "heritage of the Lord" and designed to be a blessing. But the couple must feel secure in their own relationship with each other prior to bringing a child into their lives. A couple who think the presence of children in the family will cement a shaky relationship do not understand the dynamics of life. *Children complicate relationships.* In fact, having a child during the first two years of marriage doubles the chance of divorce. Since divorce rates already claim one-half of all marriages, this means that only one in four couples could make it if all other factors are equal.

For the most part, the average couple is completely unprepared for the demands of parenthood. This lack of training creates worry and stress that most young couples are not prepared to handle. They spend the nine months of pregnancy purchasing all the darling baby clothes and furniture necessary to welcome the little one into the world. If they receive any training at all, it comes from a Lamaze class for natural childbirth, which only instructs parents on how to bring a child into the world. It does not train parents how to nurture and train a baby once it joins the family.

The suddenness with which parental responsibilities are thrust upon a young couple accentuates their lack of preparation. During the honeymoon a young couple can gradually learn about each other. When an infant arrives on the scene, there is no opportunity for gradual acquaintance. Therefore, a crisis situation dominates the marriage scene. The husband-wife relationship now competes with the parent-child relationship for time, affection, and caring. Husband and wife now grope about as they try to reorganize their relationship with each other.

What's the answer to this dilemma? Preparation . . . preparation . . . preparation—for both marriage *and* parenthood.

Knowledge alone will not solve all the problems connected with these adjustments, but it certainly will go a long way in helping intelligent couples deal with the realities before they hit.

A healthy parent-child relationship develops from a healthy husband-wife relationship. These bonds of love foster the security a child needs. The mother's emotional security to a great extent depends on the affection, security, and fulfillment she feels in her relationship with her husband. A woman's self-respect is closely tied to her feelings of being valued, respected, and cherished. Not only acceptance of herself but also her role as wife and mother heavily depend on her husband's acceptance and support. *It is the husband-wife role, then, that is the determining factor in whether both husband and wife will function at peak performance as mother and father.*

The Early Nesting Years

The childless couple's life continues much the same as it did when they were courting. Usually both continue to pursue active careers. When tensions arise and problems surface, they escape them by going different directions in the workaday world. Evenings, weekends, and vacations are free to enjoy as they see fit. However, children drastically change the scene. Suddenly they must assume the role of parents. Family patterns are disrupted. Life is no longer what the young couple has been used to.

Married life is irrevocably changed. The demanding infant's insistent cries interrupt Mom and Dad's sleep and relentlessly change their days as well. They realize, perhaps for the first time, that, as parents, they are totally responsible for this helpless person and cannot rid themselves of their responsibility.

At first a real sense of stability and pride elates the parents as they settle down with *their* baby. The infant is a visible sign to all that the couple have begun their life together in earnest. They may not have received much attention from friends and

family since the wedding, but now all gather around to welcome the new baby and voice concern for the welfare of the new parents and their future together.

And at the same time, the new parents find themselves shrouded in fears and frustrations. Sleepless nights have left both husband and wife utterly exhausted. Owing to the confinement caused by the ever-present responsibility they feel very lonely. No longer do they enjoy social and job contacts outside the home, and depression darkens their lives. The volume of household duties that one small infant has produced leaves them feeling overworked. The house that once stayed immaculately neat as both husband and wife picked up after themselves now takes on the appearance of Pig Pen Palace. Financial responsibilities increase. And every time they turn around, they face additional decisions—decisions about doctors, playmates, day care, formulas, spiritual training, and discipline.

During the early nesting years parents are also perplexed about the spacing of children. Studies show that children who are two years apart or less and of the same sex are more likely to be competitive. This may result in intense battles of sibling rivalry, but take heart. They are more likely to enjoy one another's company during times of truce. Children who are more than four years apart will have less in common and *perhaps* will not engage in as much sibling rivalry.

Of more consequence than the spacing of children are such factors as: age and health of the mother; financial obligations; the reasons why another child is desired; the emotional climate of the marriage; a unified desire to have another child; the emotional and physical ability of both parents to invest in the training and education of another family member; available space in the house for one more . . . the list is limitless.

Pressure on a marriage greatly increases when children enter the scene. When a couple are not well-matched in ideas on how to train and discipline children, conflicts are inevitable. A blending of their

194

How Do Children Affect Marriage?

The following statements will measure your knowledge regarding the effect of children on marriage stability. Respond to each statement by circling the number that most closely reveals your opinion.
1. Strongly agree   2. Mildly agree   3. Not sure   4. Mildly disagree
5. Strongly disagree

1 2 3 4 5   1. Studies show that marital satisfaction continues to decline throughout the child-rearing years.

1 2 3 4 5   2. A couple's happiness level usually reaches its lowest ebb when the children are in their teens.

1 2 3 4 5   3. Over the span of married years, the highest level of marital satisfaction is reached during the latter years.

1 2 3 4 5   4. Having a child during the first two years of marriage doubles a couple's chance of divorce.

1 2 3 4 5   5. After the children are launched from the home, a couple's marital satisfaction begins to rise.

1 2 3 4 5   6. The first year of marriage is the rockiest for most couples.

1 2 3 4 5   7. The new groom/husband suffers more severe symptoms of disillusionment following the wedding than does the bride.

1 2 3 4 5   8. The future of a marriage is determined to a large extent by the adjustment a couple makes during the first year.

1 2 3 4 5   9. Statistics show that 51 percent of all divorces occur before five years of marriage.

Read chapter 11 to discover the correct response to each. Then discuss each statement with your spouse, a friend, or parent study group.

requirements. They will be able to address the matters of children and discipline in detail rather than in such idealistic terms as, "Oh, yes! Let's have three darling babies!" They will have worked through such matters as roles, problem solving, decision making, compatibility, communication, finances, and in-laws. The couples who make the easiest adjustment have had ample premarital guidance and two or more years to adapt to each other before Baby bounces into action.

A Man As Husband

Marriage brings status satisfaction to a man. He expects marriage to provide some of the feelings of importance that he craves. When a child enters the scene, a husband quickly learns that the attention he once had all to himself must now be divided. A new father must be sufficiently mature to recognize that when his wife shares her love with his child, she does not love him any less. Father and child are not in competition for a woman's affections.

Because feelings of this nature can easily erupt, it becomes essential that husband and wife schedule occasions to be together without interference from a child. They must set aside time and money for leisure activities outside the home if they wish to maintain their identity as a couple and to rekindle the fires of romance that tend to dwindle or get lost in a myriad of complex responsibilities. A couple should schedule such occasions for themselves at least twice a month. If you absolutely cannot afford a baby-sitter, trade baby-sitting tasks with another couple. Select activities that appeal to both of you. Go for a drive, a picnic, or a swim. Enjoy yourselves, laugh, dream big dreams. Forget your problems. Hold hands and talk of common interests. Concentrate on each other. Build a better future for yourselves. You and your spouse will never regret time spent like this.

Someone has said that the most important thing a man can do for his children is to love his wife. He was correct. A good father is first and foremost a good husband. When a man respects his wife as a person in her

ideals for family living becomes necessary. If the wife grew up in the country and cherishes fond memories of the family working together in the garden whereas her city-sprouted husband has never seen anything more earthy than a tulip blossom, compromise is a must.

Sometimes the responsibilities of parenthood so weigh down a couple that they cannot see the joys of parenthood. Young parents must always keep in perspective the happiness and trials of parenthood. Children are one of the richest sources of pleasure in family life. And the happier a couple are in their growing marriage, the more capable they will be to share that happiness with their child.

It would greatly assist most couples in the early years of marriage if during their engagement period they would begin taking the steps necessary to make a good transition after marriage. For instance, a couple who thoroughly read and study *We've Only Just Begun, To Have and to Hold,* and *Train Up a Child* will have a more realistic picture of married life and its own right, when he remains sensitive to her moods, and when he regards her role in the home as important as his, the home atmosphere is sure to be friendly and cooperative. Young personalities thrive in such surroundings.

Husband, love your wife. Tell her that you cherish the way she looks and that she is as lovely as the day you married her. Express your love through small acts of chivalry, compliments, appreciation of her devotion in the home, and thoughtful remembrances such as flowers, cards, or a dinner out. Keep the spark of affection glowing in your marriage. A woman can tolerate a lot if she knows that her husband still considers her his sweetheart.

Make no mistake about it. Daily expressions of romantic attention are vital to a woman's existence. Without constant reassurance of her husband's affection, she will not be able to meet as readily the needs of the child. A father who gives this kind of emotional support will find that his efforts are well rewarded even though at times his strength may be sorely taxed.

An attentive husband presents a proper picture of a man's role to both sons and daughters. The need for a strong husband/father image is greater than ever in today's fast pace where family members are being pulled in every direction away from the home. School, church, community activities, jobs, recreational activities, peers, and the mass media all beckon for attention at the same time. The male plays a strong role in holding a family together.

A Man As Father

Preparation for fatherhood has been sadly neglected. A young girl may pick up a certain amount of experience from babysitting and later she may enroll in a family living class. But I know of no system to train fathers for their important role. Yet it is crucial that men develop an awareness of their vital role in the development of an emotionally healthy child.

During the time a young man dates and courts his bride-to-be, he maintains a certain amount of independence. Once they get married, he quickly learns to include his wife in his plans, but nevertheless he still retains a measure of independence. After a baby comes along, he loses an even greater portion of his independence and finds that his wife depends on him more heavily than previously and needs especially large doses of affection, security, and encouragement. A man must recognize this need and give this kind of support. Then the security they find by working together will be transmitted to their child.

Although the mother usually spends the most time with a child, we should not underestimate the father's role. Fathers make several contributions to a child's growth that they alone can provide. The first and most important thing a father can do is to be a man. From his father a boy learns masculine traits that he will copy and that will become a part of his personality. From him a young man learns how a man's man acts. If a father wants his son to develop a healthy attitude toward women, he must provide a model of respect, for a child will set his values by observing how Mom and Dad get along. If a son observes his father downgrading women, he will imitate this attitude. If his father is familiar with women friends of his wife, the boy will quickly pick this up and think, This is the way for a man's man to act with women.

Girls need a relationship with their fathers as much as boys do. A girl must learn the differences between the male and female roles, and her father helps her develop her own femininity. Fathers must realize that a growing girl needs her father to appreciate her. She needs to dress to please him and to act like a girl. One reason few adult women feel real closeness, comfort, and understanding in their relationships with men is because their fathers never provided them with an opportunity to develop such feelings early in life.

The type of caring relationship a young girl establishes with her father critically affects her sexual functioning years down the line. Dr. Seymour Fisher[1] of the State University of New York investigated the differences between women with high and those with low sexual responsiveness. He

Am I Ready for Children?

Here's a quick and easy method of assessing readiness for parenthood. Those preparing for parenthood as well as others may enjoy taking it. Circle the response that most closely responds to your true feelings about each statement.

1. Definitely yes   2. Probably yes   3. Unsure   4. Probably not
5. Definitely not

1 2 3 4 5   1. When children are present in a room, they gravitate to me or show that they like me.

1 2 3 4 5   2. I often pause to admire infants or talk with small children.

1 2 3 4 5   3. I enjoy holding infants and small children.

1 2 3 4 5   4. I could handle the task of infant care even if my partner refused to assist or share tasks with me.

1 2 3 4 5   5. Even though I might be awakened during the night by an infant crying, I am confident I could handle the additional stress.

1 2 3 4 5   6. I enjoy infant-care tasks such as diapering, bathing, feeding, dressing, and burping.

1 2 3 4 5   7. I enjoy toddler-care tasks such as bathing, toilet training, correcting, teaching rules as well as answering questions, and teaching numbers and colors.

1 2 3 4 5   8. I am capable of loving a child even when the child's behavior is not lovable.

1 2 3 4 5   9. I am prepared to accept either a male or female child and do not have my heart set on either a boy or girl.

1 2 3 4 5   10. I am prepared to accept my child's appearance regardless of who he might look like.

1 2 3 4 5   11. I could handle admirably the disappointment of a daughter with only average or less than average physical beauty.

1 2 3 4 5   12. I could handle admirably the disappointment of a son who was short of stature and not of a strong masculine build.

1 2 3 4 5   13. I am mature enough to handle accepting a child who is only "average" in school and other capabilities.

1 2 3 4 5   14. Our present neighborhood is suitable for children since it includes quality schools, nearby playgrounds, and good playmates.

1 2 3 4 5   15. Our home is furnished suitably for a child; no rooms are "off limits" to children.

1 2 3 4 5   16. Our present home is adequate in size and space for children.

1 2 3 4 5   17. Our income is adequate to cover the additional expenses involved in feeding, clothing, and educating a child.

1 2 3 4 5   18. We have worked out the major difficulties and sources of marital conflict and consider our marital satisfaction at a higher than average level.

1 2 3 4 5   19. I am mature enough to handle it should I have to give up an evening out with friends to care for a sick child.

1 2 3 4 5   20. I have been independent from my mother and father and other relatives for at least two years.

1 2 3 4 5   21. I have been married for at least two years before having children.

1 2 3 4 5   22. I have had the opportunity to travel and live a little before having children so that later I will not look back and say, "If only we had waited . . ."

1 2 3 4 5   23. I believe parenthood should be a choice—that it should not be engaged in just because everyone else is doing it.

1 2 3 4 5   24. I recognize that children will take time away from my spouse, and we are both prepared to deal with it.

Turn to page 239 for scoring instructions.

discovered that a woman's capacity for orgasm is very strongly tied to her perceptions and feelings concerning the dependability and trust that she has invested in people in general and in men in particular.

Women high in orgasmic response had an emotionally healthy relationship with their father during the early years. They had learned that men were there to look after a woman's best interests and to care what happened to her.

Women who had a low capacity for orgasm lacked this stabilizing factor. They felt that significant people in their lives would either go away or let them down so therefore they couldn't depend on them. They found it difficult to trust, to relax, to abandon themselves in the arms of their husbands. Their apprehension robbed them of their ability to respond sexually.

The study stated: "The lower a woman's orgasm capacity the more likely she is to describe her father as having treated her 'casually,' without elaborate attempts at control or enforcing his will, as having been easygoing rather than expecting conformity to well-defined rules. To put it another way, the greater a woman's orgasm capacity, the less permissive and the more controlling she perceives her father to be." [2]

Clearly the significant male in a woman's early years sets the pattern and tone that will greatly influence her expectations during her married years. The girl whose father in involved and interested, who invests himself in her, learns very early that a man can really care what happens to her. A little girl needs to have a father who actively sets standards in her life.

The stabilizing role a father plays goes far beyond financial support and providing for the comforts of home. When a father is separated from his family, either by physical or emotional absence, children show serious deficiencies in their social and moral relationships with their mothers, peers, and neighbors. The more direct role a father assumes in guiding and directing his family, then the more likely the family will be stable and the children will enjoy greater emotional stability.

The father who thinks he can leave child rearing to his wife has not accepted the responsibility of fatherhood. Parenthood is a two-person task, particularly in the complex and demanding culture in which we live. It doesn't take a child long to find out how well a father has accepted his role.

A Man As Leader of the Family Unit

A good father will also assume the responsibility for guiding and directing the family unit. Such a role is not merely the result of accident, custom, or tradition, but it is advocated by the inspired writers of the Bible. Study after study has indicated that where the father is respected as the leader, the family is less prone to emotional difficulties than when the father's authority is missing.

"Leadership" here, however, does not imply the dominating, dictatorial, unquestionable authority with which some men tend to rule their families. Family leadership mutually concerns both husband and *wife*. It is not as one-sided as many through the centuries have imagined. It does not mean that the husband always commands and that the wife always submits. In a mutually supportive relationship, the husband exercises "soft" leadership.

A wise husband understands his wife's position on matters and will not make unreasonable demands on her or the children. He will be sensitive to each family member's needs. He may not always give in to his wife's requests, but he will make every effort to deal fairly with her and the children. He will consider each person's feelings in matters, sympathize with their position, and recognize the person's rights in each issue. A supportive leader is respectful, fair-minded, and kind. An entire family is secure when operating under this type of leadership.

Many home problems arise when leadership roles become confused. A child who grows up in a home where the parents have reversed their roles often establishes a pattern of rebellion and delinquency. Recent studies reveal that a dominating mother figure can confuse a boy searching

for his identity. A study of unwed fathers showed that 85 percent of them came from homes where their mothers assumed the dominant role or where there were no fathers at all.

A Man and His Time

A group of 369 high school boys and 415 girls were asked to list the ten most desirable qualities for fathers. The quality that received the most votes was "spending time with his kids." The absent or frequently absent father can produce mental illness, juvenile delinquency, and homosexuality in his children. Dr. Stanley Yolles, director of the National Institute of Mental Health, states that a father has the power to reduce delinquency and also has a decided influence on his child's mental health and IQ.

In another study done by a psychologist on three hundred seventh- and eighth-grade boys, the boys were asked to keep a diary of the time in an average week that their fathers spent with them. The typical father and son were alone seven and a quarter minutes!

A father is absent if he is not home regularly. Hence, the busy doctor, the ambitious businessman, or the successful salesman who works round the clock is an absent father if he is away from home more than he is home. A good way to check up on this is to count the number of meals a week Father eats with the children.

One of John F. Kennedy's greatest attributes was that he found the time every day for his children—time to romp with them, to go boating with them, to tell them stories. Busy as he was, he tried to enter sympathetically into their lives. Contrast that with the legendary farmer who instructed his son late one afternoon to "milk the cows, feed the horses, slop the pigs, gather the eggs, catch the colt, split some kindling, stir the cream, pump fresh water, study your lessons, and get to bed." In the meantime the father rushed off to a meeting where he discussed the question: "How shall we keep our sons on the farm?"

Furthermore, the *kind* of time a father spends with his child is important. A child will remember affectionately the scenes of childhood only if the father was *really* there. Most of the time a child keeps score in terms of the time spent together more often than the place of action. He will fondly remember the day when Dad walked with him through a nearby park with more enthusiasm than the day Dad brought home a new toy. And yet it is more difficult every day for the average child to spend a significant amount of time with his dad. It seems that there is an important correlation between higher pay for Dad and less time for the family. If he'll give his child undivided attention when he asks a question, if he'll help him solve a problem the moment it arises, the child will rate it as "quality time."

Fathers who aren't around, who don't make the decisions in the house, who aren't an example for their children, will one day find themselves on the outside. These men lament later in life that their children are strangers living in their homes. Successful fathers are recognized by their children as caring, helpful, available, sometimes right and sometimes wrong, but consistently loving and approachable.

A Woman As Wife

Although the mother's role is important, the role of wife is in some ways even more important and more vital. The wife who confuses the order of things and puts her child before her husband will likely have a husband who feels neglected, and an unsatisfied husband may grow to resent any child who seems to take first place in his wife's life. Since this wife may now lack a companion and lover, she sometimes attempts to make a "substitute husband" out of her child. She may also communicate frustration and low regard for her husband to the child, which may even cause the child to develop disrespect or even hatred for the father. When women insist on being wives first and mothers second, they enrich the lives of their husbands, children, and selves.

Another basic fact a wife needs to understand is to accept her husband for what he is and not try to change him. Attempts to change a man usually end in nagging, which creates tension in the home. A wife needs to concentrate on her husband's good qualities and express admiration and appreciation for her husband's physical, mental, and spiritual capabilities. Tell your husband how smart, handsome, trim, and wonderful he looks to you. Be understanding of the heavy burdens he shoulders—the difficulties and hardships he faces in bearing the financial responsibilities for the family. Be his biggest morale booster, and make home fun to return to—a haven from the rigors of the day. Your actions will encourage him to spend more time at home with you and the children. It is almost impossible for a man to feel tenderly about a woman who is constantly criticizing him or suggesting that he change.

A Woman As Mother

The role of the mother is just as varied and important as that of the father. During the early years of child rearing she devotes a great deal of her time to homemaking tasks. It is highly important during this crucial stage of adjustment, particularly if she has just resigned from the work world, that she accept her new responsibilities graciously and with enthusiasm. If she has just left full-time employment, which is customary for a great many young women today, it is likely a profession for which she trained several years. Her career may have been rewarding and challenging. If she suddenly becomes a full-time homemaker, the switch in roles may not be easy. Her days at home may depress and bore her as she compares them to the stimulating interaction she used to find in a busy office. Co-workers may have depended on her professional opinions. Changing diapers and preparing formula or nursing baby can quickly melt from novelty to boredom.

Following childbirth a woman may find changes in her physical stamina. The process of giving birth may have sapped more of her energy than she realized. She may feel a physical and emotional letdown that only time can heal. It might be best if she and her husband postponed normal sexual relations for a few weeks following delivery. An even longer period of time may follow before she can enjoy sex to its fullest again, particularly if she wants to avoid another pregnancy. A wife needs tender, understanding support from her husband during this time.

Most important, a wife must learn to balance her role of wife and mother. The entrance of a child into the husband-wife relationship will necessitate a change in the couple's relationship. She needs to be alert to her husband's needs during this time so that the transition will go as smoothly as possible. She must be willing to leave the baby from time to time so that she can spend undivided time and attention with her husband. If at any time he begins to feel neglected, that he is playing second fiddle to a child, she is on dangerous ground. A wife who continues to meet her husband's need for appreciation, admiration, and respect will help maintain his sense of identity and his feelings of security within the relationship.

Fathers

How rich would you be if you received $100 for each behavior you practiced during the past week?

1. I greeted my child with a smile or a kiss when I came home from work.

2. I admired aloud something my child made with his hands.

3. I complimented my child on work well done.

4. I praised my child's efforts at school.

5. I had a one-on-one talk with my child.

6. I played with my child when I came home from work.

7. I went to church with my child.

8. I worked alongside my child to complete some task.

9. I listened to my child tell a story without interrupting.

10. I showed courtesy by saying "Please," "Thank you," or "Excuse me."

11. I asked permission before I used my child's things.

12. I took time to answer my child's questions.

13. I exposed my child to an opportunity to learn good music.

14. I taught my child to use tools and equipment correctly.

15. I talked with my child about sex and reproduction.

16. I showed my child's mother that I love and respect her.

The Mother As the Provider of Emotional Security

If all the babies in the world were to meet together for a convention, their main cry would probably be, "Where's my mother!" The feeling of security is more important for babies than for older children, but everyone needs to feel that he belongs to someone. In his book *Success in Marriage*, David R. Mace states, "The major cause of most serious personality disorders is maternal deprivation in early childhood" (page 61). Dr. William Glasser's book *Reality Therapy* points out that all through

our lives we must feel that someone cares just for us and that we must return the feeling. When this does not happen, we lose touch with reality and will eventually become insane or will die.

Various lines of research have demonstrated this point. Dr. Harry Harlow studies baby rhesus monkeys reared by terry-cloth dummies which had built-in nursing bottles. Although these monkeys received adequate nourishment, they did not get adequate amounts of love, since there were no monkey mothers to cuddle them. These baby monkeys grew up unable to mate with

Mothers

How rich would you be if you received $100 for each behavior you practiced during the past week?

1. I smiled at my child.

2. I read or told my child a story.

3. I tucked my child in bed with a kiss.

4. I gave my child a hug.

5. I told my child of God's love for him/her.

6. I allowed my child to help with such chores as baking, cleaning, and shopping.

7. I thanked my child for helping me.

8. I called attention to an occasion when my child was courteous.

9. I thanked my child for not interrupting when I was talking.

10. I encouraged family togetherness by planning a special family activity.

11. I disciplined my child with love even though I was angry.

12. I made mealtime fun as well as nutritious.

13. I showed respect for my child's belongings.

14. I allowed my child the privilege of making a decision rather than making it for him/her.

15. I was home to greet my child after school.

16. I showed love and respect for my child's father.

receptive monkeys of the opposite sex and showed weird mannerisms much like those observed in human psychotics.

A child's first emotional relationship with his mother forms the foundation for his emotional relationship with others throughout his entire life. If his emotional relationship with his mother is good, if he feels secure and that his needs are really cared for, he will develop a stable personality and a strong self-concept.

The Mother As a Teacher

The home is a child's first school, and the mother, his first teacher. Now, a good teacher's information can be trusted to be true without the need for constant checking and doubting by the pupil, and one of the first lessons a young child needs to learn is that he can trust the reliability of his mother's teachings. He is therefore spared the confusion of testing and doubting her every lesson and command.

The acceptance of authority is the first lesson a young child needs to learn so that subsequent lessons will be easier for him. A mother must be an authority, but don't panic. An authority is someone who knows more about a subject than the person with whom he is speaking and who has the sense to stay away from other subjects. A good teacher takes pains to establish her reliability in the eyes of her students by sticking to facts that she can substantiate. Later she can venture to present subjects harder to prove, but only after her students believe in her. A mother should always choose the lesson she wants her child to learn with no more display of emotion than befits a classroom. She need not scold, reason with, nag, or punish. She simply makes the child comply.

A good teacher will employ the use of punishment as necessary, but she views punishment not as something she does *to* the child but as something she does *for* the child. Mother's attitude toward her disobedient youngster is: "I love you too much to let you behave like this."

Consistency is also a vital part of a good teacher. Any mother will end up with a bewildered mathematician if she spends Monday and Wednesday teaching her child that two plus two equals six and equal time on Tuesday and Thursday that two plus two equals four. Inconsistency on the part of a mother's discipline produces confusion and panic within a child so that he ultimately feels like saying, "Oh, forget it!" And he will give up trying to follow any teaching. Convey to the child the same fact as many times as necessary for him to accept it. If you mean it, say it. If you don't mean it, don't say it. But when you do say something, stick to it! It is better to be consistently wrong in discipline than to be right and inconsistent.

The mother as teacher is responsible for other areas of social development. It is up to her to see that a child's talents are developed. And a child needs to be challenged with the thought that he lives not just for self-satisfaction and the joy of achievement but that he is under obligation to use his talents and abilities for mankind. He should

be educated to idealism rather than materialism. And if a mother has developed within her child a solid sense of self-worth, she won't have to worry about all the social niceties—these will come.

A mother is also responsible for the physical development of her child. Since she plans and prepares the meals, she needs a basic knowledge of health, nutrition, and physiology. Good family health practices protect a family against colds, bouts with the flu and other diseases, and dental caries. When a family is in good health, the mother has proved that she has done her job well as family nutritionist.

Last, a mother should educate her child to recognize that he is created in the image of God and that it is his duty to portray—with divine help—that image to the best of his ability.

The first five or six years of a child's life are crucial to his development as an emotionally secure and independent adult. The home atmosphere created by the parents during this time will have a tremendous impact on their child's future. Yet parenthood is thrust upon us instantly. Oh, that we could *grow* into parenthood!

That's why neither husband nor wife should take for granted a happy home life. Both should conscientiously prepare for it and nurture it. Both have everything to gain and nothing to lose from consciously doing something every day to increase the happiness of each other. In this way both will contribute more than they realize to the future happiness of the entire family.

The Mid-life Crunch

Routine marks the middle years of marriage. The romance and pride of having begun a new family have faded. Parents now must adjust to the less fascinating tasks of attending parent-teacher conferences, chauffeuring children to and from meetings, supervising music lessons, and settling fights over who gets to sit where. As the children grow older, tension between husband and wife is bound to increase. Major decisions must now be faced regarding dating, schooling, activities, peer groups, and career goals. Any dissimilarity in the couple's background, methods of discipline, or future expectations for the children now come into sharp contrast. In order to live harmoniously at this time of life, the ideals of family living must be blended into one goal. In some families this transition occurs smoothly and easily, but in other families the aims of Father, Mother, and child clash hotly. Both husband and wife must work together in order to achieve their objectives, and during this time, the mid-life crunch, marital satisfaction reaches its lowest point. How did the couple veer from their original wedded happiness?

Initially, women achieve immense personal satisfaction from marriage. They have finally reached the goal for which they have been aiming since they first understood the difference between boys and girls. But a woman's personal satisfaction has dwindled by half by the time her first child appears. This level of satisfaction continues to decline through the middle years.

Most women are extremely sensitive to

Chart based on facts reported in an article by Boyd C. Rollins and Kenneth L. Cannon in the *Journal of Marriage and the Family,* May, 1974, p. 271.

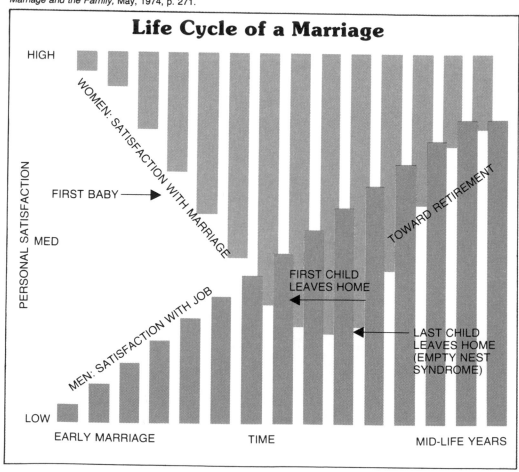

the changes that enter the marital relationship, whereas many men are totally unaware of their wife's feelings. As long as he has clean clothes to wear, meals on time, sexual privileges on demand—what else can a man want or expect? Yet, she may be "climbing the walls" from the lack of emotional support that she feels she must have from him. Men are more likely to settle for a business arrangement of sorts. Romance is an added benefit for a man and not the necessity it is for his wife.

On the other hand, during those early years while the wife's personal satisfaction is high, the husband's sense of satisfaction is low. Why? When they married, he may have been still studying for the occupation to which he would devote his talents, or maybe he had to accept a low status job in order to support his family. Gradually through the years he has worked and fought his way up. Now, as he enters his 40s, he has a position of some status and greater financial security than ever before. And while his satisfaction escalates, hers nosedives. A crisis is in the making!

Can you see by this chart when your marriage will likely face the greatest danger? Yes, it comes during the mid-life crunch. And yet husbands frequently don't recognize it because of the tremendous job satisfaction that they are experiencing. Meanwhile their wives feel extremely exasperated over how to communicate their emptiness of body, soul, and spirit. (Remember, these findings show only trends and so do not represent every couple.)

Children not only affect marriage when they come into it but also when they leave. As the child moves away from home base, husband and wife once again must adjust their marital roles. This is especially true for mothers who have devoted themselves full time to the rearing of children. When the last child leaves home, Mother literally joins the ranks of the unemployed. Loneliness, purposelessness, and emptiness can set in with devastating swiftness. The silent house speaks of many crowded, busy memories. If her identity has been wrapped up in mothering, she may now begin to question her worth. She may grieve over the loss of her children. She may question her unique individuality as a mother. The launched children will survive, but what about Mother?

Husband and wife must each prepare themselves for the time when their children grow up and leave home. For the average couple more than half of their married years together will be with an empty nest. If the well-adjusted couple will prepare for this time, it can be a highly satisfying period of life. The key is careful planning.

Parenting During the Mid-life Crunch

During the middle years parents must begin to share more and more family responsibilities with the children. One of the best ways of maintaining family solidarity during the middle years is to conduct weekly family conferences. Such meetings must take a high priority on the weekly schedule of activities. Don't neglect them because of overcommitments. The weekly conference gives each family member the opportunity to voice concerns, make suggestions, schedule activities, set goals, deal with problems, and participate in one of the best learning experiences possible.

Father or Mother might be tempted to exercise their prerogative and sit as chairperson. But the softer the role a parent plays and the more input they encourage from the children, the greater will be the end rewards. The heavy hand of a dictator will soon kill any progress. This does not mean that a child will have an equal vote on all matters, but by allowing all family members to have a vote in making decisions that affect them will build family loyalty and cohesiveness. Some families rotate leadership and allow each child on occasion to be the "captain" of the ship. Such an approach provides excellent training for the future and also cultivates a rich climate for personal growth and enhancement of positive attitudes toward each family member. (This idea alone might do more to blend stepfamilies than any other single suggestion.)

stampeding the arena for Priority One.

Wise families take inventory of their strengths and weaknesses at various intervals during the years.

Is each person in the family able to think, act, and function independently?

Is each individual emotionally healthy?

Is there a sense of teamwork among family members?

Does the family share and achieve certain goals together?

Is the family's spiritual climate relevant to everyday life?

Is conversation in the home demeaning or encouraging to personal worth?

Does each family member carry his/her share of responsibility without being overburdened?

Does the family take time to pursue recreational activities that give relief from daily tensions and promote good health and vitality?

By answering these and similar questions you will get a clearer view of where your family is at present and what you might expect in the future.

Do Broken Homes Produce Fractured Children?

Divorce and separation are rising more rapidly in families with children than among married families as a whole. Currently one out of three minor children is not living with his or her two natural parents. What is more shocking, perhaps, is that many now accept divorce as a "norm"—as "par for the course." Since 60 to 70 percent of all divorces involve minor children, the future welfare of the youngsters constitutes a key issue in child-custody cases. Many such cases drag on for two years while the parents slug it out in court, usually with bitter hatred, though sometimes with hopes of reuniting. Frequently these parents use their children to get even with each other.

Many have tried to justify their actions by saying that their children are better off in a home without conflict than in one where constant fighting and marital unhappiness reigns. However, the evidence does not support this theory.

It might also be advantageous to allow your children to observe you and your mate work through problems. Invite your child, if the subject matter is appropriate, to sit in and listen as you grapple with solutions. Through this method your child will learn that problems do not have to destroy relationships. Instead, your child will learn how to think through a problem, brainstorm solutions, and analyze and choose a proper course of action even under stress.

Each family must take stock of its priorities and guard against overcommitment. The school, church, clubs, sports, and other activities constantly compete for attention. Even when the entire family does manage to spend an evening at home, the omnipresent television mars the sacredness of the family circle. Families should neither try to isolate themselves totally from social activities nor should they attempt to participate in everything. Therefore parents must carefully guide their children in learning to choose what is most important for them to participate in. It is too easy to be overwhelmed by the multiplicity of events

How does divorce affect children? Dr. Harvey White has presented the results of one noteworthy study in his book, *Your Family Is Good for You.* "The Children of Divorce Project," as it has become known, reported findings after researchers interviewed 60 families at the time of divorce and then a year later. The investigators tried to observe such emotional problems as depression, anxiety, withdrawal, and poor functioning. The investigation revealed that the younger the child, the more severe were the effects because the younger child is most dependent on his family for security and protection. The study concluded that the children suffered "an acute crisis related to the loss of a parent and the turmoil of divorce, as well as long-term emotional problems that appeared later on."

"The two-and-a-half- to three-and-a-half-year-old group experienced regression in toilet training, irritability, whining, crying, fearfulness, separation anxieties, sleep problems, confusion, aggressiveness, and tantrums. It was noted that these symptoms occurred in children all but one of whom remained with their mother in their same home environment. Their play was 'joyless.' In play therapy interviews, they constructed unsafe worlds inhabited by dangerous animals, and they told stories of 'woebegone searching.' They were confused and frightened. Three out of nine in this age group were more troubled a year after the divorce, and it was learned that these three came from a home where the divorce conflict persisted and mothers were preoccupied much of the time.

"The four-year-olds were also severely depressed, confused, and blamed themselves for the divorce. Seven out of eleven were more depressed, more constricted in play and behavior, and expressed a greater need for approval, attention, and physical contact after the divorce. This occurred despite more loving contact and what SEEMED to be a better relationship with father on visits than existed before the divorce. It seemed to relate to a change in the mother, her pre-occupation with affairs, and her attempts to move into the father's role.

"A total of 44 percent of these preschool children were more emotionally upset one year after the divorce than they were before. The most important correlation was the emotional availability of the mother and the quality of the child's relationship with her.

"The 5- and 6-year-olds presented for the first time children who could handle divorce between their parents. Girls seemed more vulnerable at this age to loss of their fathers, and they maintained sad fantasies of recovering their fathers with their love. Visitations were almost like courtship with disappointment after they were over. The girls seemed preoccupied with their fantasies and functioned poorly at school.

"Fifty percent of the 5- and 6-year-old children seemed able to handle the divorce crisis, and 25 to 50 percent remained sad, fearful, confused about loyalties and yearned for their fathers." [3]

Even optimum visitation rights did not seem to ease the 5- and 6-year-olds' need for a father in the home. Even at this age children had to work through the loss of a parent in a relationship just as other family members were forced to. It was also found that the actual divorce proceedings are less traumatic for the child than is the adjustment process that follows.

Joan Kelly and Judith Wallerstein, the originators of The Children of Divorce Project quote a young boy who describes his parents' divorce: "It's splitting me in two." To emphasize his plight, Robert threw his hand hatchet style down the middle of his forehead.

Dr. F. James Anthony quotes another child: "I feel as if both my mother and father are inside me and are fighting, and then they are walking away from each other, breaking up my body so that I would go with them both, but if I did that, of course, I would die. I would be all broken up. I can only be a real live person if they join together again."

The effects on older children and adolescents seem somewhat less traumatic because youngsters of this age are more capable of expressing openly their feelings of hostility, anger, and bitterness, thus reducing significant emotional effects. The less involved these older youngsters are in the actual divorce proceedings, the better they can handle the situation. They are also less likely to side with one parent against the other.

This pattern of engaging children as allies against the opposing parent undercuts the normal parent-child relationship. When the mother becomes less of a mother or the father less of a father and more of a chum or friend to the child, the youngster has lost not only one parent through the conflict, but two. The child's greatest need at this point is a parent, not another chummy companion. The more distant and removed the adolescent is from the trauma of the situation, the more stable the remaining family structure is likely to be and the better the child will perform.

Research by Wallerstein and Kelly has substantiated that 25 to 50 percent of the children of divorce are seriously affected in their mood, functioning, and development for one year after the divorce. What happens after that? They followed up the group for a five year period and found that:

"Thirty-seven percent of the youngsters involved were suffering from depression that was manifested in the following: chronic and pronounced unhappiness, sexual promiscuity, delinquency in the form of drug abuse, petty stealing, alcoholism and acts of breaking and entering, poor learning, intense anger, apathy, restlessness, and a sense of intense, unremitting neediness.

"Their study found another 29 percent of the children who were making what they described as 'appropriate developmental progress' but who 'continued to experience intermittently a sense of deprivation and feelings of sadness and resentment toward one or both parents.' Thirty-four percent of the youngsters seemed to be doing well or comparable to children from intact families after the initial breakup." [4]

Fifty-six percent of the children, when asked for their opinion, said that they did not consider their present family to be any improvement over their previous family.

Other difficulties caused by the loss of a parent's presence may not surface until much later in life. Divorce is difficult enough for adults. It has an even more devastating long-term effect on children.

Despite books and articles to the contrary, divorce is rarely "creative" and almost always disastrous to everyone involved. Concerned parents will avoid it whenever possible. When divorce seems inevitable despite all efforts to salvage the marriage relationship, the parents should do everything humanly possible to minimize the damage to the children. Avoid going through divorce proceedings during the first five years of your child's life.

Unfortunately, all couples who are capable of making love are not capable of rearing responsible children. All marriages should not result in parenthood. But husbands and wives who do bring children into the world should assume the responsibility of parenthood. They should respect the privilege of parenthood enough to lay aside their own wishes and desires in order to do what is best for their children.

Divorce may seem like the only way out for a couple who face repeated frustrations and disappointments in a marriage that never measured up to their expectations. But children are the unfortunate pawns in divorce.

Your Child's Greatest Need

Your child's greatest need is not so much two parents who love him, but two parents who love each other. The most important marriage course your child will ever take is the one offered by his own family. Your sons and daughters will be observing you as models for the privileges and responsibilities of the marriage they will have someday. The ideal is not to create some type of utopia in which a child might be reared, but a warm affectionate home where consistent obedience to principles is adhered to. Perfect parents, as well as perfect marriage partners, should not be an end in themselves.

Being a successful parent is not synonymous with perfection. Rather a good parent is a conscientious person who has taken the time to become knowledgeable in parenting skills. Such parents recognize that they are never too old to change. They know that problems will not go away by pretending they aren't there. They also can distinguish between real and imaginary problems.

Even the best of parents will face problems during the years of childrearing, but they will carry their burdens lightly because they are leaning heavily on a higher power. They realize that complaining or wailing will not make the responsibilities of parenthood disappear. You will "goof" from time to time, but instead of beating yourself, accept your shortcomings as a part of the growth process.

No family can attain happiness without effort, work, and struggles. Because of the pressures of high-tension living common to most families today, both parent and child must unite their efforts so that they can realize their dreams for harmonious family living. Only continued and concentrated effort will make it possible for a family today to achieve this lofty yet attainable purpose.

Further reading you will enjoy . . .

Benson, Dan. *THE TOTAL MAN.*

Dillow, Linda. *CREATIVE COUNTERPART.*

Dobson, James. *WHAT WIVES WISH THEIR HUSBANDS KNEW ABOUT WOMEN.*

Hardesty, Margaret. *HOW TO GET YOUR HUSBAND TO FILL YOUR EMOTIONAL NEEDS.*

Mayhall, Jack and Carole. *MARRIAGE TAKES MORE THAN LOVE.*

Renich, Jill. *THE CHRISTIAN HUSBAND.*

Van Pelt, Nancy. *TO HAVE AND TO HOLD.*

Chapter at a Glance

Chapter 12

Though a Working Mom, a Single- or Stepparent—Turn Minuses into Pluses

Whether or not a mother should work outside the home during the child-rearing years is a hotly contested issue. This chapter will not discuss the appropriateness of a mother working outside the home. Instead it will explore the best ways a family can cope when the mother does have regular employment. Half of all American mothers with children under 18 hold salaried positions outside the home. An overwhelming 37 percent of mothers with preschoolers work outside the home, the majority claiming that economic necessity requires them to join the work force.[1] (Single mothers who have no other means of support have no choice. Working outside the home will be a part of their lives.)

According to a study by A. C. Nielsen, three out of five women work because the family needs the money or they want extras—a second car, a new face for the family room, or a family vacation. Only 19 percent of the women polled said they worked because they wanted to.[2] Interestingly, the husbands who participated in the survey saw things differently. Three out of five men said their wives worked because they wanted to. Only 29 percent admitted that the family needed the second income.

III. **Successful Stepparenting**
  A. The number of stepfamilies
  B. The most difficult kind of parenting
  C. Stepparenting tactics
    1. Agree on expectations
    2. Support each other
  D. What to expect from the children
    1. Children will test and retest the limits
    2. Don't expect instant love
  E. How to ease the tensions
    1. Talk out expectations
    2. Involve children in the wedding
    3. Give children an opportunity to see the stepparent under all circumstances
  4. Make children feel part of the family
  5. Arrange a special "place" for children
  6. Find commonly enjoyed activities
  F. Blending can bring mending

The Times of Working Mothers

What really separates the working mother from the rest of the world? T-I-M-E. The working mother has less time to accomplish the things she must do. Only adequate time management will allow her to survive the demands upon her. If you are a working mother, here are some quick survival tips.

Set your priorities and simplify your work as much as possible.

Enlist help from the kids—they can provide more help than you might expect.

Keep a daily "to do" list and cross off jobs as they are completed.

Plan rest and recreation away from the home and the kids (and don't feel guilty for it—since you'll actually become more productive).

Treat yourself—do it regularly and make it a habit.

Set aside one night a week as a "fun night"—no heavy work schedule, serve fun foods on paper plates and after the meal play a game together.

Save some time each week for important projects or people.

Remember, it's impossible to complete everything alone.

Many busy mothers rely on a weekly schedule with blocks of time for family activities, routine chores, errands, and leisure activities. It is wise not to schedule the days too tightly. Leave one hour a day of unscheduled time for spontaneity so that efficiency will not defeat its purpose. Buffer time is very necessary. Proper scheduling requires trial and error along with practice, but sooner or later you will work out the kinks from the system.

The biggest problem working mothers face centers on child care. Available facilities in each situation will probably narrow the possibilities. Cost will eliminate other options. Almost half the preschoolers of working mothers are cared for in their own homes, and just under a third are cared for in someone else's home. Home-based care is generally more advisable than other types of care, and in most cases it costs much less. Every mother will carefully screen all possible candidates when deciding who will care for her child. Because of the long-lasting effects of self-worth, *who* cares for the child while mother is absent takes on prime importance. And you will want to continually monitor the situation so you can check on how your child is progressing.

Authorities recommend that mothers wait to join the work force until the child is four months of age. By this time the baby has established his initial attachments, has overcome most "colic" reactions, and has settled into a routine. It is also recom-

mended that mothers avoid beginning a job while the child is between 9 and 24 months, when fears of losing mother run high.

Two women experts and champions of women's right to work, Viola Klein and Alva Myrdal, state that in order to be *sure* of a child's proper emotional security and physical development mothers should devote their entire time to a child until he turns 3. Many other experts recommend that a child should be 3 before he attends a nursery school or a day-care center. Before that age

Checklist for Working Mothers

Time for working moms is always in short supply. Working moms frequently become so involved in "doing" for their family that they neglect their own needs. However, you will be better at fulfilling your many other functions if you take some time for your own needs. Carefully go over the following list of items and evaluate if you are reserving sufficient time for yourself and making the best of your opportunities. Score yourself as follows:

1. Definitely yes   2. Probably yes   3. Unsure   4. Probably not
5. Definitely not.

During this week,

1 2 3 4 5   1. I have sorted my priorities and accomplished what was most important to me.

1 2 3 4 5   2. I have enlisted the help of the children on jobs that I might ordinarily do myself.

1 2 3 4 5   3. I have crossed jobs off my "to do" list as they were completed.

1 2 3 4 5   4. I treated myself to something special.

1 2 3 4 5   5. I set aside one night as "fun night" with the family in order to give special attention to family togetherness.

1 2 3 4 5   6. I spent some quality time with my husband and/or children.

1 2 3 4 5   7. I exhibited a positive attitude and cheerful outlook regarding my dual role as homemaker and working mother.

Discuss your feelings about each of these statements with your partner, friend, or your parent study group.

Exercise for a One-Parent Family

Losing a parent through death or divorce is a painful experience for children whether they voice it or not. Children frequently feel responsible for the loss of a parent. Helping children to acknowledge their feelings openly can help them deal with the experience. Use these open-ended sentences as discussion starters.

1. The hardest thing about living in a one-parent family is . . .

2. Sometimes I pretend that we are all together as a family and . . .

3. Sometimes I feel like crying because . . .

4. The best thing about being a one-parent family is . . .

5. When I think about what our family used to be like, I . . .

6. One of the best times I had with my other parent was . . .

7. I like our present family best when . . .

a child is not ready emotionally to leave his mother and to play with children while being supervised by a stranger.

When mothers wait to return to the work world until their children are between 6 and 11, everyone seems to adjust most easily. Mother has remained with the child during the early formative years and has fostered feelings of worth, nurtured her child, and instilled essential character traits. By the time the youngster enters school, the crucial formative years have ended. If a mother must return to the work force, it is best, then, to wait until the child begins first grade.

Although certain studies indicate that "latchkey children" (unsupervised pre-teens and early teen-agers) are not more frequently delinquent, late, absent from school, or less cooperative in behavior than their supervised classmates, it certainly is far from ideal to leave these children home alone. A multitude of emergencies might occur.

Self-supervision might groom such children for early maturity and independence, but without direction and guidance many children will fall into mischief that they might otherwise have avoided.

Mothers who work by choice often experience more guilt than those who work from economic necessity. Children are quick to sense the conflict between a mother's need to fulfill professional ambitions and, at the same time, to satisfy child-rearing responsibilities. Two contradictory needs tug at such a mother. She finds herself torn between staying at home and working outside the home. Guilt is counterproductive and causes anxiety, depression, and chronic fatigue. It will greatly impede the working mother's ability to parent. Moreover, children quickly learn how to manipulate parents who harbor guilt. A mother's reaction to leaving her child will greatly influence the child's reaction. If mother feels apprehensive, fearful, and guilt-ridden, she will convey these emotions to the child. If a mother decides to join the labor force, from the onset she should cultivate positive feelings about her decision, regardless of the child's age.

Working mothers who have arranged for the best child-care conditions tend to experience the least guilt.

The rapid increase in the number of working mothers is causing tensions in millions of marriages. Although their lives changed drastically when the mother joined the work force, most couples' perceptions of role responsibilities have not caught up with reality. They have not altered their basic assumptions on the interdynamics of marriage. They have not modified their ideas of how a mother and father should function. This produces untold conflicts. The majority of couples still think that the mother's primary job revolves around the home and children even though she may work just as many hours and just as hard at her outside job as the father does at his.

Polls conducted to determine the kind of partnership women want in marriage reveal that most women prefer a marriage in which husband and wife mutually support each other by sharing housekeeping and child-care duties. Yet, studies reveal that the working wife spends more than *forty times* as much time on housework as her male counterpart. It may not be fair, but the working wife spends an average of 26 hours a week on housework while her husband pitches in for a brief 36 minutes. A three-year-long study of 1,400 dual-career families with children under eleven showed that only one father in five helped care for the youngsters at all.[3]

Working mothers and their husbands need to think in terms of cooperative family living and *shared responsibility*. The wife will want to give top priority to helping her husband become involved in housekeeping and caring for the children. But this may not be as easy as it sounds. Some fathers don't take to such responsibility and must be eased into it gradually. Chances are, though, that a father can leave his job to pick up a sick child at school, attend a parent-teacher conference, and chauffeur children to music lessons and after-school activities just as efficiently as a mother can. Some men may need a little push and some instruction, but few will mind it once they get in the habit and develop confidence in their abilities.

Many working mothers have not fully tapped the one resource that could bring them the most help—their children. Why? Because many mothers enjoy playing the "martyr role." As "good" mothers they feel that they must "do" for everyone in the family. If you have this problem, begin parceling out household chores *and don't feel guilty about it!* Run your home on kid power—tap your greatest, most cost-efficient source of energy. Repeat the admonition, "Put your things away rather than putting them down," so often and consistently that your children will readily adopt the habit. Teach them to hang up towels immediately after their bath; to carry dirty dishes to the sink; to put the milk away after a meal; to throw empty cans into the trash container. They'll respond positively to the new routine if you hold out proper incentives. Introduce your plan with enthusiasm, and offer tangible rewards for their efforts.

Working mothers also find it difficult to spend quality time with the children. As the cliché goes, "It isn't just quantity time, it's the quality time that counts." Ironically, the mother who spends all day with her child—shopping, chauffeuring, cleaning, and marketing together—may not spend as much *quality time* with her child as a working mother might. Of course, I'm not advocating that mothers should leave the home in order to create quality time with their children!

How is it possible to create quality time even when time is in short supply? One way is to keep the television and radio off so that you can listen during the opportunities you do have. Perhaps you can be a good listener while you do sit-ups on the family room floor first thing in the morning, or while you ride bikes together, or while you drive to music lessons. Seize every opportunity of having heart-to-heart talks. Your child may be capable of handling the usual bedtime routine alone, but if you put him to bed instead, you'll rediscover that bedtime offers opportunities for quality time that are not present during the rest of the day.

As you rush around tending to everyone else's needs, are you wisely saving a little

need a constant mothering figure in order to develop proper emotional health. Perhaps we need to take a close look at the value of parenting.

A Word to Single Parents

The ideal that God sets forth is that a child should have two parents—a mother and a father. However, we function in a less-than-ideal world. Some children lose one or both parents through death, divorce, separation, or desertion. Living creatively as a single parent presents a double challenge, since the parent must accomplish the job alone.

If you are a single parent and face the prospect of raising your child without the help of a mate, you will do well to keep one fact in mind: Your child has the same needs that other children have. Your challenge is to supply those needs alone. You are not left helpless, however. You have at least two viable options—books such as this one that supply you with practical hints, and God who will provide strength and courage when you need it.

At present more than one million American children live with only one parent. Furthermore, many children who now enjoy two parents have had only one in the past or will have only one in the future. If the present rate continues, almost half of all children will live in a single-parent household before they turn 18.

Parenting alone is plainly more difficult than parenting with a partner. Responsibilities that two people once shared must now be maintained by one person—supporting the family, maintaining the car, entertaining, remodeling, and repairing the house, housecleaning, etc. Then there are all the tasks related to child care itself—nurturing; disciplining; listening; setting limits and rules; settling quarrels; transporting children to school, music lessons, and meetings; helping with homework; conducting family worship; caring for clothing; plus many other tasks. If you were to ask a two-parent family if both Father and Mother kept busy all day, both partners would insist that they had full-time jobs whether inside or outside

time for yourself? Many working mothers become so earnest about shouldering responsibilities and keeping their nose to the grindstone that they have no time to laugh, play, and be a good parent or wife. They feel guilty if they spend a little time on themselves. Interestingly enough, a working father has no problem in naming a dozen or more things he'd like to indulge in and will do so without a trace of guilt. Working mothers need leisure time too. They need an opportunity to pursue a measure of personal fulfillment for themselves—a hobby, a class, a church project, or club activities.

Women want the best of both worlds. In this liberated age both worlds are open to women, but it is very difficult, if not impossible, to have it all at the same time. No one—male or female—can be a good parent in his or her spare time, regardless of what some authors expound. Every working mom needs to examine prayerfully her priorities. If her time away from home is harming her children, then she will need to cut back on her work-load. Unfortunately, we often cannot see the danger signals until it is too late. One thing is certain: All children the home. Now, however, one partner must carry all the responsibilities. This frequently overloads the circuits. Time management takes on new meaning and should receive utmost attention.

All parents care about their children, but single parents have a special reason for cherishing their children—in most cases the youngsters are all that remains of their "family." Divorced single parents frequently hope that successful parenting can in some way compensate for the marriage failure. The widowed often commit themselves to their children in an effort to show continued fidelity to their former spouses.

Children fill the lives of single parents with special meaning. To become a successful parent, though single, becomes a primary goal. In a way, it is easier for a single parent to focus on the children's needs, because he or she does not have to divide time between a spouse and children. And so some parents become overprotective or become overly concerned if their children seem troubled. Single parents usually do have cause for concern if separation, death, or divorce has upset the family. Excessive misbehavior, insecurity, or attention-seeking behavior all signal the superalert single parent.

One of the biggest problems that faces single parents is child care. Who will watch the children when the parent is not at home? Surveys show that most single parents do not feel satisfied with their present child-care arrangements and go through a succession of possibilities before settling on one. School holidays and summer vacations present special problems in one-parent homes. Nearby grandparents or relatives can often help out.

Recent data show that about 55 percent of single parent mothers work outside the home and that another 12 percent are actively looking for work. Single mothers, more than other working women, need the nonmonetary rewards that work outside the home offers. It provides them with the financial support needed, yes, but it also provides them with a social life and much needed self-esteem. Single parents who work full-time worry about what their absence from the family is doing to their children. They often suffer intense guilt feelings—even when the children evidence no signs of problems. Single fathers seem to carry less of a guilt load about both working and parenting than do mothers in the same category.

When financial problems pile up on everything else, the single parent may feel ready to despair. Single parents who are forced to live on a reduced budget should not shudder at discussing finances with children. Level with them. Be calm and matter-of-fact. Above all, don't feel guilty for having to turn down a request for a new bike or whatever.

Single parents with small children often confront special problems. As much as a parent may adore the child, he or she may not be able to escape the child. A child's incessant claims on parental time and attention can become very irritating. Naturally this can occur in two-parent families as well, but single parents are particularly vulnerable because of the frustration generated by work problems, home responsibilities, insufficient funds, and many other stresses unrelated to the child. The parent wants to do the things all good parents do but fails, and this increases the guilt feelings.

Once the young person reaches school age, the guilt feelings connected with child care usually lessen. But new problems surface as the child enters a new social world—sports, games, birthday parties, sleepovers, and church activities.

Single parents, more than married parents, need a support system and companionship outside the home. Children alone cannot fill the void. The single parent needs outside help because he or she has no one inside the home to turn to for support. Without a partner, all responsibilities must be borne alone and all emergencies present a double challenge. Friends, neighbors, relatives, singles' groups, and the church can all provide portions of the support system—the single parent's lifeline. Such a support system becomes the key to the single parent's emotional well-being as well as to the child's.

If being a single parent has any consolations, it might be the opportunity to draw closer to the children. Since no other adult shares the house and distracts time or attention, it becomes natural for the single parent to discuss with the children the events of the day, plans for the week, menus, and many other things. Children may also find it easier to talk with a parent about their problems, friends, and school when the parent is single. Talking to children is not the same as conversing with an adult, but it is better than talking to no one!

Single parents need to recognize, however, that they must not rely on their children for sympathy or support during times of stress. Children often assume that they are to blame or attempt to help the parent solve the problem. Children cannot become emotional substitutes for a missing parent.

Another benefit to single parents is that they have no one to argue with concerning discipline. Their children have less opportunity to "divide and conquer" than other children, and because they often have to assume more responsibility they may mature a little faster.

Spiritual training should receive top priority in the one parent home. Particularly is this true when there is no father in the home. Since parents stand in the place of God in the eyes of their children, it might be difficult for a child in a fatherless home to relate to a heavenly Father. A loving, nurturing mother can help her child form a proper concept of God through her own example, by teaching the child God's Word, and by allowing him to observe godly male models.

If you face the prospect of raising your child alone, keep in mind that your child's needs are exactly the same as any other child's needs. The difference is that *you*— without the help of a mate—must see that these needs are satisfied. But God has not left you helpless even though you are alone. God can and will guide you step by step.

Managing well as a single parent involves having an adequate support system available and maintaining a positive attitude. Single-parenting will naturally produce its own kind of stresses, but single parents should recognize the contribution they are making—alone! Few other things in life are as rewarding as rearing well-adjusted, responsible children.

Successful Stepparenting—Blending Can Bring Mending

Since nearly seven million children live with stepparents today, we should briefly look at how parenting other people's children differs from parenting one's own. A leading family authority has stated that the role of a stepparent is five times more difficult than that faced by other parents. It may not always be that difficult, but stepparents do face a challenging job.

First, you will need to settle on what you should expect from the child. Both the parent and the stepparent must get their act together first so that their expectations coincide. Otherwise, they're in for chaos. Once agreed, then both parents together should discuss the matter with the youngster so that he clearly recognizes that the stepparent has become a permanent member of the team.

A stepmother particularly needs her husband's support. As the newcomer into an already formed relationship, she is usually viewed as both an intruder and a rescuer. If the father is so passive or weak that he allows the stepmother to take the initiative, the child will deeply resent it. In addition, the stepmother will likely feel completely overwhelmed by the complex problems she must confront, and many critical situations may become deeply rooted in the first few months of the relationship.

Even though everyone involved may have discussed behavior expectations prior to marriage, parents can count on opposition from the children. Each stepchild will test and retest the limits. It is part of a child's need to explore the limits of any new relationship or situation. Please note: The stepparent's response to the testing will determine how long the testing will go on. Hence, the sooner the stepparent makes his presence felt and shows that he is there to stay, the sooner the child will accept the new situation.

Stepparents should mentally prepare themselves, in most cases, for initial feelings of resentment. The younger the child, the easier he will adjust to the stepparent. However, most stepparents are not lucky enough to take on this responsibility early enough so that the child can become a part of them. Instead they must work with the child after his character and personality have more or less solidified. The die is cast. Even when an older child does feel love toward a stepparent, he is usually less likely to verbalize it or to show it openly.

If you are a stepparent, be prepared for the mountains ahead. Don't expect instant love from the child. Remember that the child has already sustained a great loss through death or divorce. Because he has just come through a devastating emotional drought, he is extremely vulnerable to hurt. As a result he may frequently act worse than he normally would. The stepparent often misinterprets such misbehavior and assumes that the child has rejected him, but this is not necessarily the case. The stepchild who only visits on occasion may never feel any "love" in the real sense of the word for the stepparent. Someone has suggested that a stepparent strike the word *love* from his vocabulary. Instead it might be better if the stepparent and child formed a relationship of respect that might lead in time to something warmer and deeper.

In remarriage, families blend best when the youngsters have been prepared for the new stepparent. The cardinal rule when forming a stepfamily is to talk out expectations *before marriage.* Each partner does not need to hold identical opinions on every subject, but it is crucial that each understands how the other person feels and reacts especially when it comes to disciplinary matters. Such preparation involves understanding the limitations of stepparenting. The stepparent has no biological ties to the child and therefore must earn the young person's respect. Nothing comes to a stepparent via position alone. The new stepparent will likely have to prove himself or herself over and over.

Many people think that stepparenting is as natural as breathing. Life is full of rude awakenings. Many stepparents figure that they are mature, that they love kids, and that they are easy to get along with. "It will be like having one of my own," they chant.

But stepparenting is very, very different. No biological ties govern the relationship. The child does not have to love you as your own child naturally would. All the love you planned to heap on your stepchild won't make any difference. The realization of this fact hits with full force within six months after marriage.

The longer a stepchild knows an incoming stepparent prior to marriage, the better the chances for working out expectations and problems. Leaving a child out of preparations when a new person is about to enter his life can have long-lasting repercussions. Wise adults generally involve the stepchild in the wedding service. One family actually mentioned the names of each stepchild when exchanging vows during the wedding service. It made the children feel part of the new family unit. This sharply contrasts to another family I have worked with. The father vehemently stated: "I married *her*, not her kids!" He refused to recognize that when children are involved, it is always a package deal.

Prior to the wedding service allow the stepchild to see the new parent's real personality under all circumstances. And the incoming parent should make every attempt to encourage the child to reveal

*"Violet has a girl and a boy from her first marriage,
a kid from her second, and three from her third.
I've got two teen-agers from my second marriage; my third wife
left me with four kids; and I have custody of two girls and
a boy from my fourth. No wonder I'm called a stepfather—
I need to watch where I'm stepping."*

what he expects from the relationship.

Becoming the stepparent to the child of a divorced person may be much different than living with a child who yearns for someone to fill the void left by a deceased parent. The longer the child has lived in the single-parent home after the death of the parent, the more rigid his memories tend to become and the more difficult the adjustment may be. The child will likely expect the new parent to take up where the old one left off, and it just isn't possible.

Every child in the newly formed family should feel a part of the family as soon as possible. The child needs to know that he has a special place. If the stepchild only visits on weekends or holidays, it is still necessary to arrange a place that belongs only to him—a bed, a drawer, certain possessions. When two sets of children must merge, it becomes even more important that each child have a space all his own. One mother who moved her two children into the home of her new husband with his two children commented, "All the children have been forced to do some adjusting. The children must share bedrooms. My oldest daughter wants a bedroom of her own, and my husband's children are whining 'Whose house is this anyway.'"

The stepparent family needs to find common ground, an activity, a sharing of jobs—that can draw them together. It might be weekend camping, a sport enjoyed by all, a love for bird watching, or perhaps leading church activities together. But it needs to be something that will help the family form bonds of friendship with one another.

No one can replace a biological parent, and no stepparent should try. However, the best thing that can happen to the child of a family broken by death or divorce is to gain the right stepparent. This child can be loved by his biological parent—yes. But to be loved by someone who has chosen to love you is something quite different. A happy "blended family" is possible if the adults are mature, patient, and persistent, and if God's love is consistently demonstrated during the blending process and beyond. Blending can bring mending.

Further reading you will enjoy . . .

FOR WORKING MOTHERS

Cotton, Dorothy. *THE CASE FOR THE WORKING MOTHER.*

Curtis, Jean. *WORKING MOTHERS.*

Greenleaf, Barbara *HELP—A HANDBOOK FOR WORKING MOTHERS.*

FOR SINGLE PARENTS

Gatley, Richard H. and David Koulack. *SINGLE FATHER'S HANDBOOK—A GUIDE FOR SEPARATED AND DIVORCED FATHERS.*

Hope, Karol and Nancy Young, eds. *MOMMA: THE SOURCEBOOK FOR SINGLE MOTHERS.*

Klein, Carole. *THE SINGLE PARENT EXPERIENCE.*

Peppler, Alice. *SINGLE AGAIN—THIS TIME WITH CHILDREN.*

Stewart, Ann. *PARENT ALONE.*

Weiss, Robert S. *GOING IT ALONE.*

STEPPARENTING

Felker, Evelyn. *RAISING OTHER PEOPLE'S KIDS.*

Noble, June and William. *HOW TO LIVE WITH OTHER PEOPLE'S CHILDREN.*

Thomson, Helen. *THE SUCCESSFUL STEPPARENT.*

Chapter 13

Family Togetherness— Wrapping Up the Entire Package

Throughout this book you have learned child-rearing principles that require genuine self-discipline to put into practice. The benefits of the effort expended will ultimately outweigh the struggle. Nonetheless, it takes a lot of hard work to be a good parent. Parenting, however, involves more than just hard work, effort, and self-discipline. An added benefit is the ability to have fun with each other, to enjoy being part of a happy family.

Too much family togetherness actually stifles growth and inhibits development, but too little does the same. The real failure of families today is overcommitment—not to the family but to overcommitment at work,

at school, at church, with hobbies, and in the community. We go through life in the fast lane! But no one can enjoy family togetherness when everyone lives at such a breakneck speed.

Many parents argue that in the long run the quality of time—not the quantity—matters most. A grain of truth lies embedded in this notion. However, any family wishing to build solidarity must experience both quality and quantity.

How can this best be accomplished? A grown child often recalls more clearly and fondly the time spent together, not the birthday when you gave him an expensive ten-speed bike. In our family we promoted

Chapter at a Glance

I. **The Challenge**
   A. Child rearing takes effort
   B. Child rearing provides fun

II. **Maintaining a Balance**
   A. Too much togetherness stifles growth
   B. Too little togetherness stifles growth
   C. Quality time must be balanced with quantity

III. **Establish Family Traditions**
   A. Traditions promote togetherness
   B. Traditions can encourage fun and creativity

IV. **Rethink Your Values**
   A. Slow the pace
   B. Establish priorities
   C. Your child needs *you*—not things
   D. Your child needs your *time*
   E. Some things are urgent; others are important

V. **Child Rearing Can Be—**
   A. Devastating
   B. Rewarding

togetherness by following certain traditions. We maintained one tradition for years—having Mexican tostadas by candlelight every Friday evening. All three children have now left home, but when they return for a visit, they look forward to tostadas on Friday night. It's traditional.

We also turned Friday evening into family night. After tostadas, we would sit around a crackling fire (in the wintertime) and read aloud. Sometimes we took turns reading aloud and so finished many books together that provided spiritual lessons and direction to our lives. Repetition cemented this into a family tradition.

Another tradition we established was sitting together in church. We tried not to become arbitrary about this, but exceptions were rare. When the children's divisions were dismissed before the 11 A.M. worship hour began, we did not need to search for our children. We sat in the same pew each week, three rows from the front. This provided the opportunity for viewing the participants up front at close range. If there is any time of the week that a family should stay together, it is when worshiping. This tradition should be established early and maintained. When our children establish their own families, I fully expect to see each family sitting together at church three pews from the front! It's traditional.

Birthday celebrations, holding hands while saying grace, regular family worship, we repeated all until they became traditions for us. Such traditions evoke a sense of belonging and closeness. A godly family should not consist of loners who share a roof. Instead, it should be a group of persons intimately involved in sharing activities that will build a fond heritage. Each family needs characteristics, values, and activities that mark it as unique and different.

Harry and I make no pretense about knowing all there is to know about parenting. But we have learned from our years of working with families that happy family members must basically enjoy one another. We have often fallen short of the ideals that we see so clearly with our 20/20 hindsight. But we thank God for the fun times that we have enjoyed with our children.

This spirit of fun and creativity must have rubbed off on our children, because for our 17th wedding anniversary they surprised us with an unannounced party. When Harry and I arrived home one Sunday evening, our house was packed with guests whom our children had chosen and invited. I was given a few minutes to pretty up, and then we were escorted to seats of honor. Carlene, the originator and director of this social event, proceeded to read:

On January the First at eight o'clock in the evening, just 17 short, full, happy years ago, there was a wedding at the home of Mr. and Mrs. Carl William Real. Their daughter

Nancy Lue.

was married to

Mr. Harry Authur Van Pelt

We would like to tonight recreate just a small part of the wonderfull, wonderfull evening. Soooo:

Yes, so on with the show! We all participated in a delightful evening of games, food, and music. Even a recording of our wedding was played for the guests. The climax of the evening occurred when our three youngsters presented us with an envelope. With eager anticipation we opened it.

Dear Mr. and Mrs. Harry A. Van Pelt,

You have just received a gift trip for two, for three days and two nights at the beautiful log cabin in Canmore, Alberta, Canada.

We hope that you will have a lovely second honeymoon, and enjoy the vacation from home, children, and the regular routine. The facilities you know well, so rest assured that you will have no trouble, only lots of fun and a very lovely time.

All the other dates you were "supposed to have" as of now are canceled. They were all fake!! There were a few people involved indirectly helping us fake you out, and they all send you all the luck in the world and the best of wishes.

The signatures of three champion children—Carlene, Rodney, and Mark—concluded the letter along with 15 dollars that they had collected among themselves. I don't know how this affects you right now, but my eyes are swimming in tears. What precious memories of fun times we now cherish as we look back upon the days when our family was all together!

The time has come for parents to rethink their values. It's time to slow the pace. Forget the new car, carpeting, or furniture for your redecorating project. Put into second or third place all the materialistic advantages you want to provide for your child. Your child doesn't need things as much as he needs *you*. He needs that personal investment of precious time which only *you* can provide.

Take time for a hand-in-hand nature walk, and answer his questions about God's creation. Take time to build a kite, and savor the delight on your child's face as he watches it race and dance on the wings of

Evaluating Family Togetherness

In order to help you sort through your priorities and evaluate the level of closeness your family is currently experiencing, circle the number that most closely describes your feelings. Use the following scale:

1. All of the time   2. Most of the time   3. Some of the time
4. Infrequently   5. Never.

1 2 3 4 5   1. We plan a family fun night together at least once a week.

1 2 3 4 5   2. It is fun to be a member of our family.

1 2 3 4 5   3. Everyone in our family participates in the chosen family activities.

1 2 3 4 5   4. Family togetherness holds a high priority in our family.

1 2 3 4 5   5. We promote family togetherness by following certain traditions, such as holding hands during table grace, et cetera.

the wind. Take time for a romp and tussle on the family room floor where all can chime in with musical giggles. Take time to listen to your child now, for tomorrow he may not wish to talk with you. Take time for all this *now*. Tomorrow carries no guarantees.

It takes *time* to be an effective parent, but I'm not suggesting that you must invest 100 percent of your energies in your child. You should sort out your priorities so that you understand the difference between the urgent and the important. The urgent matters of life always seem to take precedence while important matters lie neglected. For instance, the ringing of the telephone may have interrupted you as you were reading your child his Bible lesson. You may have spent a half-hour on the phone while your child trotted off to bed alone. The urgent won again.

SLOW DOWN CHRISTIAN MOTHER. SLOW DOWN CHRISTIAN FATHER. Take time for the important things now. Sort through your priorities. God will bless and honor your efforts.

Rearing a child can be devastating, head splitting, and nerve shredding at times. Days may come when you feel like trading your son at a swap meet! There may be days when you feel as though you have failed miserably and have done everything wrong. Despair may rush in like a flood.

Am I advocating that couples should not have a child owing to the trials and stresses of parenthood? Heaven forbid! The couple who desire children (not just the couple who expect to have kids because everyone else does) and who wish to participate with God in the thrill of procreation should thoughtfully respond to the challenge of parenthood. One of life's greatest rewards is watching your child mature and begin to return the investment you have put into him. And suddenly one day you will discover that you must have done more things right than wrong because there before you will stand a lovely human being whose character reveals the qualities you have worked hard to cultivate.

The world as a whole will probably never fully appreciate the effort expended in good parenting. But in the final judgment all will appear as God views it, and He will openly reward parents who have prepared their children for His kingdom. It will be seen then that one child, brought up in the right way, is more than just worth the effort expended. It may cost tears, anxiety, and sleepless nights to oversee the development of a child, but each parent who has worked wisely unto salvation will hear God say, "Well done, thou good and faithful servant."

Further reading you will enjoy . . .

Anson, Elva and Kathie Liden. *THE COMPLEAT FAMILY BOOK.*
Schaeffer, Edith. *WHAT IS A FAMILY?*
Rickerson, Wayne. *CHRISTIAN FAMILY ACTIVITIES* (for families with children)
Rickerson, Wayne. *CHRISTIAN FAMILY ACTIVITIES* (for families with teens).
Reed, Bobby. *CHRISTIAN FAMILY ACTIVITIES* (for one-parent families)

Footnotes

Chapter 2

[1] Kay Kuzma. *Understanding Children.* (Mountain View, California: Pacific Press, 1978), pp. 133, 134.
[2] Dr. James Dobson. *Hide or Seek.* (Old Tappan, New Jersey: Fleming H. Revell Co., 1974), pp. 23, 24.
[3] From J. B. Phillips: *The New Testament in Modern English,* Revised Edition. © J. B. Phillips 1958, 1960, 1972. Used by permission of Macmillan Publishing Co., Inc.

Chapter 9

[1] Lendon Smith, *Feed Your Kids Right* (New York. Dell Publishing Co., 1979), p. 221.
[2] *Ibid.*
[3] "Why Be a Vegetarian?" *Life and Health,* Vegetarian Supplement, pp. 14-19.
[4] *Ibid.*

Chapter 11

[1] Dr. Seymour Fisher, *Understanding the Female Orgasm* (New York: Basic Books, Inc., 1973).
[2] *Ibid.,* p. 78.
[3] Harvey White, M.D., *Your Family Is Good for You* (New York: Random House, 1978), pp. 157, 158.
[4] Onalee McGraw, *The Family, Feminism and the Therapeutic State* (Washington, D.C.: The Heritage Foundation, 1980), p. 24.

Chapter 12

[1] Dr. Joyce Brothers, "Men in Love and Marriage," *Woman's Day,* January, 1982.
[2] *Ibid.*
[3] *Ibid.,* p. 48.

Bibliography

Abrahamson, David. *The Emotional Care of Your Child.* Richmond Hill, Ontario, Canada: Simon and Schuster, Inc.

A Healthy Personality for Your Child. Washington, D.C.: Government Printing Office, 1952.

Ainsworth, Mary. *Deprivation of Maternal Care—A Reassessment of Its Effects.* Geneva: World Health Organization, 1962.

Becker, Wesley C. *Parents Are Teachers.* Champaign, Ill.: Research Press Company, 1971.

Benson, Dan. *The Total Man.* Wheaton, Ill.: Tyndale House Publishers, 1977.

Bernhardt, David K. *Being a Parent.* Toronto: University of Toronto Press, 1970.

Briggs, Dorothy Corkille. *Your Child's Self-Esteem.* Garden City, N.Y.: Doubleday and Company, Inc., 1970.

Campbell, D. Ross. *How to Really Love Your Child.* Wheaton, Ill.: Victor, 1977.

Canfield, Jack, and Harold C. Wells. *100 Ways to Enhance Self-concept in the Classroom—A Handbook for Teachers and Parents.* Englewood Cliffs, N.J.: Prentice-Hall, Inc., 1976.

Caprio, Frank S., and Frank B. *Parents and Teenagers.* New York: The Citadel Press, 1969.

Christènson, Larry. *The Christian Family.* Minneapolis, Minn.: Bethany Fellowship, 1970.

Cotton, Dorothy. *Case for the Working Mother.* New York: Stein and Day, 1965.

Curtis, Jean. *Working Mothers.* Garden City, N.Y.: Doubleday, 1976.

Dillow, Linda. *Creative Counterpart.* Nashville: Thomas Nelson Publishers, 1977.

Dobson, James C. *Dare to Discipline.* Wheaton, Ill.: Tyndale House Publishers, 1970.

———. *Dr. Dobson Answers Your Questions.* Wheaton, Ill.: Tyndale House Publishers, 1982.

———. *Hide or Seek.* Old Tappan, N.J.: Fleming H. Revell Company, 1974.

———. *The Strong-willed Child.* Wheaton, Ill.: Tyndale House Publishers, 1978.

———. *What Wives Wish Their Husbands Knew About Women.* Wheaton, Ill.: Tyndale House Publishers, 1975.

Dodson, Fitzhugh. *How to Parent.* New York: A Signet Book From New American Library, 1970.

Donovan, Frank R. *Raising Your Children: What Behavioral Scientists Have Discovered.* New York: Crowell, 1968.

Dreikurs, Rudolf, with Vicki Soltz. *Children: The Challenge.* New York: Duell, Sloan and Pearce, 1964.

Drescher, John M. *Seven Things Children Need.* Scottdale, Pa.: Herald Press, 1976.

English, Horace B. *Dynamics of Child Development.* New York: Holt, Rinehart and Winston, Inc., 1961.

Felker, Evelyn. *Raising Other People's Kids.* Grand Rapids, Mich.: Eerdman's, 1981.

Foster, Constance J. *Developing Responsibility in Children.* Chicago, Ill.: Science Research Associates, Inc., 1953.

Fraiberg, Selma. *The Magic Years.* New York: Scribner, 1959.

Gatley, Richard H., and David Koulack. *Single Father's Handbook—A Guide for Separated and Divorced Fathers.* Garden City, N.Y.: Doubleday, 1979.

Gaulke, Earl H. *You Can Have a Family Where Everybody Wins.* St. Louis: Concordia, 1975.

Gesell, Arnold, and Frances L. Ilg. *The Child From Five to Ten.* New York: Harper and Row, 1946.

———. *Infant and Child in the Culture of Today.* New York: Harper and Row, Publishers, 1943.

Ginott, Haim G. *Between Parent and Child.* N.Y.: The Macmillan Company, 1965.

———. *Between Parent and Teen-ager.* New York: Avon Books, 1969.

Gordon, Thomas. *Parent Effectiveness Training.* New York: Peter H. Wyden, Inc., Publisher, 1970.

Greenleaf, Barbara Kaye, with Lewis A. Schaffer, M.D. *Help—A Handbook for Working Mothers.* New York: Thomas Y. Crowell, 1978.

Hardisty, Margaret. *How to Get Your Husband to Fulfill Your Emotional Needs.* Irvine, Calif.: Harvest House, 1980.

Heffner, Elaine. *Mothering—The Emotional Experience of Motherhood After Freud and Feminism.* Garden City, N.Y.: Doubleday, 1978.

Herzog, Elizabeth, and Cecelia E. Sudia. *Boys in Fatherless Families.* Washington, D.C.: U.S. Department of Health, Education, and Welfare, DHEW Publication No. (OCD) 72-33, 1971.

LaHaye, Tim. *The Battle for the Family.* Old Tappan, N.J.: Fleming H. Revell, 1982.

Laycock, S. R. *Family Living and Sex Education.* Toronto, Canada: Mil-Mac Publications, Ltd., 1967.

Leman, Dr. Kevin. *Parenthood Without Hassles.* Irvine, Calif.: Harvest House, 1979.

LeShan, Eda J. *How to Survive Parenthood.* New York: Random House, 1965.

Maltz, Maxwell. *The Magic Power of Self-Image Psychology.* New York: Pocket Books, 1970.

Mayhall, Jack and Carole. *Marriage Takes More Than Love.* Colorado Springs: Navepress, 1978.

McEntire, Patricia. *Mommy, I'm Hungry: How to Feed Your Child Nutritiously.* Sacramento, Calif.: Cougar Books, 1981.

Menninger, William C., et al. *How to Help Your Children.* New York: Sterling, 1959.

Mow, Anna B. *Your Teen-ager and You.* Grand Rapids, Mich.: Zondervan Publishing House, 1967.

Murdock, Carol V. *Single Parents Are People Too.* New York: Butterick Publications, 1980.

Musson, Paul Henry; John Janeway Conger; and Jerome Kagan. *Child Development and Personality.* New York: Harper and Row, 1974.

Narramore, Clyde M. *Understanding Your Children.* Grand Rapids, Mich.: Zondervan Publishing House, 1957.

Neisser, Edith. *How to Live With Children.* Chicago, Ill.: Science Research Associates, Inc., 1950.

————. *The Roots of Self-Confidence.* Chicago, Ill.: Science Research Associates, Inc., 1954.

Newman, George. *101 Ways to Be a Long Distance Super Dad.* Mountain View, Calif.: Blossom Valley Press, 1981.

Noble, June and William. *How to Live With Other People's Children.* New York: Hawthorn Books, 1979.

Ostrovsky, Everett. *Sibling Rivalry.* New York: Cornerstone Library, 1969.

Peppler, Alice Stolper. *Single Again—This Time With Children.* Minneapolis: Augsburg, 1982.

Profiles of Children. 1970 White House Conference on Children. Washington, D.C.: U.S. Government Printing Office.

Reed, Bobbie. *I Didn't Plan to Be a Single Parent.* St. Louis: Concordia, 1981.

————. *Stepfamilies Living in Christian Harmony.* St. Louis: Concordia, 1980.

Renich, Fred. *The Christian Husband.* Wheaton, Ill.: Tyndale House Publishers, 1976.

Robertson, James. *Young Children in Hospital.* New York: Basic Books, 1959.

Ross Laboratories. *Developing Self-esteem; When Your Child Is Unruly; Your Children and Discipline.* Columbus, Ohio: Ross Laboratories, 1969.

Scanzoni, Letha. *Sex Is a Parent Affair.* Glendale, Calif.: G/L Publications, 1973.

Schuller, Robert H. *Self-love.* New York: Hawthorn Books, Inc., 1969.

Seidman, Jerome M. *The Child: A Book of Readings.* New York: Holt, Rinehart and Winston, 1969.

Smith, Lendon H. *Feed Your Kids Right.* New York: Dell Books, 1979.

————. *Improving Your Child's Behavior Chemistry.* New York: Pocket Books, 1976.

Smith, Sally Liberman. *Nobody Said It's Easy.* New York: The Macmillan Company, 1965.

Stevens, Anita, and Lucy Freeman. *I Hate My Parents.* New York: Tower Publications.

Television and Social Behavior. An annotated bibliography of research focusing on the impact of television on children. Rockville, Maryland: National Institute of Mental Health, 1971.

Tomlinson-Keasey, Carol. *Child's Eye View.* New York: St. Martin's Press, 1980.

Thomson, Helen. *The Successful Stepparent.* New York: Harper and Row, 1966.

Trasler, Gordon, et al. *The Formative Years.* London: British Broadcasting Corporation, 1968.

Van Pelt, Nancy L. *The Compleat Courtship.* Washington, D.C.: Southern Publishing Association, 1982.

————. *The Compleat Marriage.* Washington, D.C.: Southern Publishing Association, 1979.

————. *To Have and to Hold.* Washington, D.C.: Southern Publishing Association, 1980.

Homan, William E. *Child Sense: A Pediatrician's Guide for Today's Families.* New York: Basic Books, 1969.

Hope, Karol, and Nancy Young, eds. *Momma Handbook: The Source Book for Single Mothers.* New York: New American Library, 1976.

Hurlock, Elizabeth B. *Child Development.* 6th Edition. New York: McGraw-Hill Book Co., 1977.

Hymes, James L. *Teaching the Child Under Six.* Englewood Cliffs, N.J.: Prentice-Hall, Inc., 1963.

Ilg, Frances L., and Louise Bates Ames. *Child Behavior.* New York: Harper and Row, 1955.

It's Your World of Good Food. Cooking for Health and Happiness. Lessons 1-12. Glendale, Calif.: The Voice of Prophecy.

Jersild, Arthur T. *Child Psychology.* Englewood Cliffs, New Jersey: Prentice-Hall, Inc., 1961.

Klein, Carole. *The Single Parent Experience.* New York: Walker and Co., 1973.

Klein, Ted. *The Father's Book.* New York: Ace Publishing Corp., 1968.

Kuzma, Jan and Kay. *Building Character.* Mt. View, Calif.: Pacific Press, 1979.

Kuzma, Kay. *Prime-Time Parenting.* New York: Rawson, Wade Pub., Inc., 1980.

————. *Understanding Children.* Mt. View, Calif.: Pacific Press, 1978.

LaHaye, Beverly. *How to Develop Your Child's Temperament.* Irvine, Calif.: Harvest House, 1977.

Vigeveno, H. S., and Anne Claire. *Divorce and the Children.* Glendale, Calif. G/L Publications, 1979.

Wagemaker, Herbert. *Why Can't I Understand My Kids?* Grand Rapids: Zondervan, 1973.

Watts, Virginia. *The Single Parent.* Old Tappan, N.J.: Revell, 1976.

Weiss, Robert S. *Going It Alone.* New York: Basic Books, 1979.

White, Ellen G. *Child Guidance.* Nashville, Tenn.: Southern Publishing Association, 1954.

———. *Happiness Homemade.* Nashville, Tenn.: Southern Publishing Association, 1971.

White, Harvey, M.D. *Your Family Is Good for You.* New York: Random House, 1979.

Wilkerson, David R. *Parents on Trial.* New York: Hawthorn Books, Inc., 1967.

Winnicott, D. W. *Mother and Child: A Primer of First Relationships.* New York: Basic Books, 1957.

Wolf, Anna. *The Parent's Manual: A Guide to the Emotional Development of Young Children.* New York: Ungar, 1962.

Wood, Barry. *Questions Teenagers Ask About Dating and Sex.* Old Tappan, N.J.: Fleming H. Revell Co., 1981.

Woodley, Persia. *Creative Survival for Single Mothers.* Celestial Arts, 1975.

Wright, Norman, and Rex Johnson. *Communication—Key to Your Teens.* Irvine, Calif.: Harvest House, 1978.

Art and Photo Credits

Illustrations

Tim Adams: 14-15, 24-25, 52-53, 72-73, 94-95, 122-123, 148-149, 158-159, 166-167, 176-177, 190-191, 214-215, 228-229.

Ronald Hester: 16, 27, 29, 30, 33, 36, 39, 41, 42, 44, 47, 57, 58, 63, 75, 78, 83, 84, 87, 99, 101, 105, 107, 111, 113, 114, 127, 131, 132, 134, 139, 141, 154, 179, 183, 186, 193, 196, 201, 208, 210, 216, 220, 223, 230, 237.

Photography

Four by Five: Back Cover, 12-13, 22-23, 50-51, 70-71, 92-93, 120-121, 146-147, 156-157, 164-165, 174-175, 188-189, 226-227, 234-235.

Photofile: 212-213.

Robert Wright: Front Cover

David B. Sherwin: (Front and Back Covers)

Answer Key

Page 18. THE GOOD PARENT TEST

Scoring: For all odd-numbered statements, total the point value of the numbers circled:

Reverse score on even-numbered statements as follows: if the number circled reads (4) receives 1 point; (3) receives 2 points; (2) receives 3 points; (1) receives 4 points. Total and enter score here: _____

Total of both odd and even: _____

INTERPRETATION OF SCORES:

82 to 88 You are a GOOD PARENT! But you still will find help in this book.

75 to 81 You are honorable in your child-rearing knowledge. The book will encourage you.

68 to 74 You are acceptable in your child-rearing knowledge, but there is room for improvement.

61 to 67 Your child-rearing knowledge definitely needs help.

52 to 60 You have reprehensible knowledge of parent skills and desperately need help!

A score below 52 is abominable and means that you are violating the majority of principles needed in successful parenting. But take heart. Help is on the way. And there's no better time to begin than now!

After reading the book, please retake the GOOD PARENT TEST and rescore yourself to measure your improvement. See, we told you help was on the way!

Page 28. SCORING INSTRUCTIONS FOR SELF-ESTEEM EVALUATION

To find your self-esteem index (SEI), simply add scores of all Self-esteem Statements. The possible range of your Self-esteem Index is from 0 to 100. Sound Self-esteem is indicated by an SEI of 95 or more. Experience shows that any score under 90 is a disadvantage, a score of 75 or less is a serious disadvantage, and an SEI of 50 or less indicates a really crippling lack of Self-esteem.

Page 100. ARE YOU TRAINING YOUR CHILD TO BE OBNOXIOUS?

The fewer "ones" and the more "fives" scored, the less likely you are to be training an obnoxious child.

Discuss your responses with your partner, a friend, or your parent study group.

Page 128. RIGHTS vs. PRIVILEGES

Scoring: Each of the 4 items actually is a parental right. But remember every parental right must be tempered and balanced with wisdom. Read the section in the text "Parental Right VS. Teen-age Privileges" and then discuss your responses with your partner, a friend, or your parent study group.

Page 136. **TEEN-AGERS AND DISCIPLINE**
Scoring: (1) c; (2) b and/or d; (3) e; (4) b; (5) e; (6) a; (7) d; (8) a; (9) d.

Page 153. **SELF-TEST ON DRUG PREVENTION**
Scoring: If you have been able to answer TRUE to all or most of the previous statements, CONGRATULATIONS! Your chances for ever dealing with drug abuse in your family are very slim.

Page 162. **SIBLING RIVALRY TRUE OR FALSE**
Scoring: The test was "rigged." All the answers are true. The test now serves as a solid set of guidelines for handling sibling conflicts.

Page 184. **THINKING BACK: HOW IT WAS FOR ME**
The higher your score, the higher your probability of being able to pass on healthy attitudes to your children.

Page 198. **AM I READY FOR CHILDREN?**
Total the point value of the numbers circled, then score as follows:

24-35: Congratulations! If you have been 100 percent honest, according to your responses you will likely possess superior ability to parent. In all areas tested, you indicate marital stability, personal maturity, and readiness for child-care tasks. (I hope the real thing doesn't disillusion you too severely!)

36-48: You've done well! You definitely indicate above average ability to cope with the pressures of parenting. If you continue to study and prepare yourself for this demanding role, you are likely to experience success and pleasure in the parenting experience.

49-60: Take it easy! You show only average potential for parenting. If average is good enough for you, go ahead with your plans. However there are enough mediocre parents in the world. Why not slow things down and go into an intense period of study and preparation. Read some books, attend some parent education classes, and then press toward the mark.

61-89: Caution! Your score indicates a below average readiness for the demands of parenthood. It would be better if you put off thoughts of having children until some of your attitudes change. An intense period of study and preparation would be advisable.

90-120: Beware! You are definitely not ready to meet the demands of parenting. Put all thoughts of having children out of your mind until some drastic changes are made.

The Parent's Prayer

Heavenly Father,

I am overwhelmed with the enormity of the demands of parenthood. Without You constantly at my side, my efforts would be in vain. I praise You for being the source of all joy and victory, self-esteem and gratitude in my life.

Help me, Father, to instill in my children healthy feelings of worth even when my own feelings of self-worth dip painfully low. Keep me from demeaning them through name-calling, shame, or ridicule. Grant me the ability to encourage their good qualities with abundant hugs and words of encouragement.

Hold my tongue when I should be listening rather than talking. May I be ready to listen when they need me. Keep me from unnecessary nagging, and guard my tone of voice when I am disciplining them. Give me daily patience to instill character and responsibility. May I have the wisdom to grant reasonable wishes as well as the courage to withhold harmful requests.

May a smile daily light my face. May happiness and laughter fill our home. Grant me the ability to recognize when to put work aside and enjoy present-moment experiences. I am trusting You to help me build a treasure house of fond memories and family traditions for the future.

Forgive the host of shortcomings and failures that consume me from the past. Please take from me any guilt, anger, or resentment that might cripple my relationship with my children. Keep me from taking my own personal frustrations out on my children.

May I show love to my children from infancy up. May they know love because they have experienced it in our home.

My children are Your children also, Father. I commit them into Your powerful hands. May my example in serving You inspire in them a love and desire to serve You forever.

Above all gifts, Lord, grant me patience and self-control. Thank You for going before me to help me through all the difficult days ahead. I love You and thank You for answering this my prayer for the future of my children. I trust You to fulfill all our needs in Your time.

_____   _____
Date   Name